Anime and the Art of Adaptation

ALSO BY DANI CAVALLARO
AND FROM MCFARLAND

*Anime and the Visual Novel: Narrative
Structure, Design and Play at the Crossroads
of Animation and Computer Games* (2010)

*Magic as Metaphor in Anime:
A Critical Study* (2010)

*The Mind of Italo Calvino: A Critical
Exploration of His Thought and Writings* (2010)

*Anime and Memory: Aesthetic, Cultural
and Thematic Perspectives* (2009)

*The Art of Studio Gainax: Experimentation, Style and
Innovation at the Leading Edge of Anime* (2009)

*Anime Intersections: Tradition and Innovation
in Theme and Technique* (2007)

The Animé Art of Hayao Miyazaki (2006)

*The Cinema of Mamoru Oshii: Fantasy,
Technology and Politics* (2006)

Anime and the Art of Adaptation

Eight Famous Works from Page to Screen

DANI CAVALLARO

McFarland & Company, Inc., Publishers
Jefferson, North Carolina, and London

LIBRARY OF CONGRESS CATALOGUING-IN-PUBLICATION DATA

Cavallaro, Dani.
   Anime and the art of adaptation : eight famous works from page to screen / Dani Cavallaro.
      p.   cm.
   Includes bibliographical references and index.
   Includes filmography.

   ISBN 978-0-7864-5860-8
   softcover : 50# alkaline paper ∞

   1. Animated films — History and criticism.   2. Film adaptations — History and criticism.   I. Title.
   NC1765.C38   2010
   791.43'34 — dc22   2010024301

British Library cataloguing data are available

©2010 Dani Cavallaro. All rights reserved

No part of this book may be reproduced or transmitted in any form or by any means, electronic or mechanical, including photocopying or recording, or by any information storage and retrieval system, without permission in writing from the publisher.

On the cover: Artwork from the 1988 animated film *Grave of the Fireflies* (Studio Ghibli/The Kobal Collection)

Manufactured in the United States of America

McFarland & Company, Inc., Publishers
   Box 611, Jefferson, North Carolina 28640
   www.mcfarlandpub.com

To Paddy,
with love and gratitude
... and to Betsy, too, in homage to her supervisory role

Contents

Preface 1

1. The Frame of Reference 5
2. The Nightmare of History
   Belladonna of Sadness, *Grave of the Fireflies*
   and *Like the Clouds, Like the Wind* 19
3. Epic Adventure with a Sci-Fi Twist
   Gankutsuou: The Count of Monte Cristo 38
4. The Fairy Tale Reimagined
   The Snow Queen 64
5. Romance Meets Revolution
   Romeo x Juliet 99
6. A Magical Murder Enigma
   Umineko no Naku Koro ni 128
7. A Tapestry of Courtly Life
   The Tale of Genji 146

Filmography 197
Bibliography 201
Index 207

Language is an archaeological vehicle ... the language we speak is a whole palimpsest of human effort and history.
— Russell Hoban

For the world to be interesting, you have to be manipulating it all the time.
— Brian Eno

Preface

Keep on the lookout for novel ideas that others have used successfully. Your idea has to be original only in its adaptation to the problem you're working on.

To invent, you need a good imagination and a pile of junk.
— Thomas Alva Edison

This study explores a selection of anime offering adaptations of famous works of both Eastern and Western provenance. It is not concerned with assessing the so-called quality of adaptations in value judgmental terms but with appreciating their significance and appeal as autonomous textual formations. Its basic premise is that by contrast with Western animation studios, whose adaptations of illustrious originals turn exclusively to children's books and fairy tales for inspiration and always endeavor to edulcorate the sources' messages, anime studios utilizing well-known dramatic, mythical or literary antecedents are frequently drawn to stories with grave undertones or even to the realms of tragedy and epic. When they do venture into the domain of children's fiction, they often bring out its more mature themes or else reimagine the initial yarns by infusing their worlds with complex subtexts. This divergence in preferences within the particular field of adaptation can be related to a broader phenomenon: the attraction famously evinced by Eastern audiences (and cultures generally) to materials of darker texture, not solely in anime but also in other cogent facets of the performance, literary and visual arts. In the specific case of Japanese culture, that proclivity can be seen as a direct corollary of an essential facet of indigenous aesthetics tersely captured by John Reeve as follows: "Serenity and turbulence, spirituality and slaughter have often gone hand in hand in Japanese culture.... Japanese art, like Japanese religion, can provide an assurance (or illusion) of calm while also honestly reflecting the turbulence of life both outside and within" (Reeve, p. 22). This entails that the very concepts of entertainment, amusement, pleasure and fun can never be conclusively dissevered from the perception, albeit subliminal, of unruly and chaotic energies coursing at all times through the fabric of human existence. Japan's fascination with the shadowy and the somber is also beautifully documented by Junichirou Tanizaki, who enthusiastically celebrates his culture's "propensity to seek beauty in darkness" (Tanizaki, p. 47), maintaining that tenebrousness, frightening though it may be, is also instrumental in imbuing reality with "a quality of mystery and depth superior to that of any wall painting or ornament" (p. 33).

Using the propositions delineated above as its theoretical underpinnings, the book then moves onto its tripartite core interest: i. what anime contributes to the sources it adapts in stylistic, aesthetic and psychological terms; ii. how specific features of the medium impact alchemically on the original sources to bring into being imaginative works of autonomous stature; iii. relatedly, what renders an adaptation in anime form an artistic product *sui generis*. To sum up, i. focuses on "tools"; ii. on "methods"; and iii. on "outcomes." Historically, the book covers an extensive period spanning the late 1950s to the present day. It accordingly addresses a broad spectrum of series and movies drawing inspiration from varyingly eminent works in a variety of forms and styles. So as to avoid the trap of diffuseness into which a study of such scope could plausibly fall and provide instead a focused investigation, the book concentrates on specific case studies. These encompass three titles illustrating the 1970s, 1980s and 1990s, and five titles released over the first decade of the twenty-first century. The titles used to exemplify the earlier decades here covered are deemed illustrative of those times in their expression of a recurrent cultural preoccupation with the onerous legacy of history and attendant desire to reimagine official historiography. They are accordingly discussed within a single chapter as facets of one fundamental phenomenon. The rationale underpinning the decision to prioritize specifically contemporary trends in the process of cross-media adaptation involving anime is twofold. First, anime adaptations from earlier periods tend to consist of fairly loyal page-to-screen transpositions of popular literary sources and are therefore less challenging *qua adaptations* than later adaptive works in the same medium adopting a more adventurous take on their source materials. Second, the earlier anime's relatively uncomplicated stance to mediatic relocation renders them less amenable to investigation with reference to recent developments in the field of adaptation studies, and hence less appropriate objects of study for a book wishing to explore the theoretical implications and ramifications of the topic under scrutiny.

Chapter 1 opens with an assessment of the general approach to the art of adaptation evinced by anime with an emphasis on the concept of adaptation as a fluid process and on the notion that the encoding of a source in a different medium (and hence a different means of expression) generates an entirely different text of independent standing. The opening chapter then concentrates sequentially on three theoretical perspectives of axial significance to the journey from the page to the anime screen: developments in the domain of contemporary adaptation studies; philosophical debates on the concepts of originality, reproduction and simulation stretching from Plato via Walter Benjamin to Jean Baudrillard (and other relevant facets of poststructuralist thought); the impact of anime-specific codes and conventions (graphic, dramatic, cinematographical) on the adaptation process (i.e., what makes an adaptation in anime form a distinctive cultural product capable of instilling new meanings into its sources). Chapter 2 addresses the three earlier anime with a focus on the concept of history, while the ensuing chapters concentrate on later productions evincing a bolder approach to the art of adaptation and, concomitantly, greater openness to theoretical examination. The discussion highlights those anime's imaginative reinterpretation of a broad range of genres, including the Romantic novel, the fairy tale, Shakespearean tragedy, the psychological saga and the supernatural murder story, devoting special attention to the animational strategies, graphic tools, and rhetorical twists and tricks through which they impart those established modes with novel connotations or indeed subject them to generic metamorphosis. The case study addressed in the closing chapter holds a special place in the discussion and is therefore accorded particularly extensive treatment. This prominence is due to three interdependent reasons. First, the chapter brings together a number of both practical and theoretical issues pertinent to the topic of adaptation at large and hence throws into relief several of the fundamental concerns explored by the book as a whole. Second, in exploring the anime adaptation of a Japanese work that has proved immensely influential in both indigenous and global milieux over several centuries, *The Tale of Genji*, it provides a unique opportunity to examine the adaptive collusion of diverse cultures, traditions and epochs. Third, the history of the original narrative's reception and adaptation over the centuries eloquently demonstrates that the significance of a text does not solely reside with its essence but also with the expressive vehicles and adaptive situations in which it is inscribed at any one point in time.

At the same time as they engage in detail with the pivotal titles, the case studies supplied in this book make additional reference — with diverse degrees of depth and breadth depending on contextual cogency — to a wider selection of anime. The primary and secondary titles include both overt adaptations, and movies or series drawing inspiration from well-known works but reconfiguring them so radically as to render the adaptational component purely implicit or latent. The close analyses supplied in the book attend to both the anime themselves and their sources. At the same time, they examine a cross-section of approaches to the theory and practice of adaptation and appropriate critical perspectives on the phenomena of media synergy and intertextuality, alongside pertinent philosophical debates surrounding the concepts of originality, repetition and difference. Finally, the book seeks to stretch the concept of adaptation and allow it to encompass broader forms of media cross-pollination. It therefore examines its main titles in relation not only to their written sources but also to artbooks illustrating or complementing their stylistic and dramatic traits with an emphasis on the specifically visual element.

Chapter 1

The Frame of Reference

No story comes from nowhere; new stories are born of old. — Salman Rushdie

Stories, great flapping ribbons of shaped space-time, have been blowing and uncoiling around the universe since the beginning of time. And they have evolved. The weakest have died and the strongest have survived and they have grown fat on the retelling. — Terry Pratchett

Adaptations are ubiquitous in the history of anime and have accrued novel connotations over time. Despite context-bound factors affecting the nature of adaptations in different periods, one constant appears to have underpinned anime's appropriation and manipulation of sources: a tendency to underscore the status of adaptation not as a sealed product but as a process. The argument pursued in this study is fueled by the conviction that it is actually far more exciting and thought-provoking for anime viewers to reflect on the process through which an existing text has become what they see on the screen — how, in other words, it has progressively come to be translated into a work in its own right — than simply to consume the resulting show as a sealed artifact. Anime makers are well aware that adaptations have been persistently pigeonholed as coterminous with pejorative concepts such as infidelity, mindless mimicry or even downright blasphemy. In the face of this bleak legacy, they have sought to counter its negative stance by eloquently demonstrating that an adaptation does not consist of a simple binary exchange between two discrete media based on a clear subordination of the borrower to the lender but rather of a playfully promiscuous process involving forms as diverse as novels of disparate genres and formats, stage plays and puppet shows, folk and fairy tales, comics and videogames, as well as non-fiction texts drawn from the fields of history, politics, sociology and anthropology — which, cumulatively, straddle no less than a millennium.

Concurrently, the anime under scrutiny never attempt to ignore or efface the existence of the works they draw upon as entities endowed with independent reality and intrinsic weight. What they are eager to explore, in fact, is the extent to which that reality and that weight might be transposable to the domain of the animated image — either by reconfiguring them in accordance with certain technical criteria indigenous to animation itself or by externalizing visually their unique essence without interfering with their primarily verbal identity. Although the contingent outcomes of this exploration vary from anime to anime, the overall message conveyed by anime adaptations such as the ones here addressed is that no text can be transposed to a different form without altering substantially, acquiring fresh meanings and inaugurating novel perspectives. This is because the divergence of the expressive vehicle used by the adaptation from that used by its source is inevitably conducive to some difference in content and mood. That is to say, by encoding its source in a different form, the adaptation comes to constitute not merely an alternate way of saying the same thing but rather a *different text* — a radically separate way of conveying messages other the ones inherent in the source by virtue of its own formal distinctiveness. This does not automatically imply that the adaptations studied in this context always depart drastically from their sources. In fact, some of the anime echo the originals quite closely at the levels of both content and mood. Rather, it is a matter of recognizing that the "pleasure" yielded by an adaptation at its best, to cite Linda Hutcheon, entails "repetition" with "variation" (Hutcheon, p. 4).

The status of adaptations as repetitions with a variation, Hutcheon proposes, underscores their independent identity as "deliberate, announced, and extended revisitations of prior works" (p. xiv) that ought not to be regarded, therefore, as mere imitations or replications. Julie Sanders enthusiastically corroborates this proposition: "Adaptation and appropriation," she states, "are, endlessly and wonderfully, about seeing things come back to us in as many forms as possible" (Sanders, p. 160). Adaptation, according to Sanders, should frequently be thought of as "appropriation" insofar as this term more aptly describes a "decisive journey away from the informing source into a wholly new cultural product and domain" (p. 26). A cognate position is advocated by Linda Costanzo Cahir when she contends that there are significant instances in which the term "translation" would be more fruitfully applicable than "adaptation" since translation does not simply alter a form structurally to enable it to operate in an alternative context but actually engenders "a fully new text — a materially different entity" — through "a process of language" (Costanzo Cahir, p. 14).

While assessing the nature of the adaptation as an autonomous text, it is also important to appreciate that the collusion of different genres and formats poses some tantalizing questions not only about the adaptation but also about the source, challenging us repeatedly to consider what happens to the parent text when it is transposed to the screen. The anime central to this study are all adapted from texts that deploy the written word as a key communicational instrument, which renders them globally definable as literature, and therefore invite us to ponder specifically whether, when a piece of literature is transposed to the screen, it can still be called literature, should be seen to have morphed into cinema and thus left all traces of its written status behind or, more intriguingly, might be deemed to hold a dual identity as *both* literature *and* cinema. This third option entails the emancipation of the adaptation from its subservience to a supposedly privileged original and hence reflects, as Deborah Cartmell and Imelda Whelelan put it, the "desire to free our notion of film adaptations from" their "dependency on literature so that adaptations are not derided as sycophantic, derivative, and therefore inferior to their literary counterparts" (Cartmell and Whelelan, pp. 1–2). It is indeed hard to deny, as Thomas Leitch stresses, that in the realm of adaptation studies, literature has been insistently regarded as "an aesthetically sanctified field" whose value is automatically accepted "by a jury whose verdict" regarding its "film adaptations is still out" (Leitch, p. 64). In an effort to overcome this logophiliac impasse, various critics have proposed particular classificatory templates meant to differentiate specific types of adaptation.

Thus, John M. Desmond and Peter Hawkes divide adaptations into three typologies, "close, loose, or intermediate" (Desmond and Hawkes, p. 3), while Costanzo Cahir differentiates "literal, traditional, or radical" forms of adaptation. The most appealing quality of the latter's contribution to the debate, for the purpose of the present study, lies with the emphasis placed on the relative autonomy of the cinematic adaptation from its source: "The film," Costanzo Cahir maintains, "must demonstrate an audacity to create a work that stands as a world apart" so that even though it remains "related" to the original aesthetically, it is nonetheless perceivable as "self-reliant" (Costanzo Cahir, p. 263). Proposing an alternate taxonomy, Dudley Andrew has classified adaptations in terms of "borrowing," "intersecting" and "transforming" modalities (Andrew 1984; 2000). Borrowing is based on the employment of the "material, idea, or form" of a preexistent text and requires the reader or viewer to "probe the source of power of the original by examining the use of it made in adaptation." Intersection respects the source's uniqueness by leaving it "intentionally unassimilated" (Andrew 2000, p. 30), while transformation entails a more radical process of self-differentiation on the adaptation's part. In all cases, however, what matters is the adaptation's fidelity to the "spirit" of the parent text, not its mere "reproduction" of "something essential about an original text" (p. 31)—which could be effected by exclusively mechanical means. Literature and film, for Andrew, are fundamentally "separate," yet "equivalent," ways of translating ideas into signs — verbal or audiovisual — and must therefore be approached, in studying their adaptational dialogue, as two specific media forms: mediatic specificities are hence posited as a critical priority.

Kamilla Elliott, for her part, has identified six distinct categories: "psychic," "ventriloquist," "genetic," "merging," "incarnational" and "trumping." The psychic echoes Andrew's argument by underscoring the importance of preserving the spirit of the source; the ventriloquist empties the source's body of its content and lends it a new voice; the genetic sees the source and its adaptation as two versions of the same narrative deep structure; the merging upholds the reunion of two spirits beyond the boundaries of individual textual bodies; the incarnational regards a movie as the visible body toward which a novel's abstract language aspires; and the trumping, finally, views film as the mechanism performing the equivalent of a sex-change operation based on the premise that the book's spirit inhabits the wrong body and film must restore it to its appropriate shape (Elliott).

A few key issues that have tenaciously haunted the field of adaptation studies, and specifically the sector thereof concerned with filmic adaptations of literature, are here worthy of consideration for the sake of contextual accuracy. Numerous commentators are eager to ascertain whether a film is faithful to its literary parent at the levels of content, style and figurative structure, while others are more interested in establishing whether an adaptation simply transcribes its source or rather interprets it by suggesting a particular way of reading it or by engaging in speculations about issues it implicitly raises. All of the anime examined in this book as focal cases favor the second approach, capitalizing on their formal specificity to impart their originals with fresh levels of significance. A widespread concern pertains specifically to adaptations that appear to depart quite radically from their sources in which the breach in loyalty can be explained — and warranted — on the basis of their situation within altered sociohistorical milieux and related injunction to adhere to muted audience expectations and representational conventions. *Grave of the Fireflies* and *Like the Clouds, Like the Wind* are good examples of this trend. If the importance of cultural circumstances and mores is acknowledged in relation not only to the adaptation but also to the source, then it can be argued that the latter is no less context-bound than the former — and that its openness to metamorphosis and retelling is, in a sense, an ineluctable concomitant of that status. No text, in this perspective, could ever be firmly emplaced as immune to the fluctuations and whims of time. As shown in the case studies to follow, this crosscultural phenomenon makes itself manifest in the titles under scrutiny with a stunning flair for generic suppleness.

Another interesting question is whether adaptations that blatantly defy

1. The Frame of Reference 9

fidelity obliquely invite their viewers to revisit the sources in order to assess what fresh meanings these might unleash in light of their alternate retellings. It is quite feasible, for instance, that spectators already familiar with Shakespeare, Dumas or Andersen (to cite but a few authors relevant to this book) will wish to return to the originals to experience afresh their dramatic, narrative or metaphorical strengths from new perspectives inaugurated by the adaptations themselves. Several publications in the area have also focused on whether movies have at their disposal any means of replicating or mirroring their sources' distinctively literary attributes (e.g., poetic, descriptive and typographic elements) in cinematic and generally visual form. Anime's handling of graphic tools reminiscent of the written word — which is, in any case, an extraordinarily multifaceted reality in the context of Japanese language — is particularly deserving of inspection, in this respect. At the same time, this ruse lends itself to self-reflexive gestures enabling particular shows to comment obliquely on their status as adaptations.

A further issue of substantial relevance to the titles under scrutiny (given their sheer breadth of scope) concerns the significance of adaptations issuing from non-literary sources based either in popular culture or in academic writing. The use of the term non-literary requires elucidation in the present context. As noted earlier, all of the anime here studied can be said to issue from sources drawn from literature, as long as literature is broadly regarded as the province of the written word, of the letter (*litera*). In speaking about non-literary sources, the term non-literary is predicated on a more refined meaning of literary as the designation specifically applicable to a piece of narrative prose (often wholly or mainly fictional), to a poem or to a dramatic work governed by artistic rather than purely functional or utilitarian considerations. Thus, *Belladonna of Sadness* and *Umineko no Naku Koro ni* can be said to draw on literature insofar as both the cultural history text and the visual novel they respectively adapt use the written word as a key expressive medium but can also be said to utilize non-literary sources to the extent that neither of those parent texts is literary in the narrow sense of the term as defined above. This aspect of the debate contributes vitally to a salutary demotion of literary fiction and drama from the status of unequivocally privileged points of reference to that of a mere component — sizeable as this may be — of the ocean of texts from which adaptations can derive inspiration.

Likewise tantalizing are certain developing perspectives on the distinctive qualities of the kind of adaptation which, while electing one source as its principal matrix, concurrently draws from other ancillary texts or media of both verbal and non-verbal constitution. In the context of the anime at hand, for example, it is not uncommon for a series or movie based on a canonically valued novelistic or dramatic source to hybridize the parent text through the infusion of sci-fi or action-adventure motifs into its fabric — *Gankutsuou: The Count of Monte Cristo* and *Romeo x Juliet* eloquently illustrate this idea. According to Christine Geraghty, it is worth noting, "adaptations that move furthest from the original" are precisely the ones that "are often sustained by other generic expectations" (Geraghty, p. 43). Alternately, even when the source is loyally adhered to, stylistic trends typical of different epochs or cultures may be simultaneously invoked to enrich the animational brew in adventurous fashions — *Belladonna of Sadness, Snow Queen, The Tale of Genji* and *Umineko no Naku Koro ni* exemplify this trend. These are typical cases of adaptations that squarely transcend analysis by reference to the criterion of fidelity — or lack of it — by widening the horizon of the textual web through complex processes of aesthetic cross-pollination and referencing and through an intricate mix of styles, genres and settings.

While, as indicated in the preceding pages, ongoing speculations in the field of adaptation studies are directly relevant to the transformative process explored in this book, a likewise cogent point of reference is supplied by philosophical perspectives on the phenomena of reproduction and simulation. The concept of the simulacrum is especially noteworthy, in this regard. This features conspicuously in both the theory and the practice of the visual (and, by extension, performance) arts since at least Plato (fifth century B.C.). Since the early twentieth century, the concept has been steadily acquiring novel connotations and layers of speculative complexity as a result of various technological developments: first the flourishing of mechanical reproduction and then the explosion of electronic means of generating whole virtual worlds. In Plato's philosophical system, the copy is quite incontrovertibly posited as inferior to the Idea or Pure Form that is presumed to lie behind it. The Pure Forms themselves are thought of as wholly abstract and eternal entities that exist independently of any of their material manifestations, whereas the phenomenal reality we quotidianly experience as mortal creatures is merely a second-rate copy of that etherealized transcendental domain — an unreliable carousel of illusory simulacra. Artistic representations of the material world, for their part, are even further removed from the timeless reality of Pure Forms, holding the specious status of third-rate copies, or copies of copies.

More recent thinkers have proposed that copies and simulacra should not be unequivocally regarded as inferior to the reality which they are presumed to imitate or simulate. Gilles Deleuze, for example, has drawn an interesting distinction between the copy and the simulacrum, maintaining that although the copy has been conventionally branded as second-rate, it has nonetheless been deemed worthy of some respect due to its intimate connection with an esteemed original, and hence held capable of providing insights into the values hosted by the original itself. The simulacrum, conversely, does not refer to a superior reality but only ever abides by its own reality, flouting the authority of any original that may underpin its construction. "The simulacrum," Deleuze argues, "is not a degraded copy. It harbors a positive power which denies *the original and the copy, the model and the reproduction*. At least two divergent series are internalized in the simulacrum — neither can be assigned as the original, neither as the copy.... There is no longer any privileged point of view except that of the object common to all points of view. There is no possible hierarchy, no second, no third.... The same and the similar no longer have an essence except as *simulated*, that is as expressing the functioning of the simulacrum" (Deleuze 1990, p. 262).

Walter Benjamin's groundbreaking essay "The Work of Art in the Age of Mechanical Reproduction" has indubitably been the most influential contribution to the debate surrounding originality and imitation since the dawn of industrialization and concomitant mechanization of knowledge and culture alike. Benjamin argues that mechanically reproduced copies (e.g., photographs of artworks) challenge the original's uniqueness, its "aura" (Benjamin, p. 221). Thus, the original reaches people who are neither art experts nor even, necessarily, aficionados, thereby gaining novel and unforeseen meanings. The more conservative members of the public see the commercialization of art as unpalatable confirmation for rampant commodity fetishism. More liberal consumers, however, are willing to interpret the displacement of the original from its privileged position as a salutary defiance of ossified mores. Yet, as John Berger emphasizes, the dissemination of a famous work into a variety of situations and contexts rendered possible by mechanical reproduction does not automatically represent an emancipatory move insofar as it can actually serve to reinforce that work's special meaning as the putatively unique model behind a profusion of paltry copies, and hence inspire a sense of awe bound to make it the object of a "bogus religiosity" (Berger, p. 23). The positions just outlined are directly relevant to the topic under investigation in this study as alternate ways of addressing the relationship between a parent text and its brood as a complex phenomenon capable of both transgressing and perpetuating traditional value systems.

In the context of poststructuralist philosophy, a major contribution to the debate consists of Jacques Derrida's writings. Derrida maintains that in the history of Western thought, the relationship between original and copy has been conventionally perceived in purely binary oppositional terms, and that the idea of the original, accordingly, has been unquestionably upheld as the privileged value to which the copy is subordinated as a secondary derivative supplement. This hierarchical position, Derrida intimates, is quite spurious insofar as the concept of an original is unthinkable independently of the possibility of the original being copied. In other words, we can only speak of an original if we admit, albeit tangentially, to its liability to imitation or reproduction. At the same time, Derrida is keen to emphasize the inevitable imbrication of any act or process of repetition with some element of difference. There is no such thing as pure repetition, for meaning is never stably self-present but always, in fact, prone to slippage, forever in the process of shifting, erring, taking detours and digressions, folding in and out of itself (Derrida 1978). Deleuze's writings on the inextricability of repetition and difference also deserve attention, in this context. Far from ensuring stability, Deleuze maintains, repetition turns out to constitute "by nature transgression or exception, always revealing a singularity opposed to the particulars subsumed under laws, a universal opposed to the generalities which give rise to laws" (Deleuze 1994, p. 5). Derrida's and Deleuze's arguments could be read as daring attacks on conventional notions of authenticity and inauthenticity, fidelity and infidelity, insofar as, in suggesting that no seemingly repetitive act lacks an element of difference (and hence potential creativity), they implicitly allude to the possibility of something genuinely new emerging from the old — something that is rendered new by its ineradicable difference. The propositions advanced earlier regarding an adaptation's autonomous value as a corollary of its formal and discursive difference — and hence the need to transcend the tiresome preoccupation with the criterion of loyalty to the source endemic in theories of adaptation — finds a direct correlative in Derrida's and Deleuze's contentions.

Jean Baudrillard has further problematized the concept of originality by arguing that in contemporary media-saturated cultures, the simulation of reality has taken over reality itself. The postmodern age is hence marked by the omnipresence of simulacra that have replaced any presumed originals altogether, and therefore operate as ways not of masking reality but of hiding the fact that no reality actually obtains behind the simulacra themselves. "The simulacrum," the philosopher tersely states, "is never that which conceals the truth — it is the truth which conceals that there is none. The simulacrum is true" (Baudrillard, p. 166). It is no longer possible, in this scenario, to peel away the surfaces of representation to arrive at some original reality supposedly underlying (and legitimizing) it because no such thing can be held to exist any more. Addressed in relation to some of the arguments concerning adaptation pursued earlier, Baudrillard's writings would seem to suggest that everything is an adaptation of sorts for the simple reason that it could not possibly be anything else in a culture where both origins and originality have lost their traditional status and, ultimately, any meaning whatsoever.

One of the most intriguing issues posited by anime reliant on adaptation concerns the aesthetic and semiotic specificity of the anime themselves as texts encoded in a very distinctive visual language. In other words, we are enjoined to ponder not simply the general significance of the adaptation process as a journey from page to screen but also, more exactly, on the implications of the specific transposition of written materials to animated graphics imbued with unique codes and conventions. Thus, theoretical perspectives pertaining to the broad area of cinematic adaptation, while relevant to this study, should never be divorced from detailed consideration of more local perspectives with anime as such at their center of vision. Whenever we engage with an anime adaptation, we must ask ourselves what happens to the original when it enters not just the screen in general but the anime screen as a discursive domain of independent caliber. For instance, there would be little mileage in pursuing an investigation of the anime version of *Romeo and Juliet* produced by Studio Gonzo simply as a cinematic adaptation without reflecting on the particular qualities which the drama acquires as a corollary of its transformation into an anime rather than a live-action movie or an animation informed by different criteria and corresponding cultural proclivities. The detailed analyses of the anime here under scrutiny endeavor to address their distinctiveness as anime in accordance with the foregoing observations, striving to elucidate the particular ways in which anime adaptations create their own meanings.

At this stage in the discussion, some general points of a formal and mediatic nature are nonetheless necessary. On the one hand, it is crucial to focus on technical and symbolic codes affecting the screenplay, its narratorial stance and point(s) of view, its pace and rhythm, its handling of the interaction of words and other elements of the soundtrack, its use of repeated imagery and its approach to dramatic irony. On the other hand, it is equally important to attend to the social codes influencing a character's appearance and body language, alongside the ideological codes underpinning a production's impact as more or less conventional, adventurous or downright pioneering. The broad categories just outlined are, in a sense, relevant to any adaptation with a filmic outcome. Turning specifically to anime, more detailed observations are required. It is first of all vital to evaluate the import of anime-specific concepts in relation to broader preferences and trends in Japanese art and aesthetics as a whole. The pivotal ideas here at stake concern the indigenous culture's inveterate belief in the status of virtually any human practice as an art, and concomitant debunking of strict hierarchies subordinating putatively lowly artisanal activities to the ranks of so-called high art. At the same time, the intrinsic materiality of all arts is persistently upheld and this attitude traditionally results in a deeply reverential attitude toward one's materials and tools, regardless of whether one is painting an exquisitely delicate screen, say, or preparing a *bento* (the indigenous lunchbox). A frank admission of artifice, attested to by physical vestiges of the labor entailed by artistic productivity in the product itself, is no less axial an aspect of Japanese culture. Pervading these interconnected ideas is the passionate cultivation of an ethos, as hinted at in the Preface, that audaciously celebrates the coexistence of calm and turmoil as inextricable polarities of human life and cosmic balance at large.

It is no less crucial, in this context, to pay close attention to the specific incidence of anime-specific codes and conventions in four interrelated areas: graphic, compositional, animational and cinematographical. A major factor influencing anime in its handling of the adaptation process lies with the medium's distinctive approach to the task of characterization. Many viewers with even the most superficial knowledge of anime will instantly associate its character designs with somatic traits such as extended limbs, alongside heads, feet, hands and hair of blatantly unrealistic, normally exaggerated, dimensions and proportions. Such features make the characters amenable to the display of high levels of dynamism. Certain recurrent vestimentary motifs are also easily linked with anime (e.g., in the representation of ubiquitous school uniforms, and of futuristic, retrofuturistic or antiquarian costumes). The commitment to realism in fashion design contrasts dialectically with the deliberate avoidance of realism in the rendition of anatomical attributes. Where faces are concerned, oversized glossy eyes, tiny mouths and noses, and preposterously abundant (as well as typically unruly) manes of all imaginable hues are likewise conspicuous among the medium's most familiar traits. What should not be ignored, in appreciating these formulaic representational strategies, is first anime's concomitant use of relatively realistic physiognomies and second its knack of deploying facial characteristics very subtly to convey a wide range of emotions by recourse to often minuscule adjustments to the most diminutive of curves and through the diversified handling of alternately soft and angular shadows.

Overtly stylized emotive icons can also be utilized to communicate economically and wordlessly specific affective states — e.g., bulging veins to signify effort or intensity, sweat drops to express anxiety or fear, and nose bleeds to allude to erotic desire or even perverse thoughts. A similarly formulaic device readily associated with anime as a graphic discourse is the use of "SD" ("Super Deformed") versions of the characters to signal their emotive shift from normal, generally serious, dispositions to infantile, cute or parodic distortions of those basic personality types. Most crucially in the present context, characterization plays a key role in drawing the audience into the anime's adaptive universe, disconcerting though this may initially appear to viewers acquainted with the source materials, by delivering varied galleries of personae that are cogently situated within a specific and well-defined social milieu. This applies to all manner of anime actors independently of their diegetic status or prominence within the overall yarn. Characterization, therefore, is held carefully within the parameters of a particular production, helping the anime assert its aesthetic autonomy from its source. Even when bizarrely elaborate parallel universes display outlandish menageries of creatures, the anime will succeed in accomplishing that task as long as it is capable of intimating that its characters inhabit a fundamentally universal human drama.

In an anime's translation of its source's settings into a distinctive world of its own, backgrounds are of cardinal significance. In virtually all animation, and indeed cinema generally, backgrounds contribute crucially to establishing and maintaining a particular ambience and a palpable *genius loci*. In anime, however, they rise to the ranks of vibrantly animate actors in their own right in the representation of both the natural habitat and architecture. Typically, anime's backgrounds are intricately detailed and most liberal in the adoption of artistic — especially painterly — effects such as watercolor-style washes, crayon-like marks, pigment swathes and gradients. At the same time, they do not merely augment the lifelikeness of the drama's characters by enfolding their personalities and actions in distinctive atmospheres but also draw vigor from them, acquiring novel connotations and traits at every turn in consonance with the actors' shifting emotions. A meticulous approach to product design ensures that settings are consistently populated by correspondingly convincing props and accessories. At the adaptational level, an original's transposition to the anime screen is often individualized precisely by the depiction of objects intended to allude metonymically to entire cultures and lifestyles. Lighting and coloration play a key part in enhancing a background's richness, combining particular orchestrations of the play of light and shadow with appropriate chromatic palettes, modulations and gradations intended to convey distinctive moods and levels of pathos.

One of the most interesting challenges posed by the anime here examined has to do with the responses they elicit from viewers who, if they are familiar with the sources, will have already visualized certain characters and settings through imaginative picturing — a process that is always, inexorably, partial, subjective and influenced by specific cultural, historical and discursive circumstances. In seeing new versions of people we have previously visualized inside our heads leaping, trundling and dancing across a screen in the basic shapes of highly stylized figures set against gorgeously rendered scenery paintings may be experienced by some not merely as an amusing surprise but as a shock. In any case, notwithstanding the variable severity of individual reactions to the anime adaptation at hand, it is undeniable that with each alternative visualization reaching the screen, our pictorial memory will be challenged, jogged or stretched in innumerable and unexpected ways.

In the specifically cinematographical arena, it is from the repeated employment of a range of classic camera operations that anime derives much of its distinctiveness and its adaptations of disparate sources, relatedly, come most memorably to life. Anime abounds, most notably, with strategies meant to evoke the illusion of movement while economizing radically on the number of frames necessary to effect this impression. These include "sliding," where a frame is made to slide across the field of vision; "fairing," where frames are placed and distanced from one another in such a way as to convey the illusion of acceleration or deceleration at the beginning or end of a cut; and, quite famously, "panning," where the camera itself remains stationary but its focus moves from left to right (or vice versa) to capture a series of frames across a horizontal plane. In the "tilt," an analogous procedure is adopted but the focus moves vertically instead. The related operation known as "follow pan" keeps the camera locked onto one single element and follows its motion throughout the cut. With "tracking," conversely, the camera moves with the object being filmed in a side-to-side or forward-backward motion in order to concentrate on minute parts of an image. To express dramatic intensity without recourse to camera motion at all, the "fix" is also consistently utilized. "Fade in/fade out," the gradual appearance or disappearance of an image, the "dissolve," an editing technique in which one shot gently vanishes while another shot materializes in its place, and the "wipe," a procedure whereby one image seems to force the preceding image off the screen, also feature conspicuously in anime. Kinetic vibrance can be tersely achieved by recourse to the "zip pan," a strategy that uses backgrounds consisting of lines rather than of clear images so as to convey the illusion of motion. To preserve a sense of continuity between scenes presented in this fashion and those surrounding them, the basic palettes remain unaltered. In the case of the "image BG" technique, exuberant splashes of disparate colors are employed to evoke a character's affective state or to suggest a shift to an alternate reality level. In this case, overtly clashing palettes are deployed to induce a potent feeling of disorientation. Concurrently, "backlighting" is routinely adopted to create flares, blasts and flashing lights by means of "masks": cells that are painted black except for the areas to be lit, shot separately and then superimposed onto the initial cut.

Anime also resorts persistently to audacious camera angles that depart drastically from the habitual inclination to make the camera's point of view level with the human eye and display an even horizon, and play instead with perplexing perspectives. These are typically engendered by means of extreme "high-angle" and "low-angle" shots capturing actors and locations from above or below respectively; "deep-focus" shots allowing all the planes of a setting to remain in equally sharp focus; and "oblique-angle" shots tilting the camera so as to make straight lines appear as diagonals. A wide variety of interesting lenses abets anime's cinematographical ploys. These include "wide-angle" lenses able to capture wider areas than those afforded by ordinary lenses and thus evoke the impression of exaggerated perspectives, and "zoom" lenses enabling the passage from wide-angle shots to "telephoto" shots in which the lens works like a telescope. "Depth-of-field" effects are especially useful in communicating an overall sense of displacement by capitalizing on shifts of focus between the foreground and background and thus highlighting the features of contrasting portions of a scene. Finally, feelings of uncertainty, fear, anxiety or grief can be effectively conveyed with the assistance of "freeze-frame" shots, where a single frame is reiterated several times on the film strip to give the illusion of motionlessness), while confusion is effectively generated through "jump cuts," brusque transitions from one shot to another.

Viewed as an ensemble, all of the anime adaptations here explored as case studies highlight, with varying degrees of emphasis and intensity, two complementary propositions. On the one hand, they advocate the desirability of a survivalist ethos grounded on the premise that there comes a point when certain forms reach an extreme of their life cycle and, in order to escape total extinction, have no choice but to mutate into other forms, the shapes they may thus assume eluding even the most refined faculties of anticipation or prediction. On the other hand, they convey a message of organic adaptability or adjustment predicated on the idea that no matter what stage in their evolution certain forms have — or have not — reached, they are always in the process of mutating for the simple reason that they can never presume to be univocally and undilutedly *themselves* as sealed self-identical entities uncontaminated by external agencies. This is because any text (verbal, visual, multimedia) implicitly depends for its existence on *other*— real or virtual — texts. As Geraghty puts it, adaptation is essentially a "layering process" entailing "an accretion of deposits over time, a recognition of ghostly presences, and a shadowing or doubling of what is on the surface by what is glimpsed behind" (Geraghty, p. 195). Gérard Genette communicates an analogous message in emphasizing that the realm of literature is fundamentally "palimpsestuous" since "Any text is a hypertext, grafting itself onto a hypotext, an earlier text that it imitates or transforms" (Genette, p. ix). Therefore, a text ultimately *is* by virtue of what it is *not*— in virtue of all the hypothetical texts it could have been instead.

The anime under scrutiny thus remind us that any text we might experience as realized is simply a snapshot of a limitless textual web of crisscrossing images and yarns — a semiotic fragment capturing no more than an ephemeral impression of an otherwise unseizable flow of signs. In alluding to the sheer contingency and transience of all textual formations that have more or less haphazardly been extracted from that unquantifiable universe, the anime suggest that strictly speaking no one text *needs* to be what it is. The art of adaptation corroborates this idea, not only by underscoring a text's ability to become something quite different but also, implicitly, by intimating that what a text is and what it is not but might become are equally tenable ontological realities. Simultaneously, in drawing our attention to the inseparability of a text's actual and realized form from the potential forms it could have acquired or might adaptively acquire instead, the art of adaptation ultimately invites us consider a challenging possibility, which Hutcheon formulates as a disarmingly simple question: "What is *not* an adaptation?" (Hutcheon, p. 170).

Chapter 2

The Nightmare of History
Belladonna of Sadness,
Grave of the Fireflies, and
Like the Clouds, Like the Wind

> *History is a nightmare from which I am trying to awake.*
> — James Joyce

According to Julie Sanders, "The processes of adaptation and appropriation ... are in many respects a sub-section of the ... practice of intertextuality" as an "interleaving of different texts and textual traditions" (Sanders, p. 17). The theoretical study of adaptation brings into play "a wide vocabulary of active terms: version, variation, interpretation, continuation, transformation, imitation, pastiche, parody, forgery, travesty, transposition, revaluation, revision, rewriting, echo." As an ensemble, these terms are all devoted not to the programmatic celebration of "a text's closure to alternatives"—the chief objective of all disciplines pursuing ideals of semiotic self-containedness in the service of ideological stability—but rather to the assertion of the singular text's "ongoing interaction with other texts" (p. 18). There are many ways of adapting a text by casting it in an alternative genre, medium or style, as well as by redefining its boundaries through either capsulation or extension of its basic contents. No less vitally, an adaptation may comment on its original in more or less radical fashions—for instance, "by offering a revised point of view," by introducing an element of "hypothetical motivation" for actions whose causes are left unexplained in the source or by giving a voice to "the silent and marginalized" (p. 19). John Ellis has made an important contribution to adaptation studies in highlighting the gratifying implications of transtextual migration: "Adaptation into another medium becomes a means of prolonging the pleasure of the original presentation, and repeating the production of a memory" (Ellis, pp. 4–5). However, the critic is also keen to place the adaptation in a secondary, indeed parasitical, relation to the source, arguing that its function is ultimately "to efface it with the presence of its own images" (p. 3). Sanders salubriously rectifies this hierarchical approach by stressing that the pleasure of adaptation is actually an open process animated by an inveterate "sense of play," since "the adapting text does not necessarily seek to consume or efface the informing source" but can in fact be instrumental in promoting its "endurance and survival" and hence amenability to further "juxtaposed readings" (Sanders, p. 25).

> The sorceress, who in the end is able to dream Nature and therefore conceive it, incarnates the reinscription of the traces of paganism that triumphant Christianity repressed.... The feminine role, the role of sorceress ... is ambiguous, antiestablishment, and conservative at the same time.... The sorceress heals, against the Church's canon; she performs abortions, favors nonconjugal love, converts the unlivable space of a stifling Christianity.... These roles are conservative because every sorceress ends up being destroyed, and nothing is registered of her but mythical traces.
> — Hélène Cixous and Catherine Clément

The film *Belladonna of Sadness* (dir. Eiichi Yamamoto, 1973) stands out as a veritable paean to intertextuality through its integration of Jules Michelet's *La Sorcière* (1862) — itself a synthesis of cultural history and fiction inspired by the story of Joan of Arc and medieval witchcraft lore — with a plethora of artistic and aesthetic traditions, styles and trends. These include sources as varied as Tarot cards, rowdy illustrations for old tomes on medieval lore, Impressionism, Symbolism, the Pre-Raphaelites, Aubrey Beardsley, Edvard Munch, Gustav Klimt, Edmund Dulac and Arthur Rackham. Beardsley, Munch and Klimt are the film's closest predecessors where the representation of sexuality is specifically concerned. With Beardsley's art, *Belladonna of Sadness* shares a passion for undulating, curling and winding lines as ideal graphic correlatives for the rhythms of passion and desire. Munch's proclivity for images wherein pleasure and torment are often inextricably interdependent also reverberates throughout Yamamoto's film. Concurrently, *Belladonna of Sadness* partakes of Klimt's unique flair for the couching of eros in densely patterned, seemingly enameled and bejeweled surfaces of tactile luster.

No less importantly, the film proclaims its Oriental provenance, despite its profuse allusions to — and adaptations of — Western art and aesthetics, as a reflection of a stylistic sensibility which John Reeve has posited as quintessentially Nipponic. This makes itself felt in "sometimes astonishingly frank" portrayals of "the world of pleasure," allied to an assiduous cultivation of "elegance of line," the use of "strong, flat blocks of colour" and some daring approaches to "perspective and composition" (Reeve, p. 8). In its handling of chroma, *Belladonna of Sadness* specifically recalls the tendency evinced by indigenous woodblock prints to employ hues that "are not necessarily meant to reflect accurately" the palettes found in "the real world" but actually glory in their own deliberately — even flamboyantly — artificial reality. The film, moreover, harks back to that same medium's proverbial preference for extravagant ways of cropping and arranging its diverse visual components and for "strong diagonals" of the kind also adapted in their works by innovative Western painters of the nineteenth century such as Pierre-Auguste Renoir (p. 14). At times, the predilection for stylized lines foregrounded throughout by *Belladonna of Sadness* additionally brings to mind the forms of Noh Theatre.

On the graphic plane, *Belladonna of Sadness* also echoes the works of Junko Mizuno, a popular indigenous artist whose style typically blends juvenile innocence and charm with disturbing hints at horror and monstrosity — hence, its frequent description as "noir *kawaii*" or "Gothic *kawaii*" (i.e., noir or Gothic cute). Bright colors, curvaceous female forms, languorous eyes and flowing manes of the kind also witnessed in Yamamoto's movie abound across Mizuno's works. Moreover, the movie constitutes the sole extant anime adaptation in the *pinku* genre. This designates a cinematic mode pervaded by sexual and occasionally pornographic motifs. Characteristically cultivated by small independent studios, the genre burgeoned from the mid–1960s to the mid–1980s, when *pinku*'s chances of survival were sorely tested by the advent of Adult Video (AV). Yet, it never vanished altogether from the scene, being channeled by some experimentative filmmakers into the visual and symbolic exploration of the societal anomie and uncertainty bred by the reality of post-bubble Japan. In addition, *Belladonna of Sadness* is indebted to numerous musical modes, and particularly the soulful style of 1970s rock opera. This is clearly evinced by the opening segment, where the action focuses on the protagonists' wedding ceremony and the local baron's rape of Jeanne as the payment he exacts when the groom admits to not owning the required marriage tax.

Intensely, indeed viscerally, erotic throughout, *Belladonna of Sadness* does not, however, in any sense deteriorate into unsavory sexploitation thanks not only to its delicate handling of the human tragedy but also, even more crucially, to its sophisticated and strikingly original visuals. The film's refinement unquestionably owes much to the elegant harmonization of illustrator Kuni Fukai's artwork and highly imaginative animation, which appears to emanate from the images themselves, effected by Gisaburo Sugii, the movie's art director. Sugii, incidentally, has also directed the first anime adaptation of the classic eleventh-century novel *The Tale of Genji* as the 1987 movie of that title, where elements of the overall style brought to bear on *Belladonna of Sadness* are still observable. This point will be revisited in Chapter 7.

Belladonna of Sadness is most loyal to classic anime aesthetics in its passion for audacious adaptations of the metamorphosis topos — a motif that is never very far from the hearts of indigenous directors and often finds venerable precedents in the more traditional arts and crafts. The topos is most sensationally articulated with reference to the ubiquitous character of Yamamoto's devil: a protean phallic figure capable of morphing smoothly from a cartoonish imp with a jocular penchant for canine body language, through a succubus redolent of Gothic art at its most nightmarish (e.g., Johann Caspar Füssli), to a full-fledged monster of titanic proportions of Goya-tinged resonance. Morphing into a lowly handkerchief to mop up Jeanne's copious tears is not below him. Yet, as soon as soon as he has a chance of exploiting the opportunity of contact with the young woman's body — innocent as this may at first appear — as an excuse for erotic arousal, he will rapidly seize it with malicious glee. The protagonist's evolving instincts and emotions concurrently occasion some spectacular transformations, which characteristically coincide with the flooding of the screen by overwhelming expanses of color of predominantly sanguine palettes to signify both agony and ecstasy, terror and jouissance. *Belladonna of Sadness* also revels in visual juxtapositions, most pointedly by counterbalancing realistic and childlike graphics and by setting complementary hues against each other for dramatic emphasis — e.g., in the harrowing sequence where the pathos of Jeanne's flight from her persecutors starkly contrasts the green of her robe (supposedly symbolic of her witchy affiliations) and the red of the background.

This chromatic contrast, while working impactfully on the dramatic plane by communicating a vibrant sense of energy and unruly passion, also carries emotive connotations as a sensuously unsettling event. It thus succeeds in conveying with stunning economy the complex affects associated with the character of Jeanne not solely as an individual personality but also as a personification of a primordial mythical archetype. This is a figure meticulously described by Hayao Kawai in his study of the psychological undercurrents of Japanese fairy tales as a recurring presence in indigenous lore, and designated as a "woman who disappears." According to the Jungian scholar, such a character is capable of opposing the cultural propensity to repress or ignore women's status so as to perpetuate time-honored institutions and an attendant conception of order. She does so by deliberately fading away from the scene and leaving in her wake an atmosphere of profound sorrow (*aware*) and bitterness or rancor (*urami*). Such lingering emotions enable her to abide in the memories of the people she leaves behind and hence retain her abeyant power. In the domain of traditional narrative, the disappearing woman "is thought to symbolize the urge to bring something new to Japanese culture." Most importantly, in the context of Yamamoto's movie, the woman who has disappeared can be expected "to come back to this world again with a newly gained strength." Thus, "To pursue the woman who disappears from this world sorrowfully and then comes back again" can be regarded as "a worthwhile and necessary task" (Kawai, p. 25). The disappearing woman's redemptive power is elegantly communicated by Yamamoto in the finale of *Belladonna of Sadness*. First, all of the women in the crowd witnessing the putative witch's execution gradually acquire, one by one, Jeanne's physiognomy, as though to intimate the persecuted woman's undying legacy. Second, the story leaps unexpectedly to the year 1789 and the Capture of the Bastille, rendered by recourse to visuals redolent of Romantic painting, to comment on the momentous role to be played by women in the future through a focus on a crucial upheaval of unique charismatic resonance, the French Revolution. The closing frames, most felicitously, represent Eugène Delacroix's *Liberty Leading the People (La Liberté guidant le peuple)*—a painting executed in order to commemorate the subsequent July Revolution of 1830—and culminate with a close-up of the titular figure of great potency.

The movie thus celebrates the principle of textual openness upheld by Sanders along the lines traced by several of the transmutational options itemized by the critic. Especially relevant to Yamamoto's treatment of his source materials are the phenomena of continuation and transformation as intercomplementary adaptive moves, enabling the director to both perpetuate the legacy of those materials and subject them to radical reorientation. *Belladonna of Sadness* also works as a pastiche in its amalgamation of disparate visual and compositional motifs drawn from numerous cultures and periods, while verging on parody when it deliberately distorts its graphic antecedents for heightened dramatic impact. When allusions are so close to the inspirational matter as to resemble them with uncanny accuracy (as is occasionally and intentionally the case with pictorial reverberations from myriad artists), a discreet concession to the spirit of forgery also comes into play. Most importantly, in its distinctive approach to adaptation, *Belladonna of Sadness* relies on subtle echoing techniques in preference to any other modality as a sustained leading thread. In so doing, it reflects the predilection for allusiveness, in contrast with direct statement, ingrained in Japanese aesthetics for time immemorial.

At the same time, Yamamoto's film corroborates Sanders' contention that adaptation can draw on several strategies in order to reconfigure a given set of source materials. *Belladonna of Sadness* both redefines the boundaries of Michelet's text by displacing its verbal discourse and weaving instead a narrative tapestry in which graphics gain overt precedence over words and still images are repeatedly allowed to replace dynamic action per se. In this fashion, the movie proposes alternate and elliptical ways of engaging with the sorts of philosophical and ideological speculations brought into relief by Michelet that are firmly anchored in visual language as an autonomous universe. This entails the adoption of a peculiar, adaptation-specific point of view. An element of hypothetical motivation also contributes vitally to the approach to the parent text evinced by *Belladonna of Sadness*. This is tastefully inserted into the yarn in the primary guise of a desire for form, whereby the film could be said to offer an adaptation not only of Michelet's work but also of the creative process through which anime comes into being. Some of the more poignant sequences indeed consist of chains of fluid frames that incrementally record the transition from single monochromatic lines or stylized vignettes — akin to preliminary sketches or snippets of storyboards — to multidimensional and polychromatic composites of palpable richness closer to the finished product.

The onscreen development of the graphics in the direction of frames of increasing complexity obliquely emplaces in the role of unrivaled protagonist an unnamed experimental animator — a conceptual agency abstractly synthesizing the individual skills and visions of each member of the actual animation team. Moreover, Yamamoto's unscrolling visuals also function rhetorically as graphic allegories for the gradual evolution of the protagonist's own emotions and drives as an accretional process of escalating complexity and intensity. The shards of chroma, chopped lines and scrambled planes into which the screen often erupts echo metaphorically the emergence of inchoate affects which Jeanne can initially sense only in a haphazard and fragmentary fashion and must slowly conjoin into a recognizable, though illicit, identity. The tatters of color and mass assiduously foregrounded by Yamamoto's visuals hence come to symbolize the multifaceted and discordant nature of the heroine's intrinsic selfhood.

The adaptive ploys outlined above enable *Belladonna of Sadness* to enthrone with unique enthusiasm the genius of adaptation as potentially interminable play. The film, moreover, partakes of a "mode of appropriation that uses as its raw material ... the 'real' matter of facts" in the shape of actual "historical events and personalities" (Sanders, p. 139). Michelet's own parent text uses the history of witchcraft and the gruesome record of persecution embedded therein not solely out of a genuine interest in those cultural issues in relation to their times and places but also to encourage in the reader's imagination a comparison with broader manifestations of political oppression in his or her own era. Michelet outlines the authorial intentions underpinning his text as follows: "The object of my book was purely to give, not a history of Sorcery, but a simple and impressive formula of the Sorceress's way of life, which my learned predecessors darken by the very elaboration of their scientific methods and the excess of detail. My strong point is to start, not from the devil, from an empty conception, but from a living reality, the Sorceress, a warm, breathing reality, rich in results and possibilities" (Michelet, p. 326). The aim of this exploration is a frank and humane depiction of witchcraft as a popular movement intent on opposing the twin tyranny of the feudal State and the Church by means of a secret doctrine fueled by disparate elements of paganism and fairy lore. Michelet endeavors to evoke a powerful sense of the Middle Ages as an epoch of ferocious intolerance and persecution, yet also of darkly ecstatic hedonism, haunted no less ominously by feudal lords than by warlocks, demons and hobgoblins and capable of seamlessly combining unendurable squalor and luxury, anchoritic asceticism and unbridled orgiastic pleasure. Georges Bataille has devoted a section of his book *La Litterature Et Le Mal* (*Literature And Evil*, 1957) to *La Sorcière*. A series of essays also featuring discussions of Emily Brontë, Charles Baudelaire, William Blake, the Marquis de Sade, Marcel Proust, Franz Kafka and Jean Genet, the book proposes that Michelet was so passionate in his peroration of the witch's human rights and artistry as to sometimes appear veritably possessed by the topic in hand.

As Valter comments, Bataille indeed "posits that, in writing the book, Michelet was 'guided by the ecstasy of Evil'" (Valter). This intriguing contention elliptically reinforces the myth of witchcraft's infectious effect — a power associated with the broader concept of "Contagious Magic" as formulated by James George Frazer: namely, the principle from which the magical practitioner "infers that whatever he does to a material object will affect equally the person with whom the object was once in contact, whether it formed part of his body or not" (Frazer). This idea is concomitantly relevant to both sorcerous pursuits in general and the society portrayed by Michelet in particular due to its association with sacrificial rituals — a practice notoriously linked with medieval witches and obliquely dramatized by Yamamoto's film in the sequences focusing on Jeanne's influence on the people seeking her counsel and aid. Indeed, sacrifice also works in accordance with the belief system designated by Frazer as the "Law of Contact or Contagion" to the extent that it brings separate entities intimately together by a radical dismantling of individual boundaries. As Henri Hubert and Marcel Mauss emphasize, "This procedure consists in establishing a means of communication between the sacred and the profane worlds through the mediation of a victim, that is, of a thing that in the course of the ceremony is destroyed" (Hubert and Mauss, p. 97).

Yamamoto is heir to the ethical agenda pursued by Michelet and thus endeavors to articulate a cinematic event of far-reaching significance, capable of engaging in a metaphorical vein with serious reflections on contemporary formations of power — not only political in the obvious sense of the term but also political in the aesthetic sense as context-bound orchestrations of specific regimes of visuality and signification. In cultivating this cross-historical dialectics, both Michelet and Yamamoto seek to retrieve lost and occluded viewpoints that have been persistently (and conveniently) relegated to the periphery of history by imparting their promulgators with new, unsettling agencies. However, neither Michelet nor Yamamoto situate their characters as self-assertive presences explicitly parading their historical importance from the center of the text. In fact, they are eager to remind us of those people's still marginal standing in officially sanctioned versions of facts by reimagining history enough to infuse it with fresh voices, yet also emphasizing that those voices go on inhabiting interstitial or liminal pockets of the textual universe. In *Belladonna of Sadness*, this idea is most tersely communicated through the graphics themselves by means of allusions to the protagonist's physical imbrication with her natural surroundings and their protean energies. There are indeed many bewitching moments in the film when the heroine and the creatures and objects around her appear to merge in fluid mutual suffusion. It should also be noted, on this point, that although Jeanne's violation is horribly traumatizing, it also carries epiphanic connotations insofar as it is instrumental in the character's awakening not only to her dormant carnal longings but also to her true nature — thus far occluded by an enforced veneer of languid submissiveness — as an imaginative, free-willing, rebelliously resourceful and inquisitive soul.

Another anime adaptation with a venerable source at its root likewise helmed by Yamamoto is the movie *One Thousand and One Arabian Nights* (1969). Far more cartoonish than *Belladonna of Sadness*— and, at times, almost self-indulgently bizarre — this film nonetheless shares with the later work a passion for hedonistically sensuous construction. In the case of *One Thousand and One Arabian Nights,* this preference is principally evoked by the synthesis of sexual imagery of a modern stamp with time-honored forms such as Japanese scroll painting and Persian rug design. The movie drastically reimagines Scheherazade's tale-spinning venture by chronicling a 1960s salary man's escapist journey through a fantasy world replete with more or less explicit and accurate allusions to the *Arabian Nights*' original universe. Technically, the film abides in memory by virtue of its exuberantly experimental thrust, especially notable in the dexterous incorporation of live-action footage into the animated sequences, psychedelic light and color effects and astoundingly diversified morphs.

> *What is life? It is the flash of a firefly in the night. It is the breath of a buffalo in the wintertime. It is the little shadow which runs across the grass and loses itself in the sunset.*
> *— Crowfoot.*

2. The Nightmare of History

Complementing *Belladonna of Sadness* in its integration of diverse source materials, Isao Takahata's epoch-making movie *Grave of the Fireflies* (1988) offers further corroboration for Sanders' argument regarding adaptation's flair for an intertextual appropriation of multiple — and, by and large, previously neglected — voices in order to provide alternative perspectives on accepted versions of history. It does so by means of a twofold reimagining of recorded facts based on the adaptation of two very different source texts. One of these is Nosaka Akiyuki's semi-autobiographical wartime novel of the same title (*Hotaru no Haka* in the original), published in 1967 and chronicling a tragic ordeal which Takahata's film follows with overall fidelity. This source allows Takahata to focus on recent history with reference to a modern text and simultaneously pursue an educational agenda. It is worth mentioning, in passing, that another anime with a supposedly educational slant, resorting to adaptation to engage in reflection on historical and cultural realities, is *Animated Classics of Japanese Literature* (dir. Fumio Kurokawa, 1986): a TV series consisting of a collection of vignettes inspired with varying degrees of directness by famous indigenous stories.

The other source invoked by Takahata alongside Akiyuki's novel — which the writer himself claims to have deliberately echoed in his narrative — is the tradition of the double-suicide drama immortalized by Chikamatsu Monzaemon (1653–1725) in the guise of *bunraku* performances (puppet plays) revolving around the clash between societal duty (*giri*) and private sentiment (*ninjou*). The classic behind *Grave of the Fireflies* is principally Monzaemon's *The Love Suicides at Sonezaki* (1703). By recourse to this second source, Takahata is able to take a more extensive, even panoramic, approach to historical vicissitudes. With its twin adaptive constitution, *Grave of the Fireflies* follows its child protagonists, the teenage boy Seita and his younger sister Setsuko, as they struggle for survival in a world torn apart by unspeakable horrors. Deprived of both their mother and their home by a catastrophic air raid inflicted on their native city of Kobe, and further abused by a rapacious aunt entrusted with their care who is solely concerned with exploiting their services and appropriating their few remaining possessions, the two kids make an escapist attempt to find refuge in an abandoned hillside bomb shelter amid deceptively idyllic rural bliss and firefly-lit nights, only to find that the hellish reality of their times cannot be eluded and starvation is their ineluctable fate. Seita and Setsuko are no more capable of defying the intractable horrors of history than they are of fending for themselves in a world devoid of resources even for the pluckiest of adults. Seita resists this reality through an almost self-destructive cultivation of false consciousness — well-meant but ultimately pointless as all forms of misrecognition mockingly turn out to be even at the best of times, let alone in circumstances as inimical as those dramatized by

Takahata's harrowing movie. This is borne out by the vanity of Seita's effort to protect Setsuko not only from physical deprivation but also, no less poignantly, from the knowledge of their mother's death: a knowledge he believes to have safely kept from the little kid when she has, in fact, possessed and stoically negotiated it in silence all along.

It is its quintessentially tragic aura of inevitability that eventually renders even strong evaluative phrases like "graphically powerful" or "viscerally disquieting" not inaccurate descriptors per se but, quite simply, risible understatements. Indeed, *Grave of the Fireflies* does not merely *represent* grief: it consummately *incarnates* it as the sheer essence of Takahata's adaptive world — an undilutely brutal reality undisposed to translation into disembodied signifiers and eager instead to let matter speak for itself in all its troubling density. The film pithily conveys this idea right from the start, refusing to give the audience any hopeful grounds upon which the expectation of a happy ending could plausibly be erected. The opening sequence indeed portrays Seita in a state of subhuman misery, not only filthy and undernourished but also ostensibly devoid of the will to continue hanging onto the feeble thread to which his survival has been attenuated.

By a darkly ironic twist of fate, it so happens that Japan has by now surrendered. The boy's slumped form as he dies on the floor of a train station metonymically encapsulates the crushed identity of his whole nation. The film implies throughout its diegesis the close interrelatedness of the personal and the collective — so much so, according to reviewer Marc, that "this movie could be seen as a metaphor for the entire country of Japan during the war: fighting a losing battle, yet too stubbornly proud to admit defeat or accept help" (Marc). Simultaneously, the film refrains from the communication of simplistic, binary oppositional ideological messages. The Americans, for one thing, are merely referred to as "the enemy." The felicitous outcome of this stance, as Jamie Gillies emphasizes, is that the anime's "anti-war message is not overstated. There is no real mention of the fire-bombings in a political way, only in the grief experienced by the civilian Japanese people. Takahata has created an anti-war epic without resorting to finger pointing, a remarkable achievement. He accepts the consequences of the Second World War and is only showing the forgotten souls of the war, the innocents who are caught in the crossfire of destruction" (Gillies).

Seita and Setsuko are not lovers in a literal sense, in the way Monzaemon's protagonists typically are. Nor does Takahata in any way pander to gratuitously incestuous imagery or symbolism. Nevertheless, the two children's emotional proximity and the physical intimacy in which circumstances compel them to live sometimes make their relationship akin to that of erotically attached partners. The suicide topos, for its part, is brought into play by

Seita's determination to take his and his sister's fate solely into his hands — thereby refusing to help his compatriots with the war effort — even though, as hinted at earlier, it ought to be obvious that the only logical outcome of this course of action is a painful death. This motif is symbolically reinforced by the nature of the disused shelter which the protagonists elect as their fantasy home. As Dennis H. Fukushima, Jr. notes, "The term used in the dialogue to describe the hillside bomb shelters is *yokoana*, which means 'cave' 'cavern,' or 'tunnel' (literally, 'side hole'). The term is also used, however, to describe tombs which date back to ancient Japanese times.... Seita and Setsuko move into a *yokoana* both beginning a new life together and heading further towards their own death. The *yokoana* literally becomes a tomb, albeit temporary, for both their mother's ashes and for Setsuko herself" (Fukushima). There are clear indications that Takahata wished to impart an ethical lesson by drawing attention to Seita's immaturely hubristic attitude, even as he aimed to invite sympathy with his and his sibling's plight, by frankly exposing the somewhat pig-headed obstinacy with which the boy insists on doing things his own way. The boy's arrogant pride was an aspect of the drama which Akiyuki himself intended to expose in the original novel, partly to expurgate a personal sense of guilt issuing from a troubling awareness of his marginal responsibility in the death of his own sister as a result of blind arrogance.

According to Akiyuki, *Grave of the Fireflies* functions as "a double-suicide [*shinjuu*] story" in a structural, if not in an overtly thematic, fashion insofar as "the days leading up to their [the protagonists'] death are like the development of a love story," and the establishment of a sealed realm that exists "just for the two of them" is intended to give rise to something of a private "heaven." Takahata has confirmed the idea that his source text carries the distinctive stamp of a double-suicide drama but has also emphasized that what drew him most strongly to Akiyuki's narrative was precisely the concept of that evanescent "heaven," and that this was the aspect of the parent work which he strove to evoke most affectingly ("Interview with Nosaka Akiyuki and Isao Takahata"). The children's tragedy is compounded by the relative lack of information they suffer due to their almost total social isolation. Thus, they are not fully aware of the authentic gravity of the situation into which their country has plummeted. Nor can they grasp, therefore, the meaning of their neighbors' uncooperativeness and unfriendliness over the issue of food provision. By the time Seita has become better informed about the true dimensions of the crisis, and learnt the full import not only of Japan's but also of his fighting father's destiny, it is simply too late. All he can now do is to prolong ephemerally Setsuko's doomed childhood by protecting her innocence and by encouraging her lingering playfulness to the dire end.

What is most trenchantly unforgettable about Takahata's adaptation of two popular literary texts to the anime screen is his utilization of the source materials as inspiration boldly to redefine his own medium. Indeed, *Grave of the Fireflies* is by no stretch of the imagination a *typical* animated movie. Its gritty atmosphere and agonizingly cutting drama often recall, in fact, live-action Neo-Realist cinema — and particularly the works of Vittorio de Sica and Roberto Rossellini. Roger Ebert highlights this proposition, concurrently arguing that while one would not automatically "think of this as an anime subject," if *Grave of the Fireflies* had been a live-action movie, it would feasibly have been "bogged down in realism" and the final product would not, therefore, have been as "pure" and "abstract" as it actually is. The "*idea* of a little girl who's starving" was the director's chief preoccupation (Ebert): hence, the use of a flesh-and-bone child performer would have grounded it in ways that would have precluded the conceptual import of the image from shining through as effulgently as it does. Stylization, it is here implied, is Takahata's guiding principle on both the aesthetic and the ethical planes, as well as a way of eliciting powerful responses not by reflecting reality in a slavishly mimetic manner but by refining and sublimating its brute matter. Furthermore, as Gillies comments, the movie's animated status enables it to capitalize on an element of dramatic irony that could not have been derived from live-action cinema: "*Grave of the Fireflies* is one of the most painful and affecting movies you're ever likely to see, animated or otherwise.In many cases, the fact that it is animated gives simple actions and scenes a beauty and innocence that would not have existed otherwise, creating all the more contrast with the harsh and painful realities experienced by the characters" (Gillies).

The effectiveness of Takahata's method in communicating his vision is memorably attested to by the wordless montage of snapshot recollections of Setsuko flashing through Seita's brain after her departure. It is further corroborated by the recurrent sequences in which the protagonists are depicted as spectral presences beyond space and time, dexterously intercut with the main story so as to disrupt linearity and create pauses for reflection. These are emblematically singled out by the adoption of eerie lighting and coloration, suggestive of an unearthly blend of destructive napalm-fed fire and incongruously bucolic firefly glow.

An analogously unearthly mood is repeatedly conveyed by the scenes focusing on the splendidly resilient powers of nature in the face of human lunacy and destructiveness. This message is silently articulated through ever-changing prismatic skies and majestically serene seas, pastorally tranquil meadows and glistening ponds. These rival with blustering starkness the pictures of maggot-infested corpses, mutilated survivors, ash-bloated air and black rain, accompanying what have come to notoriety as some of the most devastating military operations in history.

2. The Nightmare of History 31

Dare to be naive.
— Richard Buckminster Fuller.

Like the Clouds, Like the Wind (movie; Hisayuki Toriyumi, 1990) is based on a popular novel by Ken'ichi Sakemi published in 1989, originally titled *Koukyou Monogatari* and commonly known in Anglophone circles as *Inner Palace Harem Story*. Involving as a major creative agent the late Katsuya Kondou of Studio Ghibli fame in the capacities of animation director and character designer, *Like the Clouds, Like the Wind* often brings to mind both tonally and stylistically that company's distinctive cachet even though the film was actually produced for television by Studio Pierrot. So strong is the Ghibliesque flavor of the animation as to have caused *Like the Clouds, Like the Wind* often to be mistaken for a Hayao Miyazaki work. Kondou, it should be noted, also collaborated with Sakemi on a two-volume manga retelling of the Joan of Arc story, *D'arc: Histoire de Jeanne D'arc* (1995–1996), here particularly worthy of citation because of the tangential connection with *Belladonna of Sadness*.

Set in ancient China, the story opens with the death of the seventeenth Sokan Emperor in the year 1607. As his son prepares to ascend the throne, one of the chief tasks incumbent upon his retinue is to find appropriate candidates for prospective membership to the young ruler's harem, in the knowledge that the top candidate will become Empress and hence be second only to the Emperor himself in the country's intricate and densely stratified hierarchy. Hordes of pretty girls flock to the Forbidden City in the hope of attaining to that most enviable status and among them is the film's heroine, Ginga. A tough and disarmingly frank country girl drawn to the challenge solely by the prospect of regular meals and leisure, Ginga embarks on her testing, training and schooling with no inkling of the tangle of political tensions tearing the country apart (including a fierce peasant rebellion), of suspicions regarding the actual causes of the late Emperor's demise, of lurking dissatisfaction about the heir's abilities and intentions or of the Machiavellian machinations poisoning every nook and corner of the court — let alone of the momentous role she will soon be playing in their detection and unraveling. While the protagonist's quotidian routine as she adjusts to palace customs is increasingly upset by politically motivated incidents and crimes, the crisis escalates and it rapidly becomes obvious that it is up to Ginga to make the decisive move in the fatal game of Chinese politics — a game as mind boggling and multi-layered as Chinese boxes proverbially are. In this respect, *Like the Clouds, Like the Wind* accurately captures the essence of actual Chinese history — and indeed history at large — as a bundle of forever unfinished business and forever rescindable outcomes. The finale pithily encapsulates this proposition by providing an intentionally brusque and open-ended resolution to both Ginga's personal bildungsroman and the sprawling saga of political subterfuge and belligerence.

One of the aspects of Sakemi's novel to which *Like the Clouds, Like the Wind* is most faithful — yet also imaginatively reconfigures to suit the requirements of its medium — consists of its characterization of the heroine. This resolutely eschews facile concessions to the *kawaii* mode of the kind so often seen in conventional *shoujo* anime, seeking instead to highlight Ginga's psychological and emotional ambiguity. Therefore, though unremittingly honest, shrewd and unsentimental, the girl is also portrayed, on the less positive side, as materialistic and indolent. Yet, it is Ginga's unorthodox heroism that ultimately guarantees not only the film's engrossingly entertaining action but also the gravity of the moral message discreetly delivered by its human drama. The heroine often comes across, if evaluated with reference to local aristocratic etiquette, as downright insolent, unfeminine or ill-mannered in both her iconoclastically relaxed body language and her habit of puncturing ceremonial silence with noisy ejaculations and impertinent remarks. It is incontrovertibly indicated, however, that Ginga is not simply intent on the breaking of rules as an end in itself — she is not, in other words, a stereotypically rebellious teenager hell-bent on solipsistic insouciance. In fact, the girl quizzes the status quo out of a genuine and mature mistrust of unexamined ideological assumptions and attendants codes of conduct. As a result, even though her behavior is at first met with dismay or abhorrence by the establishment's stuffily encultured guardians, it gradually begins to function as a salutary eye-opener for virtually everybody with whom Ginga comes into contact within the Forbidden City and its environs.

Little by little, many of the conventional people she meets recognize that Ginga's inquisitive attitude carries a unique power. At times, one can actually hear, metaphorically speaking, the rusty cogs and wheels of independent reasoning returning to life in their regimented heads as those characters are enjoined by the protagonist's insistent questioning to ask themselves questions that have been left unposed for far too long. Ginga's initial interaction with her dorm mates, other candidates in the imperial race, shows that she is only regarded as an object of contempt or a trigger of frustrated aggravation. However, as the girls gradually realize that the heroine operates in accordance with an ethical system of her own, conducive to selfless and ingenious action, they have no choice but to respect and admire her unique courage and spunk — and indeed jump into the fray to abet her efforts. It should also be noted, on this point, that like Ginga herself, the supporting female actors transcend established anime categories. Hence, even when they appear to conform to one-dimensional types such as the vain belle, the blue-eyed dreamer, the martial artist (*et al.*), they are engagingly individualized and could easily be imagined as fully rounded protagonists of autonomous narratives parallel to Ginga's own tale.

Like both *Belladonna of Sadness* and *Grave of the Fireflies*, *Like the Clouds, Like the Wind* foregrounds the intertextual potentialities of adaptation as an art *sui generis* by synthesizing disparate discursive matrices within its fabric. As anticipated, these include historiography, action adventure and psychological drama as primary contributors to the cumulative process of semiosis. At the same time, the film's textual web relies to a considerable degree on artistic flourishes of cross-mediatic and transtemporal significance. It is especially noteworthy, in this respect, that from a stylistic point of view, one of the most distinctive attributes exhibited by *Like the Clouds, Like the Wind* lies with the utilization of characters that look unequivocally Chinese. Relatedly, if *Like the Clouds, Like the Wind* constitutes an imaginative adaptation of the novel at its root, it also stands out — more captivatingly and with even greater originality — as an inspired adaptation of a particular chapter in Chinese art history chronologically coincident with the last part of the Ming Dynasty. The lay-out of the imperial palace and its ceremonial, administrative and residential quarters, in particular, faithfully reflects the design for the Forbidden City conceived by the Ming Dynasty in the fifteenth century.

The anime's imbrication with Chinese art history is attested to by numerous facets of its representational repertoire. The handling of space, in particular, is typically Chinese in its ability to convey an illusion of great distance and height in a limited format. This is borne out by the treatment of both architecture — from ominous war-torn ruins to resplendent palaces graced by enticing water fixtures and bustling city streets — and nature — especially its huge expanses of sapphire skies, rocky mountains and paddy fields. The anime also evinces a heightened sensitivity to the living qualities of all manner of hues and textures — a tendency shared by Chinese and Japanese art over the centuries — as well as profound deference to the evocative powers of disparate media, such as ink and watercolor. At the same time, it capitalizes to unique effect on the integration into its mise-en-scène of indigenous paintings and screens, patterns and decorative details. Also profuse are the meticulously executed elements of interior design, such as thrones, caskets, four-poster alcoves, candle-stands, draperies, glazen earthenware, myriad vessels, jars and vases, lacquer work and carved stone, and accessories such as jewels, fans and pipes. No less pivotal to the anime's aesthetic is the depiction of detailed costumes of dramatically resonant historical accuracy. The adventure's Chinese feel is additionally enhanced by the use of a soundtrack that incorporates traditional indigenous instruments, including clanging cymbals and mournful flutes.

Like the Clouds, Like the Wind is one of many anime adaptations with prose fiction as their substratum. A sensationally successful instance of novel-to-screen adaptation in recent anime history — not least due to the plethora of ancillary merchandise and adaptive spin-offs accompanying the original show — is *The Melancholy of Haruhi Suzumiya* (TV series; dir. Tatsuya Ishihara, 2006). Like Toriyumi's movie, this anime enlists the art of adaptation to the dramatization of a vibrant plot revolving around a spunky heroine inhabiting a parallel universe that comes across as both outlandishly fantastic and strangely akin to our own familiar reality. Whereas in the case of *Like the Clouds, Like the Wind* this alternative dimension carries pointedly antiquarian overtones, in that of *The Melancholy of Haruhi Suzumiya*, it is informed by a futuristic discourse woven from the development of ground-breaking scientific theories in the actual disciplines of physics and cosmology. The *Haruhi Suzumiya* series of Japanese light novels, the first of which was published in 2003, is an ongoing venture enlisting the talents of author Nagaru Tanigawa and illustrator Noizi Ito. The situation posited in *The Melancholy of Haruhi Suzumiya* contrasts nicely with the premise whence *Like the Clouds, Like the Wind* develops. Indeed, whereas Ginga initially desires nothing more than a quiet life but soon finds herself embroiled in a web of deadly intrigue, Haruhi, conversely, is defined primarily by a pathological longing for the extraordinary.

An attractive and energetic teenager inveterately disgusted with normality and hence determined to detect mysteries and anomalies in every chink and crevice, Haruhi establishes a school club — the "SOS Brigade" ("Spreading Excitement All Over the World with the Haruhi Suzumiya Brigade") — devoted to the espial of aliens, time travelers, espers and all sorts of related paranormal activities, thereby throwing her companions into a flurry of vertiginous exploits. The anime's pointedly futuristic dimension is gradually disclosed (revelation being procrastinated and obscured by the show's deliberate airing in achronic sequence) as the protagonist turns out to be a unique life force of cosmic proportions endowed with baleful potentialities, holding a pivotal part in the fabric and equilibrium of the comsos as a sprawling ocean of data. It is concurrently unveiled that the girl must be kept oblivious to her true nature if she is to be prevented from unleashing her full power. Haruhi's supposed melancholy turns out to be the prime enemy in this potentially deadly game: were the protagonist to descend into a state of depression or tedium, her mood could easily be conducive to universal annihilation — or, at least, radical transformation — by some random concatenation of energies redolent of the "butterfly effect" proposed by chaos theory. As noted, the heroine of *Like the Clouds, Like the Wind* incrementally evinces intellectual and strategic abilities that far exceed those of ordinary people. Haruhi's personality exhibits comparably exceptional connotations, here transposed to the science fictional plane, to the extent that she is putatively capable of summoning into existence any form or occurrence she might happen to fantasize about.

Other anime adaptations with novelistic credentials here worthy of notice are *The Hakkenden* (OVA series; dirs. Takashi Anno and Yuki Okamoto, 1990– 1991 [Part 1]; 1993–1995 [Part 2: *Shinsho*]) and *The Dagger of Kamui* (movie; dir. Rintaro, 1985). These shows manifestly share the attraction to the virtually inexhaustible potentialities of fictionalized historiography evinced by Toriyumi's 1990 production. The two-part OVA series *The Hakkenden* is based on the epic novel *Nansou Satomi*, penned by Kyokutei Bakin over almost three decades and published between 1814 and 1842 in no less than 106 volumes. *The Hakkenden* relies on its unique constitution as a technically adventurous blend of disparate visual and animational styles to proclaim most exuberantly its aesthetic autonomy despite its obviously adaptive standing. No less importantly, the OVA uses its distinctive medium to interrogate time-honored ethical concepts which, though still firmly enshrined in Bakin's society, might mean precious little to a contemporary audience — e.g., principles of feudal reverence, loyalty and group affiliation — while also imparting a modern twist on ancient Confucian teachings. Thus, technical and tonal originality go hand in hand in announcing the anime's self-contained caliber as both an artwork and an ideologically alert narrative. Its protagonists are eight warriors, known as the "Eight Dogs" due to the canine nature of their possessed spiritual father, who are brought together by a twin quest: finding one another and hence joining forces to combat a formidable demonic power.

Based on a novel series by Tetsu Yano, the film *The Dagger of Kamui* chronicles the life of a foundling named Jiro in the final years of the Tokugawa Shogunate (a phase of Japanese history extending from 1603 to 1868). *The Dagger of Kamui* parallels *Like the Clouds, Like the Wind* in depicting a world riven by conspiracies and bloody feuds. In this instance, a key role in the game is played by powerful ninja clans deploying their unique martial and mystic arts to fulfill their own private ambitions. Jiro is taken in by one such organization when his foster mother and her daughter are found murdered and, unjustly accused of having perpetrated the horrid crime, he leaves his village and ventures out into the big world in the sole company of the titular weapon. Once Jiro discovers the clan's true nature as a bunch of power-hungry assassins eager to take over the country in its entirety, he does not hesitate to flee once again into the unknown — now the object of the vengeful ninjas' persecution and sustained only by the possession of his dagger and by a legend surrounding the mountain of Kamui, with which his family history is supposedly connected. Stylistically, Rintaro's movie is graced throughout by fluid animation, fetchingly stylized character designs, opulent backgrounds, elegant handling of even the goriest martial sequences, intermingling of realistic action and illusions endowed with a mesmerizingly magical flavor, and full-scale epic momentum of veritable samurai gradeur. The anime also shares not only with *Like the Clouds, Like the Wind* but also with *The Hakkenden* a penchant for asserting its artistic autonomy despite its adaptive status by means of a dispassionate ethical message. This maturely assesses both the interaction and the conflict between personal aspirations, on the one hand, and national agendas on the other. In so doing, it reveals equal degrees of sensitivity to the vagaries of individual emotions and to communal notions of respect and honor.

A deliberate promotion of temporal ambiguity sustains all three of the main titles discussed in this chapter while also playing an important part in its ancillary illustrations. This is primarily borne out by the interpenetration within their respective diegetic orchestrations of past and present, on the one hand, and of the protagonists' identities and their habitats on the other. History is thereby presented as a daring encounter of fact and fiction — the French word *histoire*, in signifying at once "history" and "story," succinctly encapsulates this mission, as does the Italian "*storia*." In drawing on a broad range of visual sources, both implicitly and overtly, the three movies fully substantiate Sanders' proposition that appropriation manifestly stretches well beyond the adoption of written texts thanks to its assimilation of "companion art forms" (Sanders, p. 148). This strategy bears witness to a radical departure from "the idea of authorial originality" in favor of "a more collaborative and societal understanding of the production of art and the production of meaning" (p. 149). The perspective defined by Sanders is of immense relevance to the specific nature of anime as an art form insofar as the production of anime at practically all levels of the industry is distinguished by a marked preference for collaboration and teamwork over and above the promotion of individual talent. This principle applies to even the wealthiest and seemingly most auteur-centered of studios. With *Belladonna of Sadness*, *Grave of the Fireflies* and *Like the Clouds, Like the Wind*, it is impossible to dissever the anime's uniqueness from the cooperative effort channeled into them not solely by directors, illustrators, character designers and animation directors but also by the many more marginal members of their production crews. In flaunting with stunning experimental verve and inventiveness the status of adaptive anime as a cultural, ideological and artistic agency in its own right, the three films emphasize that no textual object is ever unequivocally monolithic. Rather, it is a matrix of potentialities, which may come to fruition only through plural and multi-branching textual permutations, interactions and interweavings. Extending

Jacques Derrida's comments on "the desire to write" to the desire to create at large, the three films here examined suggest that this amounts to a yearning "to launch things that come back to you as much as possible in as many forms as possible" (Derrida 1985, pp. 157–158). *Belladonna of Sadness, Grave of the Fireflies* and *Like the Clouds, Like the Wind* are ultimately about the pleasure of relentless launching.

Chapter 3

Epic Adventure with a Sci-Fi Twist
Gankutsuou: The Count of Monte Cristo

> *My solitude has ceased to be solitude.*
> *I am surrounded by the goddesses of revenge.*
>
> *The bitter fruits of betrayal must be plucked from the tree.*
> — Count of Monte Cristo, *Gankutsuou: The Count of Monte Cristo*

In its handling of the journey of a hugely popular nineteenth-century novel to the TV screen, Mahiro Maeda's series *Gankutsuou: The Count of Monte Cristo* (2004–2005) — where "*Gankutsuou*" can translate as "King of the Cavern" — promulgates the idea that in a satisfying adaptive process, the source text and its offspring should illuminate each other. It accomplishes this feat by showing persistently that a filmic adaptation can help us grasp a book more comprehensively or from a greater number of alternate angles, while the book, in turn, can help us assess more insightfully the adaptation's thematic and aesthetic import. Therefore, the two works benefit exponentially from parallel exploration of their respective semiotic webs — a critical venture that ultimately enhances not only our understanding of the two works as distinct entities but also of a third party: the hypothetical third text, as it were, brought into being by their dynamic interplay. If one considers, in addition, the long list of adaptations spawned over the years by the original novel, it also becomes possible — indeed pertinent — to address the intertextual dialogue between the nineteenth-century narrative and the anime with a focus on its potential impact on other previous adaptations. In other words, *Gankutsuou* could be said to redefine not only its parent text per se but also our perspective on other adaptations of that work that have preceded Maeda's own transmutational acts. Being set in a speculative time zone with a peculiar connection to the past, the anime concurrently encourages us to reflect on the historical reality alluded to by the source novel and on its future interpretations by disparate generations of both readers and adaptive agencies.

The anime draws on a major building block in the opus of one of the most prolific and popular storytellers of all times, Alexandre Dumas *père* (full name: Alexandre Dumas Davy de la Pailleterie): *The Count of Monte Cristo* (1845–1846). Proverbially associated with acrobatic swordfights and gravity-defying escapes, staged amid lavish settings and regaled with gorgeous costumes, Dumas' books are partly reflections of the author's own adventurous, indeed often reckless, lifestyle and appetite for challenging experiences, unrelentingly fed by the lure of the outlandish and punctuated by self-dramatizing flourishes so brazen as to verge on the suicidal. Drawn to revolutionary politics and, in this respect as in many others, very much a man of his times, Dumas had a firm grounding in historical circumstances of great momentum. Thus, his characters' exploits frequently revolve around actual historical events and personages: *The Three Musketeers* (1844), for example, alludes to occurrences involving King Louis XIII, Cardinal Richelieu and other famous names in seventeenth-century France. *The Count of Monte Cristo*, for its part, strikes its roots in the Napoleonic era, specifically in its dramatization of a story of iniquitous punishment and ruthless vengeance. Yet, Dumas would never lose sight of the immense potentialities inherent in fantasy and storytelling alone to which no historical record, however partial or fictionalized, could presume to aspire. In his concurrent espousal of down-to-earth political realities and the timeless realm of the imagination, the author could be said to incarnate the Romantic spirit at its boldest.

Dumas' novel comments on an especially turbulent moment in French history: namely, the immediate aftermath of the period known as the "Hundred Days." This phrase designates Napoleon's brief return to power following his escape from the island of Elba — where he had been sent into exile after his abdication as Emperor and concurrent ascent to the throne of Louis XVIII — and prior to the disastrous Battle of Waterloo (June 1815), in the wake of which Bonaparte was conclusively ostracized to St. Helena, there to meet his end six years later. Dumas' hero gets ensnared in the seditious atmosphere of that time, when anybody suspected of being a Bonapartist and hence a threat to the royalist hegemony would incur the charge of treason. The early part of the novel faithfully captures the spirit of that era of unrest, highlighting the tension between royalists and Bonapartists. It is also useful, in order to appreciate the full historical import of the original *Count of Monte Cristo*, to take into consideration the wider backdrop of the period in which it is set, since this abounds with instances of escalating political and civil turmoil bound to have far-reaching repercussions for global history — and not only the localized vicissitudes of Gallic power struggles. The epoch in question reaches back to the Revolution of 1789, the establishment of the French Republic (1792) and decapitation of Louis XVI (1793), Bonaparte's ascent to power (1799) and subsequent self-appointment as Emperor (1804) — a title he would retain until his abdication in the wake of his insanely hubristic invasion of Russia in 1812. With the so-called First Restoration, witnessing the Bourbon dynasty's return to the throne with Louis XVIII (please note that Louis XVII had never ruled, having been imprisoned from 1792 to his death in 1795), France found itself divided by the conflicting interests of the traditional aristocracy and the people. While the former was only too keen to support the restored monarchy in order to regain the lands and privileges it had lost in the Revolution, the latter by and large felt they stood little to gain from the new regime. This tension makes itself palpably evident in *The Count of Monte Cristo* at many crucial junctures. Dumas' hero does not seem to have embraced any clear-cut ideological cause when we first meet him but this only makes him all the more vulnerable to unscrupulous manipulation by his antagonists.

Dumas' novel chronicles the adventures of a young sailor named Edmond Dantès, from his unjust arrest for treason as a result of some jealous rivals' machinations and attendant imprisonment in the Château d'If, where he meets his mentor the Abbé Faria and learns from him about a legendary treasure, to his escape, discovery of said treasure and adoption of a series of disguises to wreak vengeance on his foes. The climactic persona adopted by Dantès is that of "Count of Monte Cristo" — a title chosen in homage to the isle harboring the fabulous riches that have enabled the hero to assert his status in the world and pursue his project. Deprived by the nefarious plot of both his position as Captain, to which he has recently been promoted, and his betrothed Mercédès, Dantès endures carceral deprivation so dehumanizingly severe as to make him long for death. His life takes an utterly unexpected turn when the Abbé, a fellow inmate endowed with tremendous artisanal ingenuity and scholarly knowledge, turns up in the protagonist's cell, having managed to craft tools capable of digging into the Château's formidable walls, and gradually teaches the youth everything he knows.

Upon reentering the human world, having switched places with Faria's corpse at the time of the latter's demise, Dantès quickly discovers the causes of his misfortune, and as he implacably advances toward the final goal, employs his wealth with remarkable generosity and charitableness to the advantage of various people of disparate social standing, as long as such conduct implicitly advances his personal cause. His adventures take him to numerous picturesque spots around Europe and the Mediterranean, with dramatically pivotal moments in Rome and Paris. As Dantès, in the role of the eponymous nobleman, accedes to a desirable social circle of professionals and public figures captivated by his incomparable charm, he finds that his opponents have all become powerful men whose status is erected upon all manner of crimes and misdeeds, and that one of the men directly responsible for his tragedy, Fernand Mondego, has also married Mercédès. The villains' iniquities include attempted infanticide, adultery, corruption, robbery, embezzlement, enslavement and human trading and — of course — murder. One by one, Dantès' persecutors are vanquished and many innocent creatures they have brought down in their manic quest for power and prosperity are at last relieved of their sorrow and poverty. Dantès finds love once more in the person of Haydée, a girl he has rescued from the fate of slavery imposed upon her by one of his most detested enemies: Fernand himself.

While *The Count of Monte Cristo* abounds with allusions to real historical events, it also draws on an ample network of intertextually interconnected images and motifs, including Classical and Biblical references, homages to globally renowned artists and, most consistently and enthusiastically, to the Oriental fairy-tale tradition and especially the *One Thousand and One Nights*. These are explicitly mentioned on numerous occasions (e.g., Dumas, pp. 158, 291, 390, 400), while famous characters immortalized by those tales also crop up with both regularity and symbolic poignance. These include Ali Baba (e.g., pp. 192, 198, 390) and Sinbad the Sailor (e.g., pp. 256, 280).

On the thematic plane, *The Count of Monte Cristo* is above all an extended meditation on the shortcomings of human laws. Thus, even though its intensely dynamic, multi-adventure format prevents it from ever dwelling on inactive reflection, it nonetheless lends itself to perusal as a philosophically motivated text. Central to this aspect of the narrative is its protagonist's obsessive pursuit of revenge, a task he embraces with fiery passion and calculating coldness by turns. Equal doses of ruthlessness and patience are required to feed his driving objective, and simultaneously ensure that the Count remains true to his personal sense of equanimity by rewarding his erstwhile friends no less than by bringing his enemies to irreparable ruin in both material and psychological terms. Monte Cristo is driven by the conviction that he is one of those "extraordinary beings" (p. 493) who operate on behalf of a transcendental Providence. This belief is sustained by the notion that he enjoys special insights into a deeper reality than the one pettily demarcated by human legislation and social mores. Satan is the supernatural agent to whom the Count subscribes as his chief source of inspiration, attributing degrees of beauty, nobility and sublimeness to the diabolical being that far surpass those of any conventional deity. Dumas' hero is ultimately compelled to reassess the validity of his self-appointed providential role as both his trust in the ancient law of nemesis — axial to which is the idea that the sins of the father are visited upon his progeny — and his private ethical system receive a severe blow. This coincides with the realization that the lives of totally innocent creatures are at risk of being arbitrarily sacrificed by a blind quest for revenge — providentially warranted as one may claim this to be. Doubting the legitimacy of his agenda, though still holding on to the sentiment that he has never acted solely out of self-interest, the Count must eventually accept that he is in need of forgiveness no less acutely than his oppressors are in need of punishment.

The themes of justice and revenge run in parallel to an ongoing preoccupation with the tension between love and hatred. Upon embarking on his pursuit of retribution, Monte Cristo deliberately cuts himself off from any opportunity for emotional involvement with his fellow humans, bidding farewell to gratitude and spontaneous kindness and thus remaining tenaciously detached from even the most sentimentally engaging situation. Yet, it is clear that his emotions have not been totally eliminated by experience and grief, for he is still capable of acting compassionately in extremis. This is memorably borne out by the scene where he grants Mercédès' request to spare the life of her son Albert in a duel. This moment also confirms the protagonist's newly discovered preparedness to question the tenability of his supposedly providential role, and accept that the younger generations may not deserve to be treated as objects of revenge insofar as they do not automatically inherit their ancestors' sins — as patently demonstrated by Albert's goodness despite his being the son of the abominable Fernand, now self-renamed as the Count de Morcerf.

Dumas' aesthetic is replete with Romantic leanings that eclectically manifest themselves in a variety of guises. Stylistically and structurally, *The Count of Monte Cristo* explicitly proclaims its standing as a romance-imbued historical novel and, as such, revels in the sustained interweaving of action, historical adventure and matters of the heart. The text is faithful to the conventions of the Romantic novel in utilizing a literally larger-than-life hero of unparalleled courage, bravery, intelligence and robust (though not always unproblematically admirable) moral mettle. Right from the start, Dumas' protagonist is portrayed as a man of great integrity and resolve, and his ethical credentials are thereby firmly established. His adversaries are also invested with codified personality traits — primarily, jealousy and deviousness — and do not alter much as the story progresses. It is indeed in action, rather than in psychological development, that the Romantic novel typically locates its center of interest.

From a thematic point of view, one of the original narrative's most distinctively Romantic aspects consists of its emphasis on the Faustian myth of the superior individual with diabolical affiliations. This finds expression in numerous Romantic poets and, most strikingly or even sensationally, in their enthusiastic responses to John Milton's Satan. William Blake, for example, celebrates the character as the very epitome of freedom and unrestrained desire (*The Marriage of Heaven and Hell*, ca. 1790–1799). Percy Bysshe Shelley, for his part, offers a portrayal of Milton's Devil that brings to mind with uncanny accuracy Dumas' presentation of his hero in *The Count of Monte Cristo* when he embarks on his revenge. In *A Defense of Poetry* (1821), Shelley indeed depicts Satan as "one who perseveres in some purpose which he has conceived to be excellent in spite of adversity and torture" and, most crucially, does so guided by "Implacable hate, patient cunning, and a sleepless refinement of device to inflict the extremest anguish on an enemy" (all citations from "Satan as Hero in *Paradise Lost*"). Lord Byron, relatedly, sees Satan as a far more positive force than God and regards his rebellion, accordingly, as both desirable and entirely legitimate. This fascination with the Devil is also strong in French literature, extending its influence past the Romantic age to find powerful formulation in the poetry of Charles Baudelaire, where the figure is presented as the essence of a notion of sublime beauty borne of both the power and the sadness of danger.

In its account of Dantès' abysmal "anguish," his hopelessness and gradual relinquishment of the very will to live during the time of his imprisonment and prior to the miraculous encounter with the Abbé Faria, Dumas' style strikes distinctively Romantic chords of illustrative validity. Haunted by "his sorrows" and "sufferings, with their train of gloomy spectres," the hero recalls his days as a seaman, when in the face of an impending storm, he would entertain thoughts diametrically opposed to the ones recently fostered by his bestializing captivity. "I felt that my vessel was a vain refuge," he muses, "that trembled and shook before the tempest. Soon the fury of the waves and the spirit of the sharp rocks announced the approach of death, and death then terrified me, and I used all my skill and intelligence as a man and a sailor to escape.... But I did so because I was happy, because I had not courted death.... But now it is different. I have lost all that bound me to life; death smiles and invites me to repose" (Dumas, p. 111).

No less pronouncedly Romantic in aesthetic orientation is *The Count of Monte Cristo*'s appetite for the exotic. This element brings to mind Dumas' own familial background as a man of multiracial parentage, his father being the mulatto offspring of a French marquis and a Haitian slave. Dumas' own fascination with Mediterranean and Eastern cultures, traditions and physiognomies is eloquently attested to by his portrayal of some key characters. Dantès himself is depicted at the very start of the adventure as "a fine, slim young fellow, with black eyes, and hair as dark as a raven's wing" (p. 1), while Mercédès is said to be a "young and beautiful girl, with hair as black as jet, her eyes as velvety as the gazelle's" and "arms bare to the elbow, embrowned" (p. 16). Moreover, as an integral part of his metamorphosis from the wretched

Edmond Dantès to the Count of Monte Cristo, the protagonist travels extensively in the Orient, collecting all manner of conspicuously exotic items along the way with passionate zeal. It is with Haydée that Dumas' Orientalist tastes assert themselves with arguably unprecedented lavishness. Her "arms" are described as "exquisitely moulded" and aptly enfolded by the "rich odours of the most delicious flowers" emanating from "the coral tube of a rich nargile," and her "feet" are said to be "so exquisitely formed and so delicately fair, that they might well have been taken for Parian marble." The girl's costume flaunts all the ornamental attributes one could feasibly expect of an Eastern beauty of the *Arabian Nights* variety, from the "white satin trousers" and "fairy-like slippers" to the "blue and white striped vest, with long open sleeves, trimmed with silver loops and buttons of pearls" and the seductive "bodice" allowing "the whole of the ivory throat and upper part of the bosom" to reveal themselves. However, the narrator is also eager to stress that Haydée's "loveliness"—with its "peculiarly and purely Grecian" quality proclaimed by "large dark melting eyes" and a "finely formed nose," as well as "coral lips" and "pearly teeth"— simply "mocked the vain attempts of dress to augment it" (p. 500).

As documented in detail in the pages to follow, the anime adaptation seems eager, in its often radical reconfiguration of Dumas' novel, to replicate its source text's ability to synthesize the qualities of so-called historical romance with historical fiction and even historiography, and thereby offer an alternate perspective on officially documented facts. In this matter, the anime recalls the pursuit also embraced by the films examined in the course of the previous chapter. *Gankutsuou: The Count of Monte Cristo* does not, due to its eminently futuristic relocation of the source narrative and reliance on the codes and conventions of science fiction and fantasy, replicate Dumas' historical reality in any literal sense. It is, however, deeply concerned with precisely the sorts of ideological, ethical and aesthetic issues that are thrown up by the source text and its anatomy of class-based and wealth-based power relations — and, particularly, with the limitations of human justice, the legitimacy (or iniquity) of revenge, and the eternal tug-of-war between love and hatred. Moreover, *Gankutsuou: The Count of Monte Cristo* is faithful to the dominant style adopted by the parent novel: if not in explicitly narrative, visual or rhetorical terms, certainly in its overall tone.

The prologues for each installment augment the sense of cumulative authenticity by being delivered in fluent French. On several occasions, Maeda's characters even use an overtly theatrical body language consonant with the stage conventions of the period in which the original novel was executed and in which Dumas himself enthusiastically engaged in dramatic writing. In addition, the anime flawlessly captures the essence of Dumas' France even as it thrusts it into an almost unimaginably distant future, in the visible guise of trappings, paraphernalia and status symbols typical of early nineteenth-century French aristocracy. The vehicles, specifically, tend to display an angular sci-fi construction but even this aspect of the decor feels peculiarly congruous with the show's period feel. By integrating these elements with its bizarre landscape, *Gankutsuou: The Count of Monte Cristo* manages to make the coexistence of sumptuous spaceships, giant robots, a futuristically holographic floating version of CNBC, majestic mansions, opera houses, horse-drawn carriages, public squares and boulevards seem quite credible by evoking an atmosphere of somewhat mythical timelessness. This mood is enhanced by the alternation of meticulously detailed with abstractly symbolic backgrounds, and of sequences in which motion is all-pervasive or even deliberately chaotic with sequences where movements are simplified or attenuated to convey a dramatic sense of solemnity or gravity.

Especially remarkable settings punctuate the show's most emotionally charged moments. A good example is the sequence in which the character of Héloïse de Villefort begins to lose her mind as her murderous urges are exposed by her husband, who is exclusively concerned with protecting his personal reputation and would quite welcome her suicide as a liberation. At this stage, the screen explodes into a profusion of kaleidoscopic patterns, assembling and disassembling at a hypnotizing rate. Also worthy of notice, as an additional illustration of Maeda's staging proficiency, is the constellation of cyberspace nested within the Ministry of Interior's classified database — a multilayered digital realm where each successive level becomes increasingly hazardous to penetrate by adventurous hackers in proportion to the degree of secrecy of the information it hosts. The last accessible layer is visualized as a fireball threatening to fry up the very brain of anyone seeking to bypass it. The anime's aesthetic identity will be revisited at a later stage in this chapter in light of the thematic dimension to which the discussion now turns.

Set in the year 5053, the anime opens on the Moon colony of Luna at the time of the local Carnival, dramatizing the meeting of a young nobleman, the Vicomte de Morcerf, and his friend Baron Franz d'Epinay with a charismatic self-made aristocrat — the Count of Monte Cristo. Both Albert and Franz are drawn from Dumas' novel, while a direct parallel also obtains between Luna in Carnival season and the Roman setting in which the original Count of Monte Cristo first meets the young de Morcerf and resolves to use him as a means of immersing himself in the upper echelons of Paris. The exuberantly colorful tone of the setting in which the anime's action finds inception contrasts sharply with the darkness of the source text's beginning. At the same time, however, the series conveys the tenebrous sense of mystery bound to become Monte Cristo's defining trait by means of intriguing rumors concerning the Count's background and reputation even before Albert and Franz have had a chance to meet him in person. In the novel, contrariwise, the hero is explicitly made central to the action right from page one. Albert, for his part, is depicted by Maeda as an immature, though endearing, youth unsatisfied with a life of vapid and undeserved privilege and seeking new experiences and meanings. Yet, his ingenuousness blinds him to other people's flaws despite his inherent goodness. While Albert becomes totally besotted with the enigmatic nobleman's refinement and mystique, Franz reveals a more suspicious disposition, warning his friend against their new acquaintance. Franz is indeed very protective of Albert throughout, having treasured his friendship since the day of their first childhood encounter at Franz's father's funeral.

Franz's misgivings seem justified in the light of Monte Cristo's disquietingly otherworldly — and latently monstrous — aura. When the Count first entertains Albert and Franz at the Rospoli Hotel over an exotic dinner of which he does not consume even a single morsel, he comes across as painfully human in recalling an old love consigned by events to the status of a vaporous dream. Nevertheless, the actions that soon follow intimate his inhumanity as he invites the young fellows to witness a public execution by guillotine from his terrace, draws three cards supposedly bearing the initials of the men about to be decapitated and asks Albert to pick one at random: the man thus chosen will become the beneficiary of a letter of pardon from the Cardinal which the Count claims to possess. Whereas Franz is utterly horrified by this soulless game, Albert gives in to the temptation to play God — only to save, fortuitously, the unrepentant assassin Peppino, a key member of the gang of bandits about to kidnap him. Considering how vital to Monte Cristo's advancement of his grand plan the abduction is destined to prove, one cannot help but wonder whether all of the cards might actually have borne the same letters. The fashion in which the incident is staged indeed suggests that the Count wants the intersection of Albert's fate with the band's activities to appear a product of chance when he has, in fact, arranged it no less than he has contrived to meet the young de Morcerf in the first place. Franz's anxieties augment exponentially as he proceeds to investigate the mystery of Gankutsuou, to which he is accidentally exposed in the course of a sinister soirée hosted by the Count, and thus unearths some unpalatable truths regarding the past history of the Morcerfs, the Danglars and the Villeforts. However, although Franz's reservations regarding the Count's moral standing seem perfectly justifiable, it is undeniable that Monte Cristo has a salutary effect on Albert. It is indeed through the Count that the young nobleman first realizes that his society is built and maintained by people he cannot trust to act according to any principles other than self-interest and greed.

As in the novel, Albert is instrumental in introducing the Count into high Parisian society and thus enabling him to retrace his enemies — i.e., Danglars, Villefort and Morcerf senior himself. The young aristocrat alacritously agrees to Monte Cristo's desire to accede to that prestigious circle in order to repay the Count for rescuing him from Luigi Vampa's gang of thieves and kidnappers when they abduct him and demand an exorbitant ransom for his release. Vampa himself is drawn from the nineteenth-century source. So are numerous other characters featuring in *Gankutsuou: The Count of Monte Cristo*— indeed, the majority of its cast. These include Albert's parentally chosen fiancée Eugénie de Danglars, alongside her father Baron Jullian de Danglars, France's most powerful banker, her mother Victoria de Danglars and the latter's lover Lucien Debray, one of Albert's friends. They also include the Count's attendants Bertuccio, Baptistin and Ali, Haydée, who is said to have suffered grievously at the hands of Morcerf, and the disarmingly frank and courageous Maximilien Morrel, the son of Monte Cristo's former employer, who is portrayed as the Count's spiritual son in the source text. Other important personae derived more or less explicitly from Dumas' novel are Albert's devoted mother, and the Count's former fiancée, Mercédès de Morcerf (née Herrera), his cowardly and unethical father the Général Fernand de Morcerf (a.k.a. Fernand Mondego), Franz's fiancée Valentine de Villefort, a timid and frail girl who will eventually find true love with Maximilien, her father Procureur-général Gérard de Villefort, the highest ranking judge in Paris, and her toxicology-obsessed stepmother and ruthless social climber Héloïse de Villefort, alongside Héloïse's bratty son Edouard and the illegitimate issue of an affair between Gérard de Villefort and Victoria de Danglars, the crude scheming rogue Andrea Cavalcanti (a.k.a. Benedetto).

Several of these characters undergo varyingly substantial modifications in the anime. An entertaining twist to the original cast is offered by Maeda's creation of Peppo, one of Vampa's agents, as the winsome young woman said by Franz to be a transvestite (possibly to avert Albert's interest from her). Peppo is responsible for the young de Morcerf's abduction but is later shown to care for the youth's safety and to feel sympathetic toward his emotional weakness. Furthermore, various characters drawn from Dumas' novel are subtly redefined by the show through the incorporation of notes of ambiguity that enhance to great effect their psychological complexity and dynamic significance. Albert's fiancée Eugénie, for example, is presented as acerbically critical — at times even downright spiteful — toward her naive boyfriend; yet, as the series progresses, she is seen to develop genuine feelings for Albert and to realize, much to her own surprise, that she has indeed fallen in love with him. Haydée is an even more intriguing illustration of Maeda's penchant for ironically nuanced characterization. When Albert and his mates first visit the Count in his underground wonderland — a setting often surreal to Daliesque extremes — Monte Cristo describes the exotic girl as a soulless doll programmed to satisfy his every wish. However, the Count would seem merely to be making a tongue-in-cheek concession to a familiar SF formula at this juncture since Haydée actually evinces a rich and deeply sensitive personality. Her desire to prevent Monte Cristo from being utterly consumed, and hence dehumanized, by his thirst for vengeance sorely clashes with her own longing for retaliation against the man responsible for her father's violent death and her own condemnation to a life of slavery.

Whereas Dumas' novel concentrates on the Count, Maeda's show accords greater narrative significance to the characters of Albert and his friends. Moreover, while the source text adopts a chronologically linear structure in recounting its events, the anime opens with a series of incidents that take place several hundreds of pages into the novel (where, as mentioned, they are set in Rome) and the back story is reconstructed gradually through flashbacks and hindsight as the show progresses. On this point, it is interesting to note that Dumas had initially intended, as Richard Church states, "to start his tale with the arrival in Rome of a mysterious stranger, Edmond Dantès, disguised as The Count of Monte Cristo. Happily, Dumas was persuaded by his faithful drudge, Maquet [the scholarly author with a knack of spotting appropriate materials for narrative adaptation in obscure pockets of history], to go back earlier in the life of his hero.... There followed the most famous part of the book" (in Dumas, p. xvii). In spite of its shift of perspective, however, *Gankutsuou: The Count of Monte Cristo* stays faithful to the original to a remarkable extent, especially in the rendition of its darker messages, mysteries and intrigues. Concurrently, as Theron Martin points out, the anime's use of Albert as "a framing device" makes it possible for "the viewer's perspective" to be "limited to only a little more than what Albert himself knows about the causes for the Count's motivations, which certainly helps maintain the level of suspense for anyone who hasn't read the novel. (And for those who have, the suspense is in seeing how Gonzo's going to handle various story threads)" (Martin). In addition, *Gankutsuou: The Count of Monte Cristo* leaves out quite a few digressive side plots woven by Dumas' original, supplies several of the parent characters with new destinies and elaborates quite a different dénouement. The manga, drawn by Maeda himself in the wake of the anime, focuses on the figure of Monte Cristo more closely and opts for an altogether more somber and occasionally even gruesome sensibility.

Gankutsuou: The Count of Monte Cristo deals with the themes of justice and revenge — and with interrelated tensions between the forces of compassion and greed — in its own distinctive fashion, in consonance with the broad adaptive reconceptualization of the source materials outlined above. Prominent throughout the action's most pathos-laden moments is the tendency to maximize the central adventure's apparently ancillary ramifications as intimately intertwined strands of a coherent narrative core. This enables Maeda to elaborate a tapestry of unique fecundity, inventiveness and vigor that will not fail to satisfy the palate of even the most devout Dumas aficionados. Like the original novel, the anime repeatedly indicates that the Count of Monte Cristo derives considerable pleasure from the arrangement of events and the creation of opportunities for encounters bound to prove axial to the adventure as this develops while making them seem quite accidental. This strategy is instrumental in allowing the self-made aristocrat to set in motion the various elegantly choreographed techniques by which his enemies will be progressively trapped and brought to grief. The surreptitious smirk wreathing the Count's mien when Franz desperately seeks his help — despite the boy's reservations regarding Monte Cristo's probity — neatly discloses to the viewer the premeditated nature of the character's actions from the start.

Thus, it is again suggested that Monte Cristo has planned his meeting with Albert, the youth's kidnapping by the bandits and his own seemingly miraculous rescue of the victim just as he faces death. After all, it is precisely by planning such events with the utmost care that Monte Cristo is able to make Albert feel so profoundly indebted to him as to agree unhesitatingly to usher him into prominent Parisian society and hence pave the way, albeit unwittingly, to the older man's revenge scheme. The anime also echoes Dumas' text in emphasizing the Count's determination to avenge himself as slowly and deliberately as possible. His long years of brutal incarceration have taught Monte Cristo not only science, history and languages (courtesy of the Abbé Faria) but also patience and the exquisite sophistication of the art of waiting. A speedy revenge, the Count believes, would not truly do justice to the pain he himself has had to endure. In the anime, as in the source, the slow pace at which the hero's scheme unfolds also serves to consolidate his providential image, recalling the old adage that god works in mysterious ways.

As noted, the relationship between Monte Cristo and Albert is of pivotal diegetic significance to Maeda's anime. Even though the Count finds the youth charming and guileless, he is disinclined to allow himself to get too close to Albert since, governed by the conviction that the sins of the father shall be inherited by their children, Monte Cristo can never forget that Albert is the son of one of his most abominable foes. At this stage, the Count is still firm in embracing a providential role and often hints, in conversation, at what it must be like to feel that one has godlike powers. Eventually, as Monte Cristo's ethical perspective alters in accordance with occurrences that blatantly point to its perilous limitations, he comes to recognize Albert's nobility of spirit despite his detestable paternity. Like Dumas' hero, however, Maeda's Count is implacable in his quest for vengeance and tirelessly spins its thread from the very moment he engineers the encounter with the young de Morcerf to the end. Some of his subtlest machinations bring into play various of his foes — or their immediate associates — in precise patterns, as if to suggest that Monte Cristo is not content simply to punish them but actually seeks to treat his methodical scheming as a carefully contrived work of art. As Martin comments, once the series has established the groundwork of Monte Cristo's ambitious plot, one increasingly gets the "sense of an intricate machine gradually cranking its way towards destruction and doom as the Count makes his sly first plays against the hearts and minds of his enemies." In this regard, "the writing has done a great job of capturing the spirit and character of the original novel by Alexandre Dumas.... The more you know about the original story, the more the cleverness of this writing effort shines through" (Martin). Seeing Monte Cristo's serpentinely traced plans gradually reach fruition is exhilarating and terrifying in equal measures. One of his most daring maneuvers comes with the dinner party held at a gloomy country estate once owned by the Villefort family where he cunningly deploys an ostensibly innocent game to advance his lethal plan. This is designed to lead Gérard de Villefort and Victoria de Danglars back to the scene of Andrea's adulterous conception with devastating effects for both.

Two schemata of equally calculated proportions can be seen to inform the Count's revenge. One of these is governed by the principle of symmetry — and a fearful one indeed, to echo William Blake's famously haunting phrase. This is articulated as a pattern boldly summarizable as the Danglars-Villefort-Morcerf-Danglars-Villefort trajectory, whereby Monte Cristo's two successive sets of moves against the banker and the judge frame the plan centered on Morcerf, the Count's most hated adversary. In this schema, we witness Monte Cristo's involvement of Danglars' bank in his own finances with unprecedented (and potentially extortionist) contractual implications, rapidly followed by the exposure of Héloïse de Villefort as a murderer and her husband's attendant demotion, and then by Morcerf's own public disgrace as Haydée discloses his past as a felon and slave-trader to the very assembly supposed to celebrate his ascent to absolute power, while the speciousness of his title is also revealed. The acme of Danglars' ruin is then spectacularly choreographed as the insane investments into which he has been roped by Andrea Cavalcanti — also revenge-thirsty for his own good reasons — boomerang and the Baron's entire intergalactically sprawling investment portfolio disintegrates. Danglars reacts by fleeing into space to no avail: nothing and nobody, it is ominously suggested through these scenes, can ultimately dodge the reach of Monte Cristo's vindictive hand. Villefort is also finally and conclusively disgraced and — through a sinister twist of dramatic irony when one considers his second wife's toxicomany — driven mad by poison, as Andrea exposes his horrid history of crimes, infanticide included, in the very court where the Prosecutor was wont to run his judicial tyranny unchallenged in the not-too-distant past.

The other schema includes the final and climactic assault on the already disgraced Morcerf, and may therefore be summed up as the Danglars-Villefort-Morcerf-Danglars-Villefort-Morcerf trajectory. This pattern is ruled by the principle of repetition: a trope notoriously associated, in psychoanalytical terms, with the concept of compulsion and hence eminently applicable, in that frame of reference, to Monte Cristo's compelling purpose. In the repetition-driven schema of vengeance, the sequence of events mapped out above is complemented by the dramatization of Morcerf's final retribution. While Albert and Haydée strive to nourish the Count's rapidly attenuating humanity to ensure he will not be utterly sapped by his addiction, Morcerf plays his last card by attempting a coup d'état in Paris. This part of the series is pivotal to Maeda's consolidation of the original story's political and historical significance in spite of its fantasy-imbued nature. These events are wholly indigenous to the anime and arguably mark its most dramatic departure from Dumas' novel. Another important divergence surrounds Monte Cristo's so-called conversion. In the novel, as noted, this coincides with the point at which the Count agrees to spare Albert's life in response to Mercédès' entreaties.

It would not have been logical for the anime to replicate this move since the Count's utter immunity to human emotions is posited as a major component of its adaptive fabric. Hence, in his mecha-aided duel with the younger opponent, the hero shows no restraint whatsoever. Stylistically, it must be stressed, the sequence is rendered markedly disquieting by a deliberate tonal incongruity between the retrofuturistically designed giant robots, with their synthesis of sci-fi and chivalric traits and astounding martial elegance, and the undiluted brutality of Monte Cristo's blows. This ploy serves to reinforce the Count's ruthlessness in his pursuit of revenge at any price. However, it may well be the case that Monte Cristo is aware, at this juncture, that his rival is not actually Albert — whose place Franz has self-sacrificially assumed unbeknownst to his friend — as he alludes to the young de Morcerf having "run away" from the challenge. In this reading, it could be argued that the Count is not truly turning a deaf ear to his erstwhile lover's prayers.

In his handling of the themes of legality and retribution, *Gankutsuou: The Count of Monte Cristo* repeatedly — though elliptically — calls attention to the concept of revenge as the most primitive expression of humankind's consciousness of justice, predicated upon the assumption that a wronged man has not only a right but also a duty to avenge himself. The anime also exhibits a mature awareness of the limitations inherent in this world picture by intimating that justifiable as it may at times seem to be, private blood revenge is essentially incompatible with the dictates of systematized legislation as a prerogative of the state and hence of superpersonal agencies. Thus, the series insightfully exposes the conflict between an ethical discourse that warrants revenge as a deeply ingrained tradition and a sacred rite, and a contrasting approach to justice based on modern codifications — and polarizations — of acceptable and criminal behavior.

When Maeda's Count comes close to surrendering his humanity in the service of revenge, it is also intimated that even when that goal appears most desirable and accomplishable, albeit by tortuous means, there will always be a danger of its bringing down the avenger alongside his victims. Church has vividly captured this proposition, arguing that Dumas' yarn "shows how a man, given sufficient motive through the imposition of unjust treatment, can rise to a pitch of indignation that shall make him the equal of the gods. Edmond Dantès was thrust into hell, through no fault of his own, and no sin. He refused to abandon hope. After fourteen years, during which the world had forgotten him, and love and career had withered away, he emerged having wrested a secret from that misery, which should give him unlimited wealth, and a store of wisdom, scientific and moral ascendancy, all of which he could use in his monomaniac purpose.... The major part of the novel, its backbone, is the working out of that purpose through an intricate delta of circumstances and events ... a delta which in no way delays the fury of the flood which it is to carry onward to the final serenity of justice done, and overdone. For that is the last revelation: Dantès finding himself the victim of his own intensity, and resigning at last to an authority larger than his own, or any other human agency" (in Dumas, pp. xvii-xviii).

In *Gankutsuou: The Count of Monte Cristo*, the Romantic spirit manifests itself in a distinctive manner, congruous with the anime's overall recontextualization of the inceptive *The Count of Monte Cristo*. Loyal to the governing aesthetic of the Romantic adventure story, Maeda works with deliberately one-dimensional personae a lot of the time, making it possible for the spectator to single them out immediately as objects of either admiration or repulsion. The anime is thus in a position to maximize the adventure's exciting potentialities as a piece of entertainment, without lingering excessively on character evolution per se. This is not to say, however, that in clearly aligning the forces of good against the forces of evil, Maeda precludes all opportunities for psychological development. In fact, his actors do call for attentive inspection as even the most virtuous of souls is sooner or later revealed to be haunted by both personal and collective ghosts that threaten to erode his or her rectitude. Hence, much as the adventure's noblest creatures may at first appear immune to perversion, corruption or even temptation, this is not automatically the case: it is only by undergoing arduous trials and surviving them, the series proposes, that these people can convincingly prove their true caliber. Albert is a resplendent case in point: his generosity and purity are seemingly beyond doubt, and yet his naivety is such as to cause both the youth and his associates severe distress in extremis. Monte Cristo himself is depicted as an ambiguous figure capable of experiencing with equal intensity feelings of hope and pride, on the one hand, and dark apprehensions of doubt, despondent ire and despair on the other. Fortitude and creativity, concurrently, are often seen to coexist with cynical disillusionment.

Gankutsuou: The Count of Monte Cristo also echoes its source text's Romantic passion for the exotic. This is attested to by myriad references to outlandish customs and cuisine, by the professionally executed outfits including fashion designs by Anna Sui, and by the memorable portrayals of Haydée as an enigmatic beauty from "Eastern Space" and of the Count's valet Bertuccio as a person of obviously African descent. However, it is not so much with its outlandish reveries as with its handling of the supernatural that the anime most vibrantly communicates a distinctively Romantic sensibility tinged with elements of the Gothic tradition, as well as traits of the Jacobean Revenge Tragedy (and particularly the figure of the Malcontent). The Count himself epitomizes this spirit as a being who, in order to pursue his vengeful scheme, allows the demon Gankutsuou to possess him, thereby rendering his body transparently crystalline. Insofar as the entity's origins are connected with the Château d'If and the demon is accordingly able to abet Edmond Dantès' escape from his prison, he could be said to play a role analogous to the one taken up by Faria in Dumas' novel. Yet, while the Abbé endeavors to teach the younger man all sorts of positive and constructive lessons, the demon seems governed by entirely malevolent motives. Toward the close of the anime, it manifests itself most balefully as a triple set of eyes running down the Count's mien. Monte Cristo's supernatural constitution is thrown into relief in the episode where Albert's journalist friend Beauchamp attempts to photograph and record the Count, only later to discover that nothing has been captured. The elliptical equation of the Count's physical state to a disease of intergalactic proportions contributes vitally to the suggestion that the character's vindictiveness is akin to a pathological aberration inflicted upon him by external forces over which he has no control — although, of course, there is every sign that he entered his association with Gankutsuou no less willingly than Faust embraced his own pact with Mephistopheles.

The use of locations such as the surreal city of gold stretching — seemingly endlessly — in the depths of Monte Cristo's mansion on the Champs-Élysées, alongside the adventure pivoting on a room emanating an evil aura, potently sustain the supernatural dimension of Maeda's anime with concessions to the Romantic aesthetic associated with authors such as Samuel Taylor

Coleridge. In its cumulative take on the supernatural, *Gankutsuou: The Count of Monte Cristo* captures the Romantic spirit at two interrelated levels. First, it assiduously aims to present the supernatural as quite real, in spite of its inscrutability and apparent preposterousness, through graphic depictions of uncompromising clarity, directness and precision. Nowhere is this proclivity more perturbingly evident than in the scenes where Gankutsuou abruptly surfaces to flood Monte Cristo's visage. Second, it celebrates the supernatural as the dimension in which the artist's imagination may proclaim itself most effusively, unfettered by the petty restraints of external referents that ineluctably shape the representation of ordinary reality.

The most original aspect of Maeda's adaptation, from an aesthetic point of view, indubitably resides with the anime's experimental artistry. In an imaginative handling of digital layering, compositing and rendering, occasionally so audacious as to feel almost disorientating or require some sensory adjustment, the show delivers a unique sense of kinetic tension. Pivotal to this effect is the use of static textured backgrounds over which the basic outlines of the characters' hair and clothes, as well as several other facets of the anime's visual repertoire, move normally — as if parts of the images were no less transparent than the Count's preternatural body. Hence, many of the digitally edited layers are often kept deliberately stationary even during motion. The effectiveness of this technique is gloriously borne out by the robe donned by Haydée to visit the Opera House, which can indeed be regarded as an awe-inspiring work of art unto itself. Eugénie's inwrought grand piano, in turn, stands out as that garment's equivalent in the area of interior design. The fabrics employed for the main characters' clothes range in style from the effusively Baroque design used for Franz to the contemporary, geometrically patterned casual design use for Albert, with numerous concessions to Eastern vogues peppered across the entire cast's costumes and accessories. Hair often provides the most tantalizing opportunities for experimentation: the Count's, for example, appears to be superimposed on a crepuscular sky flecked with fraying cloud banks or the muted glimmer of distant nebulae, whereas the silhouette of Haydée's luxuriant mane moves over a pattern replete with stylized and sensuously sinuous floral ornamentation. Stylistically, the anime also hints at the Jazz Age as conceived of by Francis Scott Fitzgerald — for instance, in the episode where Albert and his friends go for a ride in the countryside in their flashy automobiles. The girls' hairdos are especially consonant with the fashions prevalent in that era. The indoor scenes focusing on Albert and his male mates conversing relaxedly over vintage beverages, conversely, bring to mind the older atmosphere of fin-de-siècle decadence as dramatized by Oscar Wilde.

The palette is cumulatively bold, bright and oversaturated, frequently reveling in psychedelic effects. Opulent and intricately detailed patterns are ubiquitous: the edifices themselves are generally embossed with ornately patterned gold and silver designs regardless of whether the overall setting displays a luxurious, sparsely furnished or dreary quality. Even when they are not patterned in a literal sense of the term, the anime's surfaces are frequently marbled with shadows and drifting clouds, and bejeweled by specks of light peeping through foliage, filtering through segmented window panes or descending, as though in a gentle rain, from overhanging chandeliers. The show's interiors are almost achingly beautiful in their hues, decorative refinement and sheer tactility. They abound throughout with meticulously textured and rendered wallpaper, upholstery, draperies, carpets, rugs, soft furnishings in velvet, brocade, silk and satin, ceiling and vault frescoes, variegated marble and granite balustrades, gilded frames, cornices and plasterwork, majestic oil paintings epitomizing various characters' differing tastes and dispositions, and a profusion of exquisitely decorated tableware.

The CG work is by and large utilized in a fashion ideally suited to the maximization of the anime's sci-fi atmosphere, as is the show's highly dynamic lighting. That generic mood is also heightened by the characterization of a few major actors, including the Count himself and Haydée, as captivatingly alien — or at least futuristic. In Monte Cristo's case, there are even intimations that he might be a vampire. Dumas' own hero, it should be noted, also attracts such suspicions, though far less pronouncedly than Maeda's. The overall effect of Maeda's adventurous visuals is an impression of full perceptual immersion based on the engagement of the spectator's entire sensorium. The gorgeously compiled soundtrack abets these ruses with admirable cogency, setting off the distinctive tenor of each and every sequence. The opening theme is a gentle piano ballad meshing harmoniously with the images' nostalgic mood. The closing theme, for its part, is a sprightlier guitar piece reflecting on the Count's current schemes. The anime's soundtrack features numerous renowned pieces of classical music, including movements from Tchaikovsky's *Manfred Symphony* (1885), Donizetti's opera *Lucia di Lammermoor* (1835), Rachmaninoff's *Piano Concerto No. 2*, Schumann's *Kinderszenen* (1838), Meyerbeer's *Robert le diable* (1831) and Debussy's *Preludes deuxieme livre* (1912–1913).

Most importantly, Maeda — as a brilliant artist with a solid background in fine art — alludes to disparate European vogues spanning the period in which the source story itself is set to Art Nouveau. Gustav Klimt is clearly a major influence behind *Gankutsuou: The Count of Monte Cristo*— so much so that aspects of the artwork could be realistically described as an animated adaptation of the Austrian painter's output. A tension between naturalism and stylization, both bridged and enhanced by turns through intricately patterned multiform surfaces, contrasts of bold color and gold, silver, coral and gems, and a pervasive aura of dreamy eroticism emanating from twining or spiraling lines and waves juxtaposed with stark squares and rectangles, are among the salient aspects of Klimt's opus to which Maeda's artistry assiduously adheres. Costume and decoration are often rendered by Klimt in a style that brings to mind the image of a ghostly mosaic — an uncanny blend of minutely detailed and texturized concreteness, on the one hand, and impalpable transparence or translucence on the other. This element of the artist's work is replicated not only by the anime's approach to line and mass but also by its unique utilization of layers, as described above. It should also be noted, in this context, that Klimt himself consistently drew on Japanese visual sources, blending them in utterly unexpected ways with Byzantine, Mycenaean and Egyptian influences. Like Klimt's art, *Gankutsuou: The Count of Monte Cristo* frequently exudes an atmosphere of ubiquitous sensuality, communicating an aesthetic vision that regards images — be they paintings, hand-drawn cels or digitally generated graphics — as intensely material objects in themselves. Thus, while the anime's shimmering layers of ornamental sumptuousness might occasionally evoke an impression of almost insubstantial two-dimensionality, that vision simultaneously helps Maeda to reinforce the medium's tenacious corporeality.

The visual companion *Gankutsuou: The Count of Monte Cristo Complete* works marvels in documenting the sheer temerity of the anime's emplacement of color and pattern in the role of protagonists from start to finish. This distinctive feature of Maeda's series is immediately thrown into relief by the book's cover design. The inner cover displays elegantly patterned monochrome drawings that encapsulate in symbolic form the story's overarching preoccupation with the notion of justice and with the mutual inextricability of love and death. The passion for deep palettes, concomitantly, is luxuriously communicated by the dust jacket, with its striking portraits of Albert, Franz and Eugénie on one side and of the Count with Gankutsuou's physical form gleaming through his constitution on the other, and subtle handling of holographic effects to enhance the adventure's otherworldliness and its fascination with sophisticated textures. The anime's appetite for patterns is even more exuberantly conveyed by the three-page foldouts displaying collages of various members of the cast bearing typical facial expressions and postures, where each character is associated with a different pattern and hence with specific formal, chromatic and symbolic connotations. The predilection for Art-Nouveau linear virtuosity is reflected throughout the volume, and particularly the larger plates depicting intricate character interactions and tensions. Most memorable, in this respect, is the illustration portraying Monte Cristo and Albert, joined in an embrace intensely redolent of Klimt's art in both its composition and its lavish employment of flexuous lines, abstract ornamentation and gold.

Other notable pictures emphasize the show's symbolism. These include a number of images devoted to Monte Cristo's secret city and its surrealist penchant for single eyes and clockwork imagery, sculpted clouds, arabesques and — in a uniquely inspired synthesis of Art Nouveau, Surrealism, Symbolism and Romantic aesthetics — a profusion of exotic details.

Costumes, the book emphasizes, are deployed as an emblematic means of individualizing the various actors, with the Count's brooding garments pointing to his darkly vindictive intent and Mercédès' sculpted robes alluding to a slightly over-the-top approach to her acquired aristocratic status. Victoria de Danglars' attire is as tarty as her amorous conduct, while Héloïse de Villefort's hints at a botanical passion traversed by murky desires. Valentine's clothes are as ethereally unobtrusive as her personality, whereas Eugénie's preference for exuberantly colored prints mirrors her outgoing and adventurous disposition. Her father's garments are crudely ostentatious and instantly connotative of conspicuous consumption, which is quite in keeping with his financial and professional status. Général de Morcerf's preference for white hints at a false sense of moral purity, while Gérard de Villefort's robes echo at all times his supreme judicial role. Given the anime's fascination with fashion design, the list of examples could feasibly stretch on for several pages. In addition, the companion volume draws attention to the show's use of vehicles — by and large of a passionately retrofuturistic ilk — as character identifiers of great potency.

Over the decades, The Count of Monte Cristo has spawned countless adaptations in various media, and especially in cinematic form. As documented by the Wikipedia entry for "The Count of Monte Cristo (film)," the most notable examples include the following:

- The Count of Monte Cristo (1908 film), silent film
- The Count of Monte Cristo (1913 film), starring James O'Neill
- The Count of Monte Cristo (1918 series), starring Leon Mathot
- The Count of Monte Cristo (1929 film), directed by Henri Fescourt
- The Count of Monte Cristo (1934 film), starring Robert Donat
- The Count of Monte Cristo (1943 film), featuring Pierre Richard-Willm
- The Count of Monte Cristo (1955 film), with Jean Marais and Lia Amanda
- The Count of Monte Cristo (TV series), 1956 ITC Entertainment TV series
- The Count of Monte Cristo (1961 film), starring Louis Jourdan
- The Count of Monte Cristo (1964 series), BBC TV series featuring Alan Badel and Natasha Parry

- The Count of Monte Cristo (1968 film), with Paul Barge, Claude Jade, and Pierre Brasseur
- The Count of Monte Cristo (1975 film), starring Richard Chamberlain, Kate Nelligan and Tony Curtis
- The Count of Monte Cristo (1980 miniseries), TV miniseries with Jacques Weber, Carla Romanelli
- Veta (film), a Telugu film released in 1986, starring Chiranjeevi and Jayaprada in the lead roles, dubbed into Hindi as Faraar Qaidi.
- Uznik zamka If (English titles: The Count of Monte Cristo or The Prisoner of If Castle) (1988)
- The Count of Monte Cristo (1998 miniseries), TV miniseries starring Gérard Depardieu and Ornella Muti
- The Count of Monte Cristo (2002 film), featuring James Caviezel, Dagmara Dominczyk, and Guy Pearce. ("The Count of Monte Cristo [film]").

However, it is primarily with a literary adaptation in a different form, that of the short story with speculative leanings, that the original novel — and indeed its anime spawn — share some of the most enlightening points of contact: Italo Calvino's "The Count of Monte Cristo" (in *The Complete Cosmicomics*). This narrative suggests that a threatening outside may be kept at bay by transforming the inside into a dimension so intimately akin to an outside as to be able to oppose the actual outside. Calvino's Abbé Faria is condemned by his characteristic modus operandi to move forever from one surface to another surface, since any depth he may chance upon turns out to be yet one more superficial veneer covering up infinite layers of inscrutability. Calvino's Dantès, by contrast, relies on a reflective procedure centered not on the effort to dispel complexity but rather on the ongoing formulation of hypotheses regarding its amplification. Hence, the Abbé, in his desperate endeavor to flee the Château d'If, relentlessly digs only to discover every time that he has simply managed to access "a cell that is even deeper in the fortress" (Calvino, p. 281). In the process, "his itineraries continue to wind around themselves like a ball of yarn" (p. 283). In this vertiginous accretion of perplexities, Faria finds that each cell is separated from the outside by yet another cell. Dantès, by contrast, adopts a survivalist ethos grounded in a creative acceptance of the concept of the cosmos in its entirety as a baffling maze. Survival, according to Calvino's Dantès, does not depend on the elimination of the many obstacles blocking the way to freedom but rather on a commodious grasp of their intractable impenetrability and omnipresence. Accordingly, while Faria chases incontrovertible truths merely to unearth mysteries, Dantès chooses to multiply the riddles and insolubles around him, conjecturing ever-increasing obstacles. Paradoxically, he ends up feeling far more at "ease" (p. 282) than his companion in misfortune. Calvino's hero works on the assumption that if the speculative system he constructs in his own head is as inevasible as the material fortress is, he will at least be able to give up trying to escape and find some peace in defeat. If, however, the system he is able to imagine is even more inescapable than the Château d'If, he will then have a chance of breaking out of the real prison by surpassing its inherent intricacy in his own suppositions.

Calvino's adaptation of Dantès exhibits the characteristic traits of the kind of vibrantly speculative mind attributed by Dumas to his own hero when the yearning for death is displaced — as he perceives a sound that might denote another inmate's attempt to escape — by the urge to "think and strengthen his thoughts by reasoning." He therefore reflects: "If it is a workman, I need but knock against the wall, and he will cease to work in order to find out who is knocking, and why he does so; but as his occupation is sanctioned by the governor, he will soon resume it. If, on the contrary, it is a prisoner, the noise I will make will alarm him, he will cease, and not recommence until he thinks every one is asleep'" (Dumas, pp. 113–114). Faria's digging, for its part, is typically described thus by the character of the Abbé himself: "I was four years making the tools I possess; and have been two years scraping and digging out earth, hard as granite itself ... then to conceal the mass of earth and rubbish I dug up, I was compelled to break through a staircase, and throw the fruits of my labour into the hollow part of it; but the well is now so completely choked up, that I scarcely think it would be possible to add another handful of dust without leading to a discovery ... just at the moment when I reckoned upon success, my hopes are forever dashed from me" (pp. 125–126). Dumas' Abbé, like Calvino's, is quite simply defied by the indomitable proliferation of matter, operating as a potent metaphor for the entire world's stubborn complexity.

An especially felicitous facet of Calvino's tale is its figurative equation of Faria and Dantès to authors, and of their respective quests to manuscripts. Calvino's Faria is obsessed with conclusive and monolithic outcomes: he has set his heart on "one page among the many." Standing at the opposite end of the philosophical spectrum, his Dantès alternately seeks to record "the accumulation of rejected sheets" and "the solutions which need not to be taken into account." The proliferation of possibilities contemplated by Calvino's Dantès mirrors the status of the art of adaptation itself as a field of potentially limitless transformational and relocating strategies. In the short story, this perspective is hinted at by the hypothetical ideation of "the supernovel *Monte Cristo* with its variants and combinations of variants in the nature of billions of billions" (Calvino, p. 292).

As noted in Chapter 1, adaptations have traditionally been regarded as inferior art forms parasitically indebted to a privileged source. Gerald Peary and Roger Shatzkin have communicated this proposition with uncompromising finality, stating that "all the directorial Schererazades of the world cannot add up to Dostoevsky" (Peary and Shatzkin, p. 2). However, as Linda Hutcheon maintains, such a negative response is inadequate insofar as it does not take into account the operations through which different adaptations give ideas concrete shape (through images, music, motion) in such a way as to act imaginatively upon the texts they seek to adapt and thus generate not simply edited reflections thereof but rather independent entities: "they make simplifying selections, but also amplify and extrapolate; they make analogies; they critique or show their respect" (Hutcheon, p. 3). The galaxy of adaptations with *The Count of Monte Cristo* at their basis sonorously validates this argument by showing that the transposition of a text to a different code or medium is a creative process—not only *as well as* a derivative gesture but *over and above* such a gesture. If none of those adaptations is logically conceivable with total disregard for Dumas' parent novel, nor is it defined by that etiological affiliation as much as it is individuated by its own thoughtful interpretation of that text's themes, symbols and narrative momentum as a means of reaching out into an alternative world. An adaptation as inspired as Maeda's *Gankutsuou: The Count of Monte Cristo* professes its individuality primarily as a work of autonomous value and only in addition—importantly but not restrictively—as the vivacious brood of a venerable ancestor. When adaptations of Dumas' novel seek, each of them in its distinctive way, to be faithful to the root narrative, they do so with regard to the author's imagination and creative vision as they perceive them, not to a fixed substratum they could reliably call his one and only reality.

A vibrant symphony of dynamism, dramatic sophistication, narration, dialogue, music and—last but not least—some of the most stunningly original visuals yielded by anime throughout its history, Maeda's *Gankutsuou: The Count of Monte Cristo* proficiently demonstrates Robert Stam's thesis that cinema transforms the uniform reality of the printed page into a multidiscursive reality, as the "linguistic energy of literary writing turns into the audio-visual-kinetic-performative energy of the adaptation" (Stam, p. 46). At the same time, in inviting us to examine the anime's latent connections with a variety of other interpretations of Dumas' novel, Maeda's show intimates that familiar yarns and allusions fluidly and even fleetingly fold into one another, as settings and characters in one interpretation of a story can be perceived through other settings and characters ideated by parallel interpretations, and as events in any one version are shaped or haunted by those unfolding in other coexisting versions of the same basic narrative. Thus, *Gankutsuou: The Count of Monte*

Cristo validates another important hypothesis advanced by Stam: the idea that screen adaptations relate to several parallel works simultaneously, for they are always "caught up in a whirl of intertextual reference and transformation, of texts generating other texts in an endless process of recycling, transformation and transmutation, with no clear point of origin" (p. 66). James Naremore supports this view by proposing a shift from the concept of adaptation as "reflection" to that of adaptation as "refraction" (Naremore, p. 23) — from a notion of the adaptive text as an inert (and, by implication, unproductive) mirror to an understanding not only of the individual adaptation but also of the proliferating clan of related adaptations and interpretations wherein it is situated as a kaleidoscopic game of deflexure.

What is arguably most impressive about *Gankutsuou: The Count of Monte Cristo* is not only its ability to raise the bar for what anime can deliver at the levels of artistic quality and innovation but also its flair for embodying the very pinnacle of the diverse genres it encompasses, from action adventure to romance, from the SF saga to the revenge epic. In so doing, the show yields as engrossing philosophical meditation on some of the most powerful emotions coursing the human condition in both its noblest and its most insalubrious manifestations. Darkly melodramatic and nostalgically lyrical by turns, the series consistently succeeds in weaving its disparate strands together by maintaining throughout a fine tension between the capriciousness of fate and a world picture in which nothing seems merely an offshoot of chance and an intricate pattern of causality in fact reigns supreme.

As a reconceptualization of a well-known nineteenth-century text of Western parentage through the lenses of science fiction, *Gankutsuou: The Count of Monte Cristo* finds a precedent in Osamu Dezaki's *Hakugei: The Legend of Moby Dick* (TV series, 1997–1999), an anime that likewise engineers a tantalizing encounter between the epic-saga modality and a retrofuturistic sensibility. Even a cursory look at the show's storyline rapidly corroborates this contention. Set in the year 4699 in the aftermath of humanity's colonization — and concomitant pollution — of the galaxies, *Hakugei: The Legend of Moby Dick* chronicles young Lucky Luck's search for the legendary Captain Ahab in the desire to gain membership to his band of "whale hunters." In this context, whales are not marine mammals but abandoned spaceships and whale hunters, accordingly, are not daring fishermen but salvage teams intent on their retrieval and pillage. Captain Ahab, meanwhile, pursues a quest of his own, deriving from the injunction to lend assistance to the citizens of "Planet Moad" in their revolt against the "Federation" and its formidable whale-shaped white ship, the Moby Dick — a vessel with which Captain Ahab has entertained a traumatic relationship in the past. Enhancing the adventure's distant-future feel, Dezaki also makes the actor of the android Dew pivotal to the reconfigured narrative and to the gradual unfurling of its dark secrets, while concurrently introducing a mechanical parrot as Ahab's pirate-worthy pet.

Hakugei: The Legend of Moby Dick thus anticipates *Gankutsuou: The Count of Monte Cristo* in generic terms. Yet, it could hardly differ more substantially from the later anime in its specific approach to the art of adaptation. Indeed, whereas *Gankutsuou: The Count of Monte Cristo* remains loyal, albeit elliptically, to Dumas' novel, Dezaki's show only retains from Melville's novel some character names and a man's monomaniacal obsession with whaling — and even when it comes to whaling, as noted, the concept is radically adapted to the requirements of the new text. Most importantly, from a stylistic point of view, Dezaki's anime often displaces Melville's gravely philosophical speculation with a bouncy and exuberant ride, replete with martial set pieces allowing the reconfigured and much more cheerful Ahab to indulge his hearty appetite for action. Even though, as the story develops, opportunities for serious reflection become more frequent, the overall mood evinced by *Hakugei: The Legend of Moby Dick* is substantially sunnier than the original novel's own tenor.

In the domain of adaptations of nineteenth-century classics, a unique case is offered by *The Stingiest Man in Town* (special, Katsuhisa Yamada, 1978) — a U.S./Japan co-production involving one hundred and fifty people and employing an impressive total of 72,000 frames adapted from Paul Coker, Jr.'s original designs. The Japanese version was broadcast as a Christmas Special on Christmas Eve 1978. Based on Charles Dickens' classic *A Christmas Carol*, first published in 1843, *The Stingiest Man in Town* was created by Arthur Rankin, Jr. and Jules Bass and is essentially a remake of another popular adaptation, the live-action musical released in 1956 and starring Basil Rathbone of Sherlock-Holmes fame as part of the series *The Alcoa Hour* (TV series, dirs. Kirk Browning, Herbert Hirschman *et al.*, 1955–1957). In the 1978 animation, Scrooge's story is recounted from the perspective of B. A. H. Humbug, a narrator named after the Dickensian miser's famous catch phrase. Scrooge's voice actor is Walter Matthau and his physical appearance is accordingly modeled on that of the actual performer in an inspired integration of reality and fantasy of the kind which only the medium of animation is ultimately at liberty to accomplish with unmatched verve.

The show is faithful to the source text in highlighting Scrooge's brutally tenacious aversion to charitable conduct and objection to anything merry — let alone Christmas itself. The character's avarice and general callousness run so deeply as to even make him disinclined to share a festive repast with his kind-hearted nephew Fred. The adaptation also follows Dickens in presenting the character of Jacob Marley, Scrooge's late associate and a proverbial miser in his own right, as instrumental in the quest to reform Scrooge and as the harbinger of successive — and increasingly troubling — spectral visitations.

Exposed to the immensity of the pain caused by his possessive rapacity, the animated incarnation of Dickens' Scrooge ends up, like his literary antecedent, embracing a novel lifestyle blessed by generosity, conviviality and cheerfulness. The show is especially effective in conveying the idea that the ghosts haunting the protagonist are not merely fantastical presences of the kind so dear to a Victorian Yuletide mentality but also, indeed more importantly, unwholesome emanations issuing from his own poisoned psyche. The animation tends to soften the original ghosts' more doomful connotations on a purely visual plane, partly not to alienate or disturb the younger members of its Western audience. Yet, it evokes an atmosphere of pervasive darkness right through to the end by recourse to the most unsettling rhetorical tool of all: irony. Thus, even the less somber, or indeed partially comical, moments exude a lingering sense of foreboding. These serve to remind us of the ubiquitousness of the shadow closing in on humans at all times even as they strive to lick away at its edges with fire.

This is obviously not the right context in which to embark on a detailed evaluation of adaptations of Dickens' famous novella—given, as Fred Guida has punctiliously documented, that these are tremendously copious and diverse in both format and mood, ranging from stage and radio plays to films for both cinema and TV, parodic opera retellings, modernized versions and sequels. One exemplary instance is nonetheless worthy of note due to its tonal affinity with Yamada's adaptation: namely, Christian Birmingham's illustrations for the Kingfisher edition of the tale. (Birmingham is an artist who has also played a special role in the vast domain of adaptations of Hans Christian Andersen's opus and will accordingly be returned to in next chapter.) The most salient similarity between the animated adaptation and Birmingham's take on the novella resides with their shared employment of irony. In Birmingham, as in the show, portentous intimations of evil traverse even the jolliest scenes, thus alerting us to the unabated incidence of dark and unpredictable forces. This is especially evident in the plates devoted to the Cratchits' imaginary Christmas dinner and to Fred's party, where the unlit portions of the colorfully convivial tableaux appear to be impregnated with a silent aura of menace, and the inanimate objects on the dusky periphery of the rooms come across as disquietingly alive. Birmingham is also responsible for creating some of the most original interpretations ever witnessed in the realm of illustrations of Dickens' specters. On this count, too, the artist parallels the animated version under investigation, though with blatant stylistic divergences. The "Ghost of Christmas Past" is particularly memorable in capturing Dickens' own portrayal of the preternatural figure through its amalgamation of juvenile and hoary attributes. The character's glittering eyes, moreover, anticipate Birmingham's depiction of the Snow Queen.

Chapter 4

The Fairy Tale Reimagined
The Snow Queen

> *Only those who truly love and who are truly strong can sustain their lives as a dream. You dwell in your own enchantment. Life throws stones at you, but your love and your dream change those stones into the flowers of discovery.... People like you enrich the dreams of the worlds, and it is dreams that create history. People like you are unknowing transformers of things, protected by your own fairy tale, by love.*—Ben Okri

An apposite point of entry to the assessment of Osamu Dezaki's reworking of a time-honored fairy tale in his anime version of *The Snow Queen* (TV series, 2005–2006) is supplied by Julie Sanders' observations regarding the relationship between the art of adaptation and the realm of fairy tale and folklore. The critic proposes that these supply a set of "archetypal stories available for re-use and recycling by different ages and cultures.... One of the reasons fairy tale and folklore serve as cultural treasuries to which we endlessly return is that their stories and characters seem to transgress established social, cultural, geographical, and temporal boundaries. They are eminently adaptable into new circumstances and contexts" (Sanders, pp. 82–83). Dezaki would no doubt have felt pointedly drawn, in consonance with both the general predilections of indigenous culture and his own personal vision, to the more somber subtexts of Hans Christian Andersen's familiar tale — to the dormant underworld of spectral, inchoate, monstrous and rapacious forces seething beneath the narrative's crystalline purity, just as they are wont to do in the oneiric domain beyond the conscious mind's control.

A primary reason for the enduring appeal of a text like *The Snow Queen* to an anime director like Dezaki, given its standing as a fantasy construct amenable to adventurous adaptation and relocation, is evidently its coming-of-age dimension. This is an aspect of fairy tales at large deemed by Bruno

Bettelheim to be pivotal to their psychological and ideological significance: "fairy tales," the author maintains in his seminal book *The Uses of Enchantment*, "depict in imaginary and symbolic form the essential steps in growing up and achieving an independent existence" (Bettelheim, p.73). In revisioning *The Snow Queen*, Dezaki has been especially keen to question the authority of the happy-ending formula so often associated with the fairy tale tradition — especially in the wake of its Disney adaptations. In so doing, the director tersely advocates that stability is not a desirable objective for an individual tale any more than it can be reliably presumed to govern the lives of texts across disparate epochs and cultures. Quizzing the story's closure, Dezaki thus implicitly alludes also to the inevitable openness of the universe of textuality as a whole — which is indeed the prerequisite of the eclectic art of adaptation. Dezaki's anime, in this respect, faithfully reflects Jack Zipes' contention that revisionist renditions of fairy tales at their most dispassionate constitute "not recuperation but differentiation, not the establishment of a new norm but the questioning of all norms" (Zipes, pp. 157–158). Concomitantly, Dezaki's stance brings to mind Angela Carter's playfully irreverent evaluation of the fairy tale as a form: "The chances are, the story was put together in the form we have it, more or less out of all sorts of bits of other stories long ago and far away, and has been tinkered with, had bits added to it, lost other bits, got mixed up with other stories, until our informant herself has tailored the story personally to suit an audience ... or, simply, to suit herself" (Carter, p. x). Carter is here elliptically hinting at the very etymology of the verb "to adapt," the Latin *adaptare*: i.e., "to make fit" or "to make appropriate."

Although *The Snow Queen* constitutes an unprecedented accomplishment in the universe of adaptations of fairy tales to anime, it must nonetheless be noted that Andersen's tales were previously utilized as source materials by the series *Andersen Stories* (dir. Masami Hata, 1971). A highly imaginative interpretation of Andersen's world in the recent history of anime consists of Hayao Miyazaki's movie *Ponyo on the Cliff by the Sea* (2008), a loose adaptation of *The Little Mermaid* treated with vertiginously exuberant visual verve from beginning to end. As *Ponyo* lures us into its colorful filmic ride by recourse to electrifying graphics keen on foregrounding their emphatically hand-drawn status, its overall atmosphere emanates an aura of infantile candor which might at first induce the viewer to categorize it univocally as a children's movie. Although it is true that *Ponyo* is one of Miyazaki's most pointedly child-oriented productions to date, it must also be noted, however, that the work strikes grave and thought-provoking chords in its reconceptualization of the venerable tale in terms of a disquieting environmentalist message of tremendous political significance and corresponding animational pathos.

Miyazaki's fascination with Western fantasy literature well predates *Ponyo*, as attested to by his adaptations of *Three Thousand Miles in Search of Mother* (TV series, 1975) and *Howl's Moving Castle* (movie, 2004), as well as his devotion to the study of children's stories from an early age and involvement in the Children's Literature Research Society while studying politics and economics at Gakushuin University. Miyazaki's adaptations tend to take considerable liberties with their sources, leading to free-standing narratives of globally acclaimed stature. Miyazaki has also experimented with the adaptation of Japanese children's fiction with *Kiki's Delivery Service* (movie, 1989), in this case incurring the ire of the creator of the original story (1985), Eiko Kadono, due to his adventurous departure from the parent text. Miyazaki is not alone in treasuring fantasy literature of Western provenance intended primarily for kids as a copious wellhead of inspiration. Other notable adaptations in the genres of the fairy tale and the folk tale include *Puss in Boots* (movie, dir. Kimio Yabuki, 1969), *Aesop's Fables* (TV series, dir. Eiji Okabe, 1983) and *Cinderella* (TV series, dir. Hiroshi Sasagawa, 1996).

In the areas of child-oriented action adventure and the bildungsroman, some of the most remarkable accomplishments encompass *Heidi, Girl of the Alps* (TV series; dir. Isao Takahata, 1974), *A Dog of Flanders* (TV series; dir. Yoshio Kuroda, 1975), *Rascal the Raccoon* (TV series; dirs. Hiroshi Saitou, Seiji Endou, Shigeo Koshi, 1977), *Anne of Green Gables* (TV series; dirs. Isao Takahata and Shigeo Koshi, 1979), *The Adventures of Tom Sawyer* (TV series; dir. Hiroyoshi Saitou, 1980), *Swiss Family Robinson* (TV series; dir. Yoshio Kuroda, 1981), *The Story of Pollyanna* (TV series; dir. Kouzou Kuzuha, 1986) and *Tales from Earthsea* (movie; dir. Goro Miyazaki, 2006). Most of the titles in the second category — alongside the aforementioned *Andersen Stories* and *Three Thousand Miles in Search of Mother*, as well as several other less well-known productions — belong to the long-running Japanese series *World Masterpiece Theater*: a veritable galaxy of adaptations of famous stories of principally Western origin. *Gulliver's Space Travels: Beyond the Moon* (movie; dir. Yoshio Kuroda, 1965) and *Animal Treasure Island* (movie; dir. Hiroshi Ikeda; 1971), for their part, offer generic repositionings of classic narratives by Jonathan Swift and Robert Louis Stevenson, respectively.

Returning to Andersen, there are arguably several reasons for which his oeuvre might appeal specifically to a Japanese sensibility. One of these is that his stories never demur from exposing the dark side of fairy tale, the real-life sorrow and fear metaphorically encapsulated in their classic tropes — and most typically, as Naomi Lewis phrases it, in their "terrible trials, forests of thorns, unscalable glass mountains." Hence, Andersen's world view would be quickly grasped by a Japanese spirit eager to acknowledge the coexistence of calm and turmoil throughout the universe. No less vitally, the Danish author's unflinching belief in the sentience of all things is quite congruous with the lessons of

Shinto. According to Lewis, it was Andersen's father that "gave his child the thought that every non-human creature or *thing*—a leaf, a beetle, a darning needle—has a character of its own." (The example of the needle is especially apposite to the suggestion of a latent analogy between Andersen's stance and the Shintoist approach to life insofar as a widespread custom in traditional Japanese culture is precisely the habit of extending one's gratitude to needles for their services when they are no longer effective and must therefore be discarded.) While many of Andersen's contemporaries, suspicious of his humble origins as the son of a pious washerwoman and an iconoclastically rebellious cobbler, dismissed his tendency to endow inanimate entities with speech as absurd, the writer never lost faith in the immense narrative potentialities inherent in every being and object—in the lesson, also inculcated by his unconventional dad, that "stories lay all around—in an old trunk, a toy, a bundle of matches" (in Andersen 2004, "Introduction"). This idea is paradigmatically conveyed by *The Flying Trunk*, where the humblest kitchen accessories rise to the status of competent storytellers, from the "bundle of matches" upset about their demotion from the aristocratic ranks to which they belonged as long as they were part of "an ancient pine tree" by the woodcutter's axe — what they call "the Great Revolution"—to the "iron pot" that likes nothing better than "a sensible chat with friends" once "the business of dinner is over"; from the ladylike "earthenware pot" with highly refined narratorial talent to the "big tea urn" that is not "in good voice" unless she is "on the boil"; from the "kettle," the "kitchen's chief vocalist," to the "shopping basket" responsible for bringing in "news" about the outside world (Andersen 2004, pp. 117–119).

One of the most tantalizing things about Dezaki's *The Snow Queen* is that at the same time as it audaciously reconceptualizes Andersen's tale of this title, it also alludes to other stories by the same author—in tone, if not in content, and especially in its handling of humor. The wit exuded by several of Dezaki's scenes is of the kind one senses in a narrative like *The Princess and the Pea*, for example, where the prince traveling far and wide to find a real princess worthy of his name repeatedly discovers that although "Princesses were there in plenty, yet he could never be sure that they were the genuine article" (p. 14). Likewise memorable, in this regard, is the titular protagonist of *The Steadfast Tin Soldier*, who refrains from crying out "Here I am!" when he accidentally falls out of the window and gets stuck in the paving stones below because he does not "think it proper behaviour to cry out when in uniform" (p. 88). Andersen's own narrating voice indulges in ironically facetious asides, as exemplified by *The Goblin at the Grocer's*: "There was once a student, a proper student; he lived in an attic and owned nothing at all" (p. 202).

Throughout Dezaki's anime, one also perceives echoes of Andersen's irreverent take on conventional ethics, as a result of which his tales have often been seen to lack a moral in the classic sense of the term. In Dezaki's world, as in Andersen's *The Tinder Box*, heroes are not stereotypically noble and tend to retain, regardless of their actual age, a refreshingly childlike disposition — a proclivity that is paradigmatically conveyed, in that same tale, by the protagonist's standing as a seasoned soldier who nevertheless cherishes "sugar pigs, tin soldiers, whipping tops and rocking horses" (p. 22). Moreover, kids frequently provide the only honest voices, as borne out by *The Emperor's New Clothes*, where an innocent child is indirectly responsible for exposing the gross lie by which both the ruler and his courtiers live as a result of their unquestioning acceptance and valorization of dogmas that have speciously managed to acquire a patina of truth.

Dezaki's passion for the tiniest visual details often recalls Andersen's own flair for regaling the fairy tale world with pulsating life by recourse to delicate and minutely depicted descriptive items — the walnut-shell bed in which Thumbelina sleeps, the soup-bowl pond where she rows a tulip-petal boat using "white horsehairs as oars" (p. 33) and the "hammock" she weaves "out of blades of grass" (p. 36) are resplendent cases in point. Andersen's meticulous recording of seasonal change — in *Thumbelina* and in *The Ugly Duckling* with particular prominence — likewise resonates throughout Dezaki's *The Snow Queen* thanks to the director's unique sensitivity to the mutating landscape and ability to capture its metamorphosis as the seasons roll by through incisive graphic motifs. Architecture is no less lovingly and punctiliously portrayed — as demonstrated, for instance, by the description of "the mer-king's Palace" in *The Little Mermaid*: "Its walls are of coral, and the long pointed windows are the clearest amber, while the roof is made of cockleshells, which open and close with the waves. That's a splendid sight, for each holds a shining pearl; any single one would be the pride of a queen's crown" (p. 58). A delicious architectural touch of lyrically refined purity is the image used by the protagonist of *The Flying Trunk* to woo the princess, as he claims that while her "forehead" is comparable to "a snowy mountain," within it are "wonderful rooms and galleries, with the loveliest pictures on the walls" (p. 115).

Animals, in both Andersen and Dezaki, are a source of infinite visual delight, as well as rhetorically sophisticated personae, regardless of whether they use human words or body language. Their somatic and sartorial attributes serve to individualize them to great effect: no matter whether the detail is as hyperbolic as the dogs' preposterously oversized eyes in *The Tinder Box* or as subtle as the pompously wealthy mole's "black velvet coat" in *Thumbelina* (p. 37). Animal behavior is also a prominent topos — as evinced by the portrayal of the three dogs sitting at the table alongside the wedding-feast guests and rolling their formidable eyes at them in *The Tinder Box*. Likewise delightful, in an analogous vein, is the following vignette from *The Steadfast Tin Soldier*:

"Now the toys began to have games of their own [as humans have retired for the night] ... there was such a din that the canary woke up and joined in the talk — what is more, he did it in verse" (p. 87).

Many traces of Andersen's more disturbing tales can also be sensed in Dezaki's show. Some of these veer toward the horror lurking at the heart of the bloody hunting scenes in *The Ugly Duckling*, of the finale of *The Nightingale* in which Death comes to fetch the Emperor of China but is held in check by the loyal bird and, more pointedly and pervasively, of the entire fabric of *The Little Mermaid*: a horror "deeper than any anchor has ever sunk" (p. 58) and punctuated by violent death, mutilation and bloodshed, endless trials and the malicious whims of chance. Other disquieting moments in the anime gravitate toward a more sedate, even stoical, contemplation of the inextricability of good and evil in both the human and the supernatural dimensions. *The Snow Queen*, hailed by countless readers and critics as Andersen's masterpiece, unquestionably marks the apotheosis of the second typology. This story, like *The Little Mermaid* before it, is concurrently pervaded by the sense of mystery inherent in human beings' encounter with intractable alterity — with an Other so inscrutable as to exude equal, and equally enormous, measures of fascination and dread.

In *The Little Mermaid*, this sensation is most economically, yet disorientingly, conveyed by the revelation that "a mermaid has no tears" and that this is exactly what "makes her feel more grief than if she had" (p. 63), as well as the notion that when a mermaid dies, all that is left of this supposedly soulless creature is "foam on the water" (p. 68). This tale is also worthy of consideration, in the present context, insofar as in epitomizing Andersen's penchant for ambiguous bittersweet endings, it also mirrors anime's preference for the same dramatic strategy — an aspect of the form which Dezaki himself champions with arguably unparalleled gusto. Indeed, while the Little Mermaid's torments are rewarded with her assumption to the ranks of spirits of the air that may ascend to an eternal realm once their three-hundred-year trial is over, there is no clear endpoint to her waiting for the final reward: with every good human child she gazes upon, her odyssey will be shortened, but with every naughty child whose misdeeds she witnesses from high above, it will be ineluctably lengthened. In addition, the idea that the creature's redemption depends not on her own but on other people's goodness further curtails her free will. A comparably double-edged conclusion crowns the ordeal of the titular hero in *The Steadfast Tin Soldier*, while the ending of *The Little Match Girl*, though wrenchingly tragic at one level, ushers in a decidedly mystical sense of hope that allows for a more optimistic reading.

In tonal and stylistic terms, *The Snow Queen* finds especially close predecessors in the tales of *The Flying Trunk*, *The Ugly Duckling* and *The Wild*

Swans. A few of these stories' most salient themes, images and narrative devices therefore deserve attention at this stage. *The Flying Trunk* foreshadows *The Snow Queen* in its acute sensitivity to the realities of irretrievable loss, separation and neglect — feelings that pervade the earlier story's finale, despite its predominantly vivacious tenor, once the protagonist realizes that he will never be able to return to his bride and all he can do — somewhat like Andersen himself — is to go "wandering round the world, on foot, telling fairy tales" (p. 121). In *The Snow Queen*, it is with the character of the reindeer Bae that those affects find the most striking formulation. *The Ugly Duckling* also anticipates *The Snow Queen* in its own fashion through its heartrending portrayal of extreme loneliness and isolation (exacerbated by temporary amnesia in the case of *The Snow Queen*), counterpointed by no less intense expressions of generosity and forgiveness. Andersen's textual power to evoke delicate pictorial strokes is most patent in the tale of the stranded cygnet and this is undoubtedly an aspect of the Danish author's art to which Dezaki would have felt instinctively drawn when planning his adaptation of the later fairy tale.

It is in *The Wild Swans* that *The Snow Queen* finds its closest narrative relation. Sensitivity to minute visual details, bound to reach its stunning culmination in *The Snow Queen*, already makes itself palpably evident in *The Wild Swans* with some highly unusual visual touches. A case in point is the scene where Princess Elisa, sent off to live in poverty with a peasant family by her heartless stepmother, plays with "a green leaf— the only toy she had. She pricked a hole in it and peeped through at the sunlight. The brightness made her think of the bright eyes of her brothers" (p. 97). At the same time, *The Wild Swans* preludes *The Snow Queen* in its passion for bold metamorphic flourishes — especially in the depiction of "the cloud Palace of the fairy Morgana" where "Sea, air and sky are ever in motion" and "no vision ever comes to the watcher twice" (p. 103). These are framed by harrowing dramatic complications exuding a tenebrous halo of almost intolerable foreboding and by the diegetically pivotal obligation to embark on a perilous voyage with no unequivocally foreseeable outcome or destination.

The Snow Queen likewise glories in variations on the transformation topos, varying their magnitude from the glamorous to the minimalistic. The former typology is ushered in right at the beginning with the image of the devilish mirror that makes all hideous things seem beautiful and all comely and virtuous things, conversely, appear repulsive. Shattered into countless fragments that cause any being that comes into contact with even the tiniest of shards to become calculating and cold-hearted, the mirror provides the point of departure for the saga of woe, endurance and love with Gerda and Kay as its protagonists. Although the mirror's impact is momentous, it is from elegantly restrained descriptive notes that Andersen exposes most memorably the effect which one of the stray splinters has on Kay's personality, thus confirming the author's dexterity in the handling of subtle particulars. Hence, the boy's deterioration from a gentle, sensitive and nature-loving soul into a callous creature is neatly summed up by the observation that when terror seizes him upon his abduction by the Snow Queen, "all he could remember was multiplication tables" (p. 162). Another nice touch bearing full witness to Andersen's knack of evoking whole scenes through single lines of narrative comes later with the description of the Finmark woman, poring "so intently" over parchment covered with cryptic marks that "sweat ran from her brow like rain" (p. 185).

Going back to the metamorphosis topos, a striking example of its use in a deliberately nonsensational vein is the scene where Gerda's tears fall onto the very spot where a rose tree has been swallowed by the earth, causing the plant to spring up again in glorious bloom. The most dazzling instance of transformation occurs when Gerda at last manages to enter the Snow Queen's garden and snowflakes in charge of guarding the domain morph into creatures endowed with the most preposterous of forms: "Some were huge wild hedgehogs; others were like knotted bunches of snakes writhing their heads in all directions; others again were like fat little bears with icicles for hair." Gerda, with characteristic resourcefulness, succeeds unwittingly in vanquishing the formidable guards as the cloud of "her own breath" takes the shape of "bright angels" capable of dispelling "the dreadful snow-things" (p. 187).

Climactic and seasonal effects, already central to *The Wild Swans*, play an even more conspicuous role in *The Snow Queen*. A tangible sense of the passing seasons is conveyed from an early stage in the narrative, as the protagonists' relationship is framed precisely by reference to the different activities in which they engage according to seasonal shifts. In the summer, they sit together for hours in the miniature rose-cocooned garden placed at the meeting point of their attics' sloping roofs, chatting and playing in the fragrant warmth of the brief spell of clement weather blessing the northern region. In the winter, they interact by warming up coins and pressing them on the frosty window panes so as to create peepholes through which their eyes may gaze out into the snow-clasped world. A touching example of Andersen's descriptive genius in the chronicling of the changing seasons is provided by the scene in which Gerda, still in the relatively early stages of her quest, suddenly realizes, to her utter dismay, that "summer" is "over." Although she has witnessed "no signs of changing time" in the "enchanted garden" where she has resided practically since her departure from her hometown in search of Kay, time has in fact moved on at an alarming rate: "The long willow leaves had turned quite yellow and wet with mist; they dropped off one by one.... Oh, how mournful and bleak it was in the wide world" (p. 171).

A scintillating instance of Andersen's power to make the weather a veritable stage hero is offered by the sequence in which the Snow Queen takes Kay to her northern Palace. The sequence's frantically accelerating momentum is harmonized with the correspondingly rampant severity of the elements as the Snow Queen's sledge rises over the stormy clouds and the wind heaves and roars, reminding Kay of "ballads of olden times" (p. 163). Every single aspect of the environment responds at once to the raging weather and to the Snow Queen's passage over lakes, lands and woods as though to evoke the seamless collusion of the animal, vegetable and mineral kingdoms in a universe where protean flux reigns supreme. It is in *The Snow Queen*'s climax, however, that Andersen's passion for atmospheric drama reaches an apex of sublimity, as the protagonists emerge from the Queen's icy and eerily resounding Palace and the cutting winds suddenly die out while the sun breaks through as if to welcome them both and, most importantly, reward Gerda's stoical resilience. The topos of the voyage, already seen to play a prominent role in *The Wild Swans*, is so cardinal to *The Snow Queen* as to be realistically definable as its narrative lynchpin. The theme is enthroned as a major player early on with Kay's abduction by the titular character, which could readily be described as the most tantalizing passage in Andersen's whole oeuvre.

Like many (indeed most) of Andersen's other narratives, *The Snow Queen* also evinces a refreshing sense of humor. Therefore, even if instances of pain, deprivation and even violent death pepper the tale, the author's playful side never relinquishes the scene altogether. The character of the Raven and his sweetheart/wife-to-be are responsible for a substantial proportion of the tale's humor. This is clearly demonstrated by the scene in which the Raven, having complained that his mastery of Gerda's language is inadequate and he will therefore have to keep his tale down to the bare bones, then launches into an extraordinarily detailed and ornamented piece of rhetoric. Even more overtly amusing is the scene in which the Raven and his partner, having been asked by the Princess who wishes to reward their generosity whether they would prefer freedom or a permanent appointment as Court Ravens accompanied by limitless access to leftovers from the royal kitchens, cautiously espouse the latter option because they feel they must "think of their old age" (p. 178). The erection of the birds to the status of comic figures does not, however, exempt them totally from the darker realities of Andersen's vision and in the dénouement, we indeed learn that the male has died since Gerda made his acquaintance, leaving behind a plaintive widow. Another fine touch of humor is provided by the portrait of the hounds kept by the robbers — brutes that look as though they could easily devour a human with no effort but refrain from barking for the simple reason that it "was forbidden" (p. 180).

As elsewhere in Andersen, architectural descriptors are no less lovingly handled than natural ones. In *The Snow Queen*, a paradigmatic illustration is supplied by the castle where, at one point, Gerda believes she may have located Kay at last: each hall through which the girl passes is described as more majestic than the previous one and the ceiling of the royal bedchamber is said to be shaped "like the crown of a palm tree, with leaves of rarest crystal" (p. 177). One of the entire tale's most imaginative sequences is the one in which Gerda moves from flower to flower in the bewitched garden to glean information regarding Kay's whereabouts but only hears each flower's personal story, vision, song or dream. These ultimately amount to potential fairy tales in their own right, which renders the sequence as a whole a capsulated version of Andersen's distinctive universe in a nutshell. The oneiric element, already axial to this portion of the narrative, asserts itself with mesmerizingly haunting beauty in a later passage which many readers of all ages have not hesitated to single out as their most abiding memory of the whole tale. This is the one where Gerda perceives "a flight of shadows on the wall" of the staircase leading surreptitiously to the royal bedroom — namely, the silhouettes of "horses with thin legs and flowing manes, huntsmen, lords and ladies on horseback"— and the Raven informs her that they "are only dreams" that "come and take the gentry's thoughts on midnight rides" (p. 176).

As noted earlier, and specifically with reference to *The Emperor's New Clothes*, Andersen frequently presents children as people endowed with a sensitivity, wisdom and resourcefulness unknown to adults. *The Snow Queen* celebrates this proposition by declaring that no additional force which the heroine might aspire to gain, magical or otherwise, could ever be greater than the one which she already possesses: that is to say, the strength that issues from her very heart and, as the Finmark woman puts it, from being an "innocent child" (p. 186). Furthermore, *The Snow Queen*'s truly happy ending, one senses, does not simply reside with the protagonists' reunion or their safe return to their hometown but rather with the revelation that although by the time the story reaches its conclusion Gerda and Kay are no longer "young children," they are nonetheless "the same children still at heart" (p. 193). As foreshadowed, *The Snow Queen* elliptically points to the inseparability of good and evil, thus ushering in an atmosphere of potent ethical ambiguity. This is most tersely (in a literal, as well as figurative, sense) communicated by the eponymous character. The Snow Queen is neither good nor evil: she forcibly takes Kay under her wing and keeps him bound to her Palace by means of an unaccomplishable task, yet cannot be blamed for the misfortune that has befallen the boy in the first place. In fact, it could even be opined that the glacial lady simply takes advantage of the situation, recognizing in the ice-hearted kid a kindred spirit and securing his company out of sheer loneliness. Most crucially, the Queen's motives are never explicitly stated in the tale and this is undoubtedly one of its greatest strengths. It is also, no less vitally in this context, what Dezaki seeks to bring to the fore in his own version of the classic narrative.

The anime asserts its atmospheric distinctiveness by deliberately displacing the marked sense of enclosedness characterizing the opening segment of Andersen's story by means of an expansive landscape. This is foregrounded from the start through panoramic views of the protagonists' hometown. Moreover, the kids themselves are first introduced in the context of a rural late-summer excursion, as Gerda leads Kay to the meadow flooded with white and red roses which she has recently discovered. A remarkable example of Dezaki's broadening of the original tale's spatial scope is the deep forest, unique to the anime, reputed to harbor an ancient church whence the sound of the bell to which Gerda feels mysteriously drawn seems to issue. It is when Gerda and Kay enter the menacing woods against the adults' desires (and the girl at one point even tumbles down a Carrollian hole symbolic of a transition to some alternate realm) that the protagonists first come into contact with a magical dimension presaging the Snow Queen's advent in their lives.

Another aspect of Dezaki's anime evident from the show's inceptive moments consists of its painstaking attention to the representation of inanimate objects. This is most sensationally attested to by the Snow Queen's horse-drawn carriage: an entity that literally materializes out of nothing and comes to life whenever the lady requires transportation. The accompanying sound and lighting effects — a crystalline jingle of invisible bells, effervescent trails of ice dust, shades redolent of the Aurora Borealis — majestically abet the vehicle's depiction. In this respect, the adaptation professes utter fidelity to its antecedent insofar as Andersen's universe itself is proverbially defined by an unsurpassed ability to make the everyday reality of seemingly lifeless things proclaim its aliveness with both energy and charm. According to Jackie Wullschlager, this quality is a natural corollary of Andersen's personality, which accommodated throughout his life a "child's instinctive empathy with objects and people, and an unbridled infant egoism which enabled him to see his own story in all things." Whether or not explicit correspondences obtain between Andersen's imagination and Dezaki's, there can be little doubt that the two artists share a passionate devotion to attentively individualized actors, vivid settings and a flair for integrating the portrayal of fantastical items with a piquant take on the ludic. A major source of jocularity is supplied, in the anime, by the red and blue trolls employed in the capacity of attendants at the Snow Queen's Palace. Paradoxically, despite their role as dispensers of boisterous comic relief, these characters are also responsible for shattering the mirror from which the saga's core drama derives. In addition, Dezaki is faithful to Andersen in the studious recording of the passage of the seasons, and related attention to ritualized activities connected with both seasonal and diurnal cycles, from the autumn "gleaning" that takes place in the aftermath of the summer harvest, to the kneading of dough, weaving at the loom or carving of wooden clogs.

It should also be noted that Dezaki draws some discreet parallels between the story of *The Snow Queen* itself and Andersen's life, presenting Gerda as a washerwoman, like Andersen's mum, while Kay's dad is cast as a cobbler with a knack of creating wonderful wooden toys: Andersen is said to have learned from his father the art of constructing toy theaters. The Danish author himself finds an apposite alter ego in the persona of the itinerant minstrel Ragi, who travels from land to land in the company of a lone she-wolf and a wee monkey and is employed by Dezaki as the character charged with the task of chronicling the saga for our benefit. Increasingly, Ragi ascends to the status of a major character, accompanying Gerda in many of her most challenging adventures and incrementally revealing an intricate personality and history of his own beneath a seemingly hard surface of imponderable self-composure. It should also be noted, in this regard, that Dezaki's introduction of a narrator providing a substantial (yet not overbearing) voiceover in the guise of a weighty and somber commentary on Gerda's ordeal serves to evoke the impression that the anime is not merely replicating a story that has already been written and told but actually creating and divulging a narrative as we watch its unfolding. This engaging sense of immediacy and performative presence enables the show to speak to the feelings, anxieties and desires of a contemporary audience without seeking refuge in antiquarian fidelity as its top priority. The character of Hans Alexander Holmes parallels Ragi as a further intradiegetic Andersen avatar, being an actor, a street entertainer and, above all, an ardent bricoleur and inventor. Andersen himself indeed harbored a legendary passion for engineering and mechanics.

Furthermore, as Wolfgang Lederer points out, the very idea of the rooftop garden — as significant in the anime as it is in the source narrative — mirrors Andersen's own childhood experience since "He had just such an arrangement of flower boxes when he was a little boy (though he always played there alone)" (Lederer, p. 9). Dezaki's use of aspects of the writer's life is quite pertinent if one accepts, at least partially, Lederer's contention that Andersen, like Kay, was trapped and inhibited by his very personality and gradually developed the conviction that for a boy to transcend adolescent self-alienation and reach manhood, he needs "redemption through the love of a woman" (p. 182). This psychological evolution, argues Lederer, is something which Andersen longed for but was powerless to achieve: "Andersen started as an ugly duckling and became the resplendent swan of the *salon* and the house party; but, contrary to the ugly duckling of his famous story, he never truly *believed* that he was being accepted by the other swans." In the circumstances, however, he found marvelous ways of giving life to his dreams of acceptance and human warmth through his art: "it was from his very failures," Lederer touchingly comments, that "Andersen — poor, lonely oyster that he was — created the pearls he has left us" (p. 179).

Some figurative motifs that are of cardinal importance to the tale and its animated version alike require some consideration at this stage in the discussion. The image of the magical mirror is prominent in fairy tales and fantasy literature generally as a gateway to other worlds, as documented by narratives as diverse as *Snow White*, *Beauty and the Beast* and *Through the Looking-Glass, and What Alice Found There*. *The Snow Queen* lends the motif an original twist, on which the anime depends to great effect and with some truly inspired reorientations, by intimating that such a portal can compel people to recognize the world's ugliness and evil for what they truly are and, by implication, to see the unpalatable facets of their own individual natures which they strive to ignore or repress. According to Moira Li-Lynn Ong, the image of the "shattered mirror" can also be read as a "metaphor for depression" insofar as its penetration, as a mere shard, of a person's heart can be conducive to precisely the kind of "irritability," "negative thoughts" and "numbness" one encounters in depression. Moreover, just as depression ruptures an individual's emotional equilibrium, the accursed fragment's hold on Kay's heart leads to the fracture of the composite soul which his own self and Gerda's self appear to constitute at the start of the tale into two separate entities, disjoined by more than just space in a purely physical or geographical sense of the term. (In Dezaki's adaptation, the complementarity of the two protagonists' souls is symbolically encapsulated by the likewise interdependent values upheld by the image of the red rose associated with Gerda and that of the white rose associated with Kay.) The schism caused by the diabolical mirror's impact on the characters' lives inevitably means that both the overt victim of the curse and his complementary soul mate are equally deprived of their initial state of harmony — hence, Gerda's urge to embark on a perilous journey to restore not only her friend's but also her own natural integrity.

Furthermore, there is an obvious similarity between Kay's residence at the Snow Queen's Palace and Gerda's sojourn in the Enchanted Cottage, for both experiences constitute rites of passage in which subjectivity is held in abeyance and inactivity functions as a means of giving the mind and the emotions room to evolve: a Dark Night of the Soul without which no further motion would be possible. "When depression strikes," Ong comments, "we often become increasingly bitter and self-hating, growing so alienated that we seem lost from ourselves and others." This condition is mirrored by Kay's predicament as he becomes estranged from Gerda and his familiar environment until he is literally "whisked away by the Snow Queen." Gerda's journey, in this scenario, constitutes a metaphor for the "healing" process as a quest "into the most frightening limits" of the psyche (Ong). Mary C. Legg highlights the sheer magnitude of Gerda's task as a voyager by contrasting the girl's attitude to the world with the path chosen by the Old Woman who shelters Gerda in her magical cottage shortly after the beginning of the long journey. "Andersen insists that the woman is not a bad witch," Legg notes "but still a witch who can order the arrangement of her garden to suit her needs, manipulating the memory of Gerda. The one is childless from old age-and also possibly selfishness.... In comparison, Gerda began her journey by casting away her new red shoes. Although the gesture is foolish, the reader sympathises with someone so selfless as to endure discomfort in hopes of recovering a lost love.... The selflessness of Gerda is further contrasted with the stories of the flowers who are filled up with self-admiration. Each is absorbed in its own small story" (Legg 2004).

Lederer proposes an alternate psychoanalytical reading of the tale, focusing on Kay's metamorphosis as an allegory of male psychosexual development. In growing "intolerant of sentimentality and 'childish' stories" and deeply resenting "idealizing romanticism and piety" (Lederer, p. 26) in favor of "mathematical skill" and "more knowledge of the scientific kind," while also preferring outdoor boyish activities to female companionship, Kay "behaves, in short, like the typical adolescent" (p. 27). According to Anna Freud, this type of coldly rationalizing attitude is a defense mechanism of vital significance to adolescents (Freud, pp. 172–180). Dezaki amplifies Kay's unsentimentally technological disposition by presenting the boy as a skillful puzzle-maker from an early stage in the anime, developing this character trait over Kay's residence at the Snow Queen's Palace, where he is shown to carve and assemble effortlessly an exquisite ice castle replete with mechanisms of great refinement, as well as skates, skateboards and a flute on which he ritually performs a melody of his own conception. Lederer also suggests that the Snow Queen's kisses consign Kay to a state of "defensive-protective hibernation of the emotions during adolescence" (Lederer, p. 30). The icy lady consciously refrains from dispensing too many tokens of her attachment to the boy so as not to endanger his survival in the unfamiliar otherworld: when, on the way to the Palace, she tells Kay that were she to give him any further kisses, he would die, her aim is feasibly to ensure the boy's transition to a liminal developmental state whence he may emerge more mature and resilient.

Dezaki throws the tale's psychological dimension into relief while concurrently corroborating Legg's proposition that one of *The Snow Queen*'s principal assets lies with its ability to draw us into a world which, though outlandish, uncannily comes across as somehow familiar. This effect is enabled by Andersen's descriptive flair: "he begins the narration of *The Snow Queen*," as Legg notes, by associating the pernicious glass fragment with the homely image of "an eyelash or hair caught in an eye," and thus "creates the credibility of the story" insofar as practically anybody is likely to be acquainted with "the sharp pain" caused by "particles grating against the tender surface of the eye." This paves the way to further recognition of the suffering endured by the protagonists since, at a basic psychological level, many of us are also likely to have experienced an affliction comparable to "the tingle of numb hands and the screaming pain of swollen frozen fingers" (Legg 2003).

At the same time as he brings into play images tapping into both psychology and physiology to engage the audience in his adaptation, Dezaki also alerts us to the symbolic tension between two well-known fairy tale types: the Princess and the Queen. The figure of the Princess is traditionally associated with the concept of regal dignity and with femininity as embodied by a character that stands symbolically for the hopes and aspirations of the inner infantile self in all of us and thus alludes to a sense of promise and to prospects of future fulfillment. The figure of the Queen, conversely, represents a mature incarnation of power connotative of self-realization — though not in unequivocally positive terms given that fairy tale Queens may be cast not simply as nurturing and tender protectors but also as malicious, envious and dominant presences. On the whole, whereas the Princess type tends to emblematize the innocent delight of springtime, the Queen signifies the reliability and vigor of summer climes. The figures of the Princess and the Queen are not necessarily to be understood as mutually exclusive binary opposites for a Queen does not have to surrender her Princess self altogether but may, in fact, retain it while also incorporating an additional role into her overall personality. What Andersen enjoins us to ponder, in the light of these reflections, is the significance of a Queen figure that stands not for summer warmth but for the deepest and most intractably forbidding winter one could ever ideate — so much so that *The Snow Queen* has come to represent virtually all over the world the very spirit of dazzling iciness and many readers will readily claim that the story *has to* be read when it is cold and dark outside. *The Snow Queen*, in other words, has come to be considered the quintessentially wintry tale — even more so than the "sad tale" of "sprites and goblins" which Shakespeare's Mamilius deems "best for winter" (*The Winter's Tale*, Act II, Scene I).

It could be argued that Andersen's story actually redefines the fairy tale idea of Queenness by positing the titular character as a pre–Princess figure that has not yet attained to the innocence and joy of spring, on the one hand, and as a post–Queen being that has already exhausted the strength and confidence of summer on the other. If this interpretation were espoused, it could further be maintained that Andersen's Snow Queen is both immature and hoary, both childlike and ancient beyond imagining and that in this composite personality, multiple and discordant roles are able to coexist. The character's treatment of Kay substantiates this reading insofar as she is never overtly portrayed as either a surrogate sibling or a protective bride (roles that would be consonant with the Princess modality) or as a mother or stepmother (roles pertinent to the Queen type) but rather as a weird amalgamation of these and other possible roles in ways that defy human understanding and strict classification. Dezaki revels in this ambiguity, invoking it to create an intensely relativistic universe consonant with the proclivities intrinsic in both his own distinctive world view and the ethics of anime at large.

It should also be noted, on this point, that the figure of the Snow Queen is an important member of a larger and widely revered clan of Winter and Christmas Fairies originating in Pagan lore and then varyingly appropriated, distorted, demonized — or, quite simply, *adapted*— by Christianity. As Louise Heyden explains, "One of the major faerie queens, the Snow Queen is both faerie and sky goddess. At Winter Solstice she rides through the snowy skies, making the snow fall by shaking the pillows on her icy chariot. Her company, known as the Wild Hunt, ride through the skies until Twelfth Night, creating snowstorms in their wake" (Heyden). Japanese lore has its own memorable version of such a creature in the mythical persona of *Yuki-onna* (literally, "Snow-woman"). As the *Wikipedia* entry devoted to this figure points out, "Yuki-onna appears on snowy nights as a tall, beautiful woman with long black hair and red lips. Her inhumanly pale or even transparent skin makes her blend into the snowy landscape.... She sometimes wears a white kimono, but other legends describe her as nude, with only her face and hair standing out against the snow.... She floats across the snow, leaving no footprints (in fact, some tales say she has no feet, a feature of many Japanese ghosts), and she can transform into a cloud of mist or snow if threatened" ("Yuki-onna").

Yuki-onna closely parallels Andersen's portrayal of the Snow Queen in her moral ambivalence, having indeed been depicted as preternaturally evil in some legends and as vulnerably human in others, as a vampiric soul-sucker, succubus or child-snatcher in her maleficent incarnations and as a magnanimous, gentle or vaporously spectral force in her unharmful manifestations. Yuki-Onna also echoes Andersen's Snow Queen on the iconographic plane insofar as she often appears in the form of a glacial wave traversing the environment with tempestuous intensity in the deceptively soft embrace of a frosty mantle. This imagery pervades Dezaki's rendition of the Snow Queen's recurrent forays into the human world to regale it with winter, control storms or visit its inhabitants through fleeting apparitions. In his adaptation of the famous tale, and particularly in sequences such as those, Dezaki assiduously reminds us that it is possible to relate intimately to fantastic adventures as reflections of the hidden landscapes of human personality and hence as formative myths capable of sustaining individual journeys of maturation and self-understanding. Accepting the metaphorical veracity and psychological relevance of a fairy tale even as one recognizes its empirical otherworldliness is akin, ultimately, to accepting one's own unfolding life story as a web of endlessly intricate motivations, expectations, choices and dreams coated with rich layers of seemingly unfathomable symbolism.

Even the most devoted or fastidious Andersen fan would plausibly be willing to concede that Dezaki's show does the original story full credit. This does not only apply to those aspects of the anime that follow the source text most faithfully. In fact, it is also true — ironically, even truer at times — of those facets of the adaptation that emanate entirely from the director's own imagination and could therefore be regarded as its unofficial components. These include both episode-long digressions, shorter sequences and even mere vignettes, some of which are tangentially inspired by other fairy tales issuing from Andersen's pen. At times, we encounter obvious references to iconic Andersen props — e.g., the magical flying trunk. At others, Dezaki offers substantially original adaptations of narrative and symbolic motifs immortalized by the Danish author. In the process, several Andersen tales are revisited. These include *The Ugly Duckling*, *The Pea Blossom*, *The Traveling Companion*, *She Was Good for Nothing*, *The Red Shoes*, *The Little Match Girl* and *The Little Mermaid*.

Dezaki's adaptation of *The Little Mermaid* within the wider tapestry of his anime is worthy of consideration as an illustrative instance. The episode in question thrives on the interleaving of Andersen's original story, narrated by Hans as a miniature puppet show with the assistance of a toy theater of just the kind the Danish author would have loved, with gorgeously painted still plates and regular animated sequences recording Gerda's exploration of a mermaid-themed coastal town of picturesque charm. The place is so iconographically obsessed with the hybrid figure that mermaids of all shapes and sizes feature ubiquitously as shop signs, fountains, decorative motifs for tableware and biscuits (among several other available configurations). The Gerda-based strand of the adventure chronicles the heroine's interaction with a latter-day mermaid that has also, like Andersen's doomed protagonist, gained access to the human world and acquired a pair of legs. Although the climax of this installment is by no means as harrowing as the finale of Andersen's tale, it nonetheless carries a markedly bittersweet and ambiguous message consonant with the ethos cultivated by the art of anime at large and Dezaki's opus in particular. Thus, while Dezaki's mermaid has her longing for human friendship briefly fulfilled, she must ineluctably return to the aqueous domain where people like Gerda and wonderful adventures like Gerda's quest are intractably alien.

Returning to Dezaki's *The Snow Queen*, it should be noted that one novel element proposed by the anime that deserves special attention consists of the narrative change that makes the obnoxious glass fragments issue from the Snow Queen's very Palace, where the shattering of the magical mirror is said to have occurred. When the red and blue trolls in the Snow Queen's service are temporarily possessed by the mirror's demonic maker, they are instantly seized by an irresistible urge to drop the artifact. This serves to lend the Snow Queen's decision to snatch Kay away from his familiar world fresh levels of meaning. For one thing, it suggests that the knowledge of a direct connection between the shard that has pierced the boy's eye and heart and the Snow Queen's own domain is what draws the preternatural creature to Kay as a human whose destiny is viscerally bound to her being. Additionally, if the icy lady could be credited with the possession of ethical standards of a kind a human can grasp, it could be surmised that what has led her to rehome Kay in her world is a sense of responsibility for his misfortune. She indeed promises Kay that as long as he is a "guest" at her Palace, where "eternal beauty" and "silence" that "transcends time" reign supreme, his damaged heart "will feel no pain." What he will have to surrender "in exchange" is his "past." This reading seems to be validated by the Snow Queen's efforts to make Kay happy in her realm — much to the confusion of the trolls hosted therein, who do not appear to have witnessed this kind of conduct on their mistress' part before.

In addition, it is important to recognize that the Snow Queen likewise plays a benevolent role in several later scenes. At one point, her sheer presence within the landscape appears responsible for the materialization, against the logic of the bitter season, of the "liverwort" shoots needed to cure Gerda's grandmother when her raging fever endangers her very life. There also intimations of the Snow Queen's kindness in the adventure where her appearance — riding a snowy steed and accompanied by the Aurora — over a treacherous sea route seems indirectly instrumental in the redemption of a corrupt Captain. Nevertheless, these hypothetical attributions of morality should not induce us to forget that for Dezaki, as for Andersen, the Snow Queen is ultimately an amoral being — an entity *beyond* morality as one might conceive of that concept in ordinary terms and as remote as the land "beyond the giant glaciers of the North" where, according to the words spoken by Gerda's grandmother in the screenplay, her Palace stands. As Nicky Raven points out in his introduction to the Templar edition of Andersen's narrative, "The character of the Snow Queen sits beautifully on the edge of the story; not good, but not pure evil either. Unlike the villains of most conventional stories, she doesn't need to be defeated for Gerda and Kay to triumph" (in Andersen 2005, p. 12). Dezaki knows how to depict full-fledged villains when he is so inclined and it is no coincidence that in a show that abounds with such types, he should have chosen to suspend judgment on the titular persona herself.

A genuinely inspired adaptive move on Dezaki's part is the dramatic revelation that even once the mirror seems to have been healed and the fiend to have been consigned for good to an unfathomable chasm by the heroes' concerted efforts, the villain remains capable of resurging as long as the shard lodged in Kay's eye is still missing from the mirror. It is up to the long-suffering Gerda, at this point, to call on Kay's dormant emotions in order to trigger the boy's tears and thus the expulsion of the last hateful fragment. Another interesting mirror-related variation on the original theme dramatized by Dezaki's anime consists of the Snow Queen's desire to see the magical looking-glass reassembled. The trolls she employs are at one point enjoined to undertake the Herculean task of collecting all of the numberless specks into which the portentous surface is held to have dispersed and piece them together again. However, the niveous lady seems to harbor little faith in the ostensibly inane creatures' willingness, let alone ability, to accomplish such a feat. Accordingly, while in Andersen's story Kay is instructed by his patron to arrange a set of ice shards so that they will spell the word "Eternity" (the choice of this particular word is left unexplained), in Dezaki's anime, Kay's task is to work on a puzzle whose completion is the key to the restoration of the shattered mirror, and hence to the conclusive banishment from the Snow Queen's realm of the mirror's diabolical artificer. As long as the puzzle is incomplete, the demon will be able to avail himself of even the tiniest fissure in the texture of the icy looking-glass to reenter the Palace and go on threatening the entire cosmos with portentous waves of volcanic fire.

Another interesting departure from the original is the introduction of a mythical figure of Dezaki's own ideation as the demonic archenemy's double: a character endowed with powers comparable in magnitude, if not in intent, to those of the titular persona — the "Father of the Wind." The Snow Queen clearly mistrusts this character (who, in turn, endeavors to befriend Kay and ensure his visits to the Palace remain a secret) because she is well aware that the snow she dispenses upon the land, while not hazardous in itself, is bound to be a cause of intense suffering for all creatures if it is combined with unruly squalls and noxious heat currents. This would seem to confirm the existence of kindly streaks in the Snow Queen's personality as conceptualized in the show, while also subtly alluding to environmental issues of great topical relevance. Dezaki's portrayal of the Snow Queen as a potentially — or liminally — benevolent individual is confirmed by his preparedness to engage with dark themes when their need or dramatic appropriateness arise. This is testified by the fact that he does not demur from a frank confrontation of strife, sorrow, violence and death, even through the overt employment of stark martial contents and imagery. Such a proclivity emerges in the flashbacks to Ragi's exploits as a wartime commander, the Snow Queen's duels with her demonic antagonist (where she dons stupendous armor in genuinely chivalric style), and the installment where Gerda and Ragi visit a barren land haunted by the phantoms of ancient warriors slaughtered in horrible battles.

Dezaki's handling of the four key adventures forming Andersen's original tale deserves some attention at this stage. In his treatment of Part 3, which pivots on the Enchanted Cottage in Andersen, Dezaki is quite loyal to the source text in dramatizing Gerda's forceful adoption by the Old Woman, temporary amnesia and eventual reawakening to the reality of her situation. However, the anime turns the captor into a more customary fairy tale witch and accordingly imparts the character's portrayal with far more overtly ominous connotations. The heroine's retrieval of her memories and resultant resolve to break free, relatedly, lead to intense dynamism appropriate to Dezaki's medium, with Gerda's rescue of the roses trapped by the enchantress in a dungeon-like cave marking the culmen of the girl's heroic stamina. With the adaptation of the adventure developed in Part 4, revolving around the Prince and Princess of a marvelous realm in the context of the original text, the anime adheres to the spirit of the original in the depiction of the stupendously loquacious Raven, of the magnanimity of the royal couple and of the sumptuousness of its Palace. Once again, Dezaki relies on his medium's unique strengths: in this instance, not so much in favor of ebullient action as in the service of lavishly painted natural and architectural locales. The golden carriage and luxurious clothing with which Gerda is presented by her benefactors stand out as veritable anime gems.

Part 5, centered by Andersen on the Robber Girl, offers a radically novel take on the robbers, now portrayed as a semi-demonic tribal society governed by a complex hierarchy, set of customs and rules of conduct, simultaneously expanding the scope of the adventure and underscoring the Robber Girl's bravery in her efforts to abet Gerda's quest and generosity in the flashback to her rescue of the reindeer Bae, destined soon to become a major actor in the story. With the adaptation of Part 6, where the source narrative concentrates on the personae of the Lapland Woman and the Finmark Woman, Dezaki indulges in some flamboyant revisioning moves, depicting the two characters as elderly ladies endowed with outlandish sartorial tastes, a prodigious palate for theatrical make-up and quite unexpected acrobatic skills. At the same time, the show is faithful to Andersen's text in the treatment of narrative details—e.g., the Lapland Woman's use of dried fish inscribed with esoteric letters to communicate with the Finmark Woman, the depiction of the large bush with red berries marking the critical spot upon which Bae must put Gerda down to ensure she will proceed alone in her quest and the tearful farewell occurring at that juncture. Like Andersen's Finmark Woman, Dezaki's does not initially seem too willing to support Gerda's mission but gives in when she recognizes the girl's strength as the sole weapon through which the Snow Queen's power may be challenged: in other words, the pure determination of an honest and resilient child.

In the anime's climax, Dezaki conclusively imparts his show with remarkable artistic autonomy through formal and stylistic shifts no less than content-oriented changes. The cinematic icon of the Snow Queen's Palace, mantled in crystal gleams and emerging epiphanically from the impenetrable darkness around it, is felicitously deployed by Dezaki as the point of entry to the anime's final installments. The first of the formal shifts here worthy of note is Dezaki's interpretation of Gerda's battle against the Snow Queen's guards, which are rendered with a hearty appetite for multifarious monstrosity and abetted by an obstacle course of astounding aesthetic refinement: for instance, in the representation of the grid bearing snow-crystal patterns over which Gerda leaps like a seasoned Olympic hurdler. An arresting structural reorientation following these scenes consists of the involuted set of circumstances in which the Snow Queen decides to allow the girl into her domain. This move ushers in opportunities for two interrelated chains of dramatic ramifications. On one level, we see the heroine interact with the trolls who, in the process, retain their carnivalesque function but also rise to the status of mindful and self-determining agents with credible feelings. On the other, we are encouraged — or rather, challenged — to speculate about the Snow Queen's modus operandi and attendant ethics. While it is not preposterous to surmise that the Snow Queen, in keeping Gerda locked up in a sparsely furnished and inevitably chilly chamber and barring her access to Kay, is effectively holding the girl captive and hence behaving like a standard evil sorceress, it is also tempting to speculate that the mythical figure is actually protecting Gerda from the pain and sadness she knows the girl is bound to feel upon realizing that her playmate has no idea who she is.

The climax escalates with Kay's possession by the Snow Queen's archenemy — who has by now relinquished altogether the suave semblance of Father of the Wind and taken on the appearance of a full-fledged colossal fiend that graphically amplifies the tenor of Andersen's own description of the mirror's manufacturer as "the Devil himself" (Andersen 2004, p. 154). Surrounding this baleful event are the no less spectacular arrival of the lone wolf Olga at the Palace bearing Ragi's hat and the Snow Queen's decision to rescue the hapless minstrel from his glacial tomb. The glistening lady's encounter with Ragi at this stage in the adventure mirrors a prior meeting between the two characters — hinted at by earlier flashbacks — in which matters of snow-triggered death, survival and redemption were likewise central. Whereas at the time of the first rendezvous Ragi appeared to long for death as the only possible reprieve from a destiny of guilt-laden survival and the Snow Queen unwilling to comply with his desire, Ragi is now given a chance, having sampled the reality of death, to appreciate the true magnitude of the Snow Queen's implied message — namely, the idea that life should never, however unpalatable the alternative may seem, be casually thrown away.

The relationship between Ragi and the Snow Queen is very complex and woven from a special but largely inscrutable bond that appears to defy time and space, concurrently obfuscating the boundary between the story's here-and-now and an ancestral era steeped in myth. Dezaki's articulation of that relationship eloquently demonstrates the director's flair for sophisticated psychological analysis. At the same time, the two characters' alliance — staunchly abetted by Olga — in the final battle against the Devil could be seen as an epic adaptation of the profoundly collaborative spirit underpinning the art of anime in its entirety. With the battle, Dezaki also enjoys unprecedented scope for sensational action sequences that deploy to great effect stark chromatic contrasts (especially between icy and fiery palettes) and for the representation of martial gear of medieval and classical resonance, matched by winged steeds (akin to the ones found in *Romeo x Juliet*, here studied in Chapter 5). As anticipated, it is with the postponement of the heroes' victory, occasioned by the stubborn attachment of the very last mirror fragment to Kay's person, that the anime adaptation proclaims most sonorously its autonomous standing vis-à-vis its source. The visual parallel established by Dezaki between the tiny fissure in the mirror through which the villain may easily vanquish humanity in one fell swoop and the physical torment endured by Kay as the sole remaining victim of the curse encapsulates both the raw human drama and the cosmic dimension of the story with remarkable cinematic conciseness.

Dezaki's anime is intensely loyal to its European source — even as it proclaims its independent caliber and often departs from it with radical audacity — through the painstaking adoption of a narrative form and storytelling stance that remain true throughout to the quintessential spirit of old fairy tales. This is most pointedly the case with the numerous episodes in which Dezaki digresses from the parent text to weave quite independent substories alongside the substories already drawn from Andersen himself. The fairy tale's distinctive spirit is never ignored or obfuscated but is actually emplaced as the adventure's implicit hero by the use of a visual style vividly redolent of Scandinavian lore. In other words, the anime does not merely pay lip service to an ancient tradition to which an Eastern audience would feel attracted just because of its exotic alterity: in fact, it genuinely and consummately embodies it at the most intimate aesthetic level. It is also noteworthy that the introduction of additional stories enables Dezaki to communicate a key facet of fairy tales at large: the crucial importance of trials as inevitable vicissitudes to be endured and overcome by a heroine or a hero even if they are not explicitly linked to her or his main quest. Trials are ultimately what makes characters what they are, what invests them with recognizable identities, and are hence instrumental in helping them prove the validity of those identities holistically rather than simply on the basis of some contingent achievement. Gerda, specifically, is made what she is by each and every adventure she experiences along the way — not solely by her rescue of the boy she treasures out of love, generosity and perseverance, admirable though these qualities indubitably are.

Andersen's chosen form and medium compel him to individuate the different locations in which *The Snow Queen*'s seven parts are staged by recourse to carefully selected descriptive details capable of evoking multiple impressions in the most economical fashion imaginable. The anime mold allows Dezaki to experiment with a wide array of meticulously diversified settings. These range from balmy seaside towns to terrifying glaciers and stormy oceans, from homely village yards to magical forests, from idyllic flower-strewn meadows and sleepily winding rivers to portentous waterfalls and impervious mountain ranges. Concurrently, the series dwells by turns on palpably material edifices and evanescently refined conceptual realms, romantic vistas wherein a wilderness of shaggy trees and weather-beaten rocks seamlessly coexists with green valleys and graceful nostalgic visions, pastel-hued turrets and castles of the first water. The pictorial strategies used to portray these richly varied scenarios are numerous and, by and large, technically sophisticated. Visual effects redolent of forms as diverse as watercolor and oil painting, crayon and chalk sketches, woodcut illustrations, engravings and stained glass (among others) persistently communicate a passionate desire to grasp the beauties of both nature and architecture on the basis of patient contemplation and visionary interpretation. Mimetic imperatives are never allowed to constrain or dilute fantasy's striving for alternate worlds that may capture elemental emotions and states of mind most faithfully by following the mysteries of the world rather than endeavoring to domesticate them through slavish imitation. Harmony and balance, ironically, may be suggested through deliberate distortion while turmoil, conversely, may be evoked by means of emphatically ordered forms rendered unsettling by an excess of equilibrium. A number of scenes from Gerda's onerous voyage exemplify the former approach, whereas some of the more disquieting moments occurring in the Snow Queen's Palace at the end illustrate the latter.

Throughout the anime, it is evident that for Dezaki and his team, the force of an image — regardless of its dramatic amplitude — depends mainly on its colors: on chroma per se as well as on the trails of light and shadow left by various shapes as they are reflected and refracted by their surroundings. Swathed in shrouds of radiant light or somber shadow one moment and emitting multi-tinged haloes the next, such shapes are able to convey with arresting succinctness both serenity and violence, swirling unrest and majestic stillness. When gay hues are brought into play, their warmth and mellowness are something one does not easily forget even after the show is over, and when the shadows thicken, their incumbence feels so menacing as to be likely to impress the most seasoned of anime viewers. In marrying his dedication to color with a contemporary take on the fairy tale form, Dezaki's *The Snow Queen* would appear to validate Debbie Olson's contention that "Color is the language of modern fairy-tales." This, the critic maintains, is largely a corollary of the inscription of such stories, especially in the guise of "animated films," in "capitalist consumer culture," where color is accorded pivotal significance as "the language of advertising" and the films themselves constitute primarily a set of commodities to be publicized through the stimulation of consumer desires. In other words, color can be regarded as the common code which contemporary fairy tales and advertising share as an expressive medium, and this commonality is sustained by the status of the film as a product amenable to commercial promotion alongside a plethora of ancillary merchandise. Crucial to this strategy is the promotion of "product identification" through the association of childhood with specific palettes (Olson, p. 32) promulgating the nostalgic notion of childhood as an age of innocence and purity. Children's attraction to palettes which they associate with a film they cherish will induce them to desire analogously colored objects (e.g., toys, clothing, stationery) "that allow them to revisit the utopia of the film world." An adult, concurrently, will plausibly respond to commodities "packaged and advertised in the same color palette as the film" as an opportunity to reaccess an "idealized childhood" (p. 33).

Ironically, Dezaki corroborates Olson's argument in reverse gear insofar as *The Snow Queen*, though connected with commercial spinoffs, does not seek to foster stereotypical idealizations of childhood through product identification meant to perpetuate ideological expectations. This is demonstrated by Dezaki's refusal to associate childhood monolithically with a single palette. Thus, depending on the action's circumstances, mood and tempo, children may come to be associated by Dezaki with both cool and warm hues, gentle pastels and bold primaries, as well as colors traditionally deemed incompatible with juvenile fantasy: e.g., black, the hue typically connected with sepulchral gravity but in fact attached by the anime to the immensely positive character of the Raven so pivotal to Gerda's adventures, and gold, the hue deemed to emblematize a strictly adult notion of authority, yet used by Dezaki as a symbolic connector between Gerda and the youthful royal couple.

The artbooks documenting the series' most salient moments by means of strings of imaginatively edited stills and original character designs bring out all of the major stylistic, symbolic and thematic preoccupations evinced by the anime with commendable formal economy but no dearth of visual opulence and dramatic pathos. Dezaki's sensitive approach to lighting effects is repeatedly brought to the fore. This is borne out, for example, by the early still depicting the protagonists as they run excitedly through the late-summer rural settings, where the shafts of light touching grass and rocks with subtly graded variations communicate a potent sense of spatial expansiveness, dynamically enhanced by the horizon's curvature. It is with the forbidding winter light pervading the scenes dedicated to Kay's funeral *in absentia*, and throwing into relief Gerda's and Kay's dad's inconsolable grief in the guise of sharp shadows and chiseled expression lines, that the atmosphere most starkly gives in to darkness. With the image recording Gerda and Ragi's first encounter, by contrast, the light exudes an uplifting sense of numinous solemnity that anticipates symbolically the importance to be acquired by the two characters' relationship in the course of future events.

With the glacier sequence, the power of the elements at their most ominous is uncompromisingly, even brutally, exposed as the eye is invited to travel from the protagonists' overawed contemplation of the ice barrier before them to the increasingly arduous climbs and inclement nights which they have to endure in their pilgrimage and, beyond that critical point, to the catastrophe of Ragi's fall into a seemingly bottomless ravine. Throughout the sequence, emphasis is laid on the contrast between the human actors' puniness and nature's titanic magnitude. Another good example of Dezaki's passion for contrasts is the sequence focusing on the mirror's destruction by the possessed trolls. In this instance, we witness the frame-by-frame deterioration of the two creatures' conduct from playful banter, through heated exuberance (marked by their fire-flooded eyes), to downright malevolence, dynamically enriched by the contrast between the glowing lights and hues expressing the trolls' disturbance and the Palace's crystalline ambience. Marginal frames devoted to the gargoyles, unicorns and other sculptural hybrids adorning the many turrets, intent on commenting caustically on the trolls' actions, further enhance the sequence's distinctive tenor.

Simultaneously, pronounced emotive disparities emanate from the artbooks' juxtaposition of images of Gerda and the Snow Queen — both explicitly, as in the facing frames of the girl lying in the snow amid a portentous blizzard in a state of utter helplessness and of the titular figure's austerely immaculate mien, and overtly, as shown in the later still portraying Gerda's confrontation of the mighty ruler and highlighting the opposition between the girl's pugnacious fervor and the Queen's impassivity. Gentler instances of

Dezaki's fascination with expressive diversity come with the montage of photos focusing on the disparate responses to Kay's portrait exhibited by various kids Gerda meets along the way — ranging from disaffected skepticism in the case of the match-selling urchins, through chary curiosity in that of the young mermaid, to puzzlement in that of the magical-pear-tree crew. The Raven, patently not a human child, is the only character to exhibit frank interest in Gerda's search and to appear willing to take the drawing as a useful investigate lead. This is quite consistent with Dezaki's sensibility: as noted, the director is loyal to Andersen in the characterization of animal actors as pivotal presences. The artwork confirms this idea with great accuracy, especially with the frames foregrounding the protective attitude toward the heroine evinced by both the miniature monkey Amor and the lone wolf Olga during her illness and those devoted to Bae from his first appearance in the robbers' lair, through his part in the embedded adventure pivoting on the Robber Girl, to his vital contribution to the advancement of Gerda's quest in its climactic stages.

Linda Hutcheon argues that an adaptation should not be examined in hierarchical terms, which inevitably leads to the valorization of the source text as somewhat superior to the adaptation itself, insofar as "Multiple versions exist laterally, not vertically" (Hutcheon, p. xiii). At the same time, it is crucial to recognize that "the different media and genres that stories are transcoded to and from in the adapting process are not just formal entities." In fact, "they also represent various ways of engaging audiences" (p. ix). In moving across different contexts and traditions, moreover, adaptations pick up novel meanings through a process of "*transculturation* or *indigenization*" (p. xvi). Dezaki's *Snow Queen*, with its fairy tale source and diverse renditions and pictorial interpretations thereof, eloquently corroborates the three interrelated propositions outlined above. Andersen's story, Dezaki's anime and the numerous illustrated editions of the original tale accompanying different translations and retellings constitute parallel realities, not a hierarchical system, for each has a distinctive way of eliciting the reader's or viewer's participation in the narrativizing act and each brings into play different meanings as a result of its impact on a particular cultural milieu. It is worth noting, in commenting on a text issuing from the imagination of a widely translated author, that translation itself can be seen as a form of adaptation influenced by local cultural priorities or even prejudices. Lewis amusingly throws this idea into relief with reference to the tale of *The Princess and the Pea*: "The first English translators could not understand Andersen's humour or his subtlety. One pea? That was absurd. Three might be more credible. The museum is ignored. [This is the place where the legendary legume is held to have been housed following the events recounted in the tale.] Sadly, some of these early versions are still in use. Look out for those rogue peas" (in Andersen 2004, p. 13).

In looking at the matter of audience involvement and the effect exerted upon it by a particular form or medium, it could be argued that the original story engages us primarily through narration; the anime, through performance; and different illustrated versions of the relevant Andersen text (in isolation or in conjunction with other associated stories), through interaction. Indeed, these invite us to play with the text by mediating, both sensuously and intellectually, between its written narrative and its visual import. For the purpose of this discussion, a selection of radically different artistic styles used in illustrating the story of *The Snow Queen* are examined as a means of reflecting on how parallel versions of a text may involve their audiences in substantially diverse fashions. Thus, the tale's universe can be seen to unleash a plethora of laterally coexisting texts capable of magnetizing their receivers in ways that alter according to their cultural situation and perception.

Joel Stewart's illustrations for the 2004 edition of a selection of Andersen stories thrives on the principle of defamiliarization, radically debunking the romanticized conception of the fairy tale form that so often leads to soporifically saccharine drawings. Stewart's style is gritty and utterly unsentimental, and his characters are often intentionally represented as ungainly, stocky, even downright ugly. Yet, they ooze with vitality and personality, largely thanks to the artist's ability to convey a whole nexus of feelings and character traits simply through the way in which a figure's eyes are slanted or its jaw is set, through a tiny facet of body language or a hint at dynamism and drama. For instance, a few subtle adjustments to the witch's expression in the illustrations for *The Tinder Box* are sufficient to evoke a potent aura of fake innocence, modesty and charitableness, especially with the transition from a noncommittal look to an unmistakably shifty glance. In addition, characters described as exquisitely beautiful — such as the eponymous heroines in *Thumbelina* and *The Little Mermaid* and the female lead in *The Wild Swans*— are often portrayed as plain, homely, caricatural or cartoonishly stylized. Kings and queens, for their part, are unceremoniously depicted in full consonance with Andersen's unorthodox attitude to authority as down-to-earth people who do not hesitate to go and open the doors of their castles in the middle of s stormy night and take it upon themselves to arrange their guests' bed linen (*The Princess and the Pea*) or else busy themselves with humble chores such as chasing around the capital in search of their daughter's clandestine suitor (*The Tinder Box*). Just as *The Snow Queen* constitutes the apex of the Danish author's sustained engagement with thorny ethical issues, so Stewart's pictures for that story could be realistically posited as the culmination of the artist's vision as communicated by the aforementioned selection of Andersen tales.

In his portrayal of the titular character and her domain, Stewart explicitly emphasizes the concept of glacial impenetrability, succinctly encapsulating the idea in the Snow Queen's crown as a set of four prongs, extending straight out of the skull with no obvious demarcation between the physical body and the royal endowment, that brings to mind both inverted icicles (stalagmites of sorts) and the candid fangs of some wild polar creature. To heighten the sense of forbidding impregnability associated with the character, Stewart resorts to an almost entirely monochromatic palette, barely punctuated by the gentlest touches of purple and green shading. The Snow Queen, notably, is both one of the most stylized figures in Stewart's entire Andersen gallery and one of the most (possibly *the* most) stylized depictions of that character in the history of *The Snow Queen* at large. In Stewart, the character does not come across as overtly intimidating but rather as unapproachable. Stylization renders her pointedly non-human, so that even though she is by no means unattractive, she is not sensuously desirable either insofar as she is bled of any possible vestige of corporeal warmth. In this respect, Stewart's graphics loyally capture Andersen's own description of the Snow Queen as "wonderfully delicate and grand" but made of "ice all through, dazzling, glittering ice" and endowed with "eyes" that "blazed out like two bright stars" but harbored "no peace or rest" (Andersen 2004, p. 158). To label Stewart's depiction of the Snow Queen simply effective would be to do it an unpardonable injustice for sublime is arguably a far more apposite term.

With Christian Birmingham's illustrations for the single edition of *The Snow Queen* (Andersen 2007), we enter a completely different pictorial discourse in which the dreamworld atmosphere one could readily associate with the domain of fairy tales is predominant. Yet, Birmingham has his own distinctive way of fostering defamiliarization — in this case, through the graceful establishment of a stylistic tension between the ethereal and visionary feel of the settings, palettes and lines, on the one hand, and the unsettlingly photorealistic credibility of the characters' physiques, and faces in particular, on the other hand. The aesthetic conflict between dreaminess and photorealistic accuracy implicitly asks us to ponder the reality of the fairy tale world we have accessed, obfuscating the barrier between realism and fantasy and situating the tale in a liminal realm where neither its fictionality (as a piece of entertainment) nor its veracity (as a metaphysical speculation) can be taken for granted. Furthermore, the sense of remoteness conveyed by the green, slightly glazed eyes of Birmingham's Snow Queen renders even her tender smile ineffably intimidating. The character's body language, in this visual version of the tale, is made particularly intriguing by suggestions that she is peeking into the human world from an alien realm. These are chiefly communicated by images in which the Snow Queen appears to be parting the icy cloak that inexorably accompanies her excursions into the human realm in an effort to gain access to it. The tentativeness of the gesture intimates that Birmingham's

Snow Queen does not regard her infiltrations of our reality as an automatic prerogative or right but rather as adventures to be embarked upon with graceful restraint, modesty and even a modicum of surreptitiousness.

P. J. Lynch's Snow Queen (Andersen 2009), by contrast, comes across as the kind of *femme fatale* one would expect to encounter in Pre-Raphaelite and Victorian art, at one point overtly bringing to mind J. W. Waterhouse's *Circe Invidiosa*. What lends Lynch's figure pictorial uniqueness is the replacement of the sultry and exotic connotations often carried by those antecedents with total, immaculate and impenetrable whiteness, punctuated by waves of evanescence or translucence. These traits of Lynch's Snow Queen are notable in all the plates featuring this character — from her general portrait, through the depiction of her first visit to Kay's home and subsequent abduction of the boy, to her climactic presentation in the midst of the lake at the heart of her Palace as Kay vainly labors to assemble pieces of ice so that they will spell the word "Eternity." Edmund Dulac's rendition of the Snow Queen (Andersen 1911) anticipates Lynch's in the image devoted to the character's first visit, where her body is so ethereal as to appear to merge with the astoundingly atmospheric turret-crested background. In Dulac's general portrait of the mythical figure, however, other features of the artist's unique signature come more explicitly to the fore. These include a passion for subdued but softly gleaming hues, as well as figures gently outlined in black but not so dependent on neat ink boundaries to define shapes and hold them together as on the colors themselves. The keenness on texture and pattern, as well as on minute details, that is notable across Dulac's illustrations for *The Snow Queen* bears witness to the influence on his style of Persian art, the Pre-Raphaelites and, most vitally in this context, Japanese prints.

A Japanese feel is also evident in Kay Nielsen's illustrations for the tale (Andersen 1924a) — most prominently, in the plate portraying the protagonists' escape from the northern castle into the warm glow of a regenerated world where stylization, the evocation of dynamism through vibrant undulating lines and the symbolic use of vegetation play pivotal roles. An intriguing variation on the theme of the Snow Queen's first visit is offered by Adrienne Segur (Andersen 2001), who depicts the character as a diminutive angelic being, as though to evoke her fundamentally benign or even celestial nature. In this image, Segur employs a monochromatic bluescale palette, favoring an intimate and subdued mood of diamond purity. The same style is adopted in the rendition of the scene in which Gerda enters the royal abode at night in the company of the Raven — in this case, a forceful sense of the heroine's vulnerability in an utterly unfamiliar environment is symbolically conveyed by her portrayal as a minute doll-like figure amid majestic architectural structures and decor. A monochromatic palette is also utilized in the portrayal of the protagonists' return to their hometown where the architecture is rendered, conversely, as a comfortable stage set. Elsewhere, Segur's illustrations for *The Snow Queen* exhibit the artist's customary preference for a rich and jewel-toned style oozing an exquisite Rococo feel. Opulence is unquestionably the dominant trait in the depiction of Kay in thrall to his captor. Just as Segur departs most unexpectedly from the vogue prevalent among illustrators in her depiction of the Snow Queen's initial appearance outside Kay's window, so Anne Anderson invests the scene chronicling the Snow Queen's ride through the skies with the boy in a strikingly original fashion (Andersen 1924b). The image comes across as simultaneously homely and sublime, familiar and menacingly alien. Thus, while the white birds are ideated as rather prosaic farmhouse chickens, and the howling wolves resemble a pack of reasonably well-trained German Shepherds, the racing cloud banks and tempestuous waters emanate unbridled fury. This impression is reinforced by the anthropomorphic presentation of the raging wind as a bleak Angel of Death and of the Snow Queen's sledge-prow as a skull-like structure worthy of Hans Holbein's anamorphic experiments.

If Birmingham and Lynch highlight the tale's most resonantly otherworldly dimension through an emphasis on the oneiric and the timeless respectively, with T. Pym (the pseudonym adopted by the late Victorian illustrator Clara Creed), we enter quite a different adaptive domain (Andersen 2002). Pym's images bring to mind the medieval art of illumination in their knack of encapsulating a densely layered world in a single picture rendered in brilliant hues and subtle textures. At the same time, they exude a nostalgic mood in the evocation of an old-style world on the brink of collapse, alongside a sentimentalist strain in the idealization of childhood. With Bernadette Watts, it is a preference for primitivist and folk styles that reigns supreme in the representation of Andersen's world (Andersen 1997). The artist's dedication to the loving depiction of flowers and animals is often redolent of Marc Chagall's oeuvre, as attested to by the plates portraying the abduction, the magic garden and the encounter with the reindeer. A tangible sense of the balmy breeze pervading the more idyllic moments and of the glacial stillness accompanying the more pathos-laden ones are terse definers of Watts' aesthetic cachet. One of the most cherished editions of recent years is undoubtedly the one retold by fiction author Nicky Raven and illustrated by Vladislav Yerko (Andersen 2005). The almost addictive dedication to details exhibited by the artist's pictures makes several of his plates so magnetizing as to suggest a feeling of disorientation, drawing the eye into an optical machine of hallucinogenic power. Yerko's art reveals the influence of disparate sources and invariably demonstrates unique adaptive capabilities in their handling. These include late Gothic and Renaissance Flemish art, with its keen sense of observation, attention to minutiae, bright colors and debt to the tradition of manuscript illumination; Pieter Bruegel the Elder's unsentimental depiction of village life (especially in the abduction scene); late medieval and early Renaissance Italian art influenced by International Gothic, particularly Simone Martini and Benozzo Gozzoli; and, last but not least, Ukrainian jewelry art as a form that has assiduously shaped Yerko's original culture since prehistoric times.

It is vital, at this point, to examine what aspects of the various illustrators' styles and moods are most strikingly paralleled by Dezaki's own adaptation. What deserves attention is not merely the repertoire of broadly *visual* correspondences or discrepancies involved at the basic iconographic level but rather the symphony of echoes reverberating across the distinctive art forms cultivated by those illustrators and by Dezaki himself that somehow convey comparable visions. Thus, in exploring Dezaki's work, it is important to assess how affinities and divergences between the anime and the illustrations are captured specifically in cinema and, even more specifically, in anime. In developing an individual artistic code over the years, Dezaki upholds the specificity of his medium insofar as his use of techniques characteristic not just of anime but also of cinema generally in tandem with visual and animational tropes distinctive of anime as such reminds us consistently that what he accomplishes through anime could not be achieved in the same fashion or to the same degree in any other medium. In this respect, Dezaki's style corroborates the view, put forward by André Gaudreault and Philippe Marion, that "Each medium, according to the ways in which it exploits, combines and multiplies the 'familiar' materials of expression"—i.e., "rhythm, movement, gesture, music, speech, image, writing" can be seen to harbor "its own communicational energies" (Gaudreault and Marion, p. 65).

Dezaki's cinematography is principally distinguished by a visual style reliant on arresting effects and makes regular use of the split-screen technique: the partition of the screen into two or more simultaneous images with or without explicit boundaries. This strategy contributes to the radical disruption of mimetic realism by shattering the illusion fostered by that ethos, according to which the screen is supposed to provide something of a transparent window on reality. This defamiliarizing ruse on Dezaki's part finds an apt equivalent in the likewise estranging pictorial ploys utilized by Stewart and Birmingham. The director is also famously keen on the use of stark lighting as a means of evoking unsettling dramatic effects capable of jarring the audience out of any possible temptation to indulge passively in a comfortable consumption of the action and visual. At the same time, Dezaki resorts assiduously to crayon freeze frames, which he has evocatively described as "Postcard Memories" in the audio commentary accompanying the OVA *Black Jack* (2006), helmed by Dezaki himself and Fumihiro Yoshimura. Typically, a freeze-frame shot consists of a shot in which a single frame is repeated several times to evoke the semblance of a still photograph. Dezaki lends this technique a distinctive twist by concurrently employing the freeze-frame shot as a means of chronicling *en abyme* the key moments of the anime-making process, causing a detailed and relatively realistic frame capturing characters and settings as they do in the finished artwork to fade regressively to a frame akin to a painting, drawing or even rough sketch encapsulating the anime's early stages of production in an eminently allusive, even cryptic, fashion. This particular ploy echoes Birmingham's synthesis of photorealism and dreamlike fantasy in his art.

One of the most effective instances of Dezaki's utilization of freeze-frame shots of the type described above is offered by the key sequence in which the baleful splinter penetrates Kay's eye. The same technique is later deployed to capture the emotional repercussions of the ocular violation, culminating with the moment when the boy maliciously destroys the flower pots containing the red and white roses he and Gerda have been lovingly tending thus far. The scene's symbolic poignance remains memorable even after one has watched subsequent episodes dramatizing more pointedly spectacular incidents. There are also some memorable occasions in which Dezaki makes artistic production integral to the action in depicting artists in the process of sketching, drawing or painting. A good example is supplied by the sequence in which Ragi executes a stunningly accurate portrait of Kay at Gerda's behest. Another instance is the episode featuring Orinette, the hapless lover of a magnanimous monarch who turns abruptly into a belligerent monster as a result of wearing a pair of spectacles made out of shards of the malefic broken mirror. Both the king and Orinette are said to be competent painters and to have spent many happy hours together at their art prior to the man's degeneration into a brute. Orinette's room is still replete with testaments to her and her lover's talent, displaying numerous paintings created in a style reminiscent of the one employed in several of Dezaki's most remarkable freeze-frame shots.

While Dezaki parallels both Stewart and Birmingham in his handling of defamiliarization, and Birmingham specifically in the integration of contrasting visual moods, his style concomitantly recalls Stewart's passion for stylization and stark solemnity and Lynch's dispassionate, yet dramatic, naturalism, with occasional forays into the realm of nostalgic antiquarianism of the kind one encounters in T. Pym. At the same time, Dezaki shares with Watts a profound attraction to natural details, allied to a tendency to foreground their vitality through overtly hand-drawn graphics. This is most palpably evident in several of the director's distinctive freeze-frame shots. Yerko's surreal dimension, finally, finds an animational correspondence in the sequences of Dezaki's anime where curiously magnified details are accorded dramatic prominence at the expense of more realistic aspects of the settings. A brilliant example is the installment set in a prosperous town hosting an annual festival where local shopkeepers advertise their business by means of gigantic floats that portray iconic artisanal trademarks. The clocks, shoes and fish (among countless other items) parading through the streets are so alive as to dwarf the elegant real-life architecture around them to the status of a secondary stage set.

Adaptations of Andersen's *The Snow Queen* to all manner of media have been so numerous and diverse that presuming to supply a comprehensive list of them in the present context would be entirely inappropriate. A few examples seem, however, worthy of mention for contextual reference (and, possibly, further exploration by the keen reader). In the realm of animation, *The Snow Queen* has given origin to the Soviet film *Snezhnaya Koroleva* (dir. Lev Atamanov, 1957), the American short *The Snow Queen* (dirs. Marek Buchwald and Vladlen Barbe, 1992), the British productions *The Snow Queen* (movie; dir. Martin Gates, 1995) and *The Snow Queen's Revenge* (movie; dir. Martin Gates, 1996), the BBC television film *The Snow Queen* (dir. Julian Gibbs, 2005) — in turn adapted from an operatic concert held in London at the Barbican Arts Centre in 2003. Live-action adaptations have also abounded, particularly notable instances being the Soviet film *Snezhnaya Koroleva* (dir. Gennadi Kazansky, 1966), the BBC production *The Snow Queen* helmed by Andrew Gosling (1976), which integrates live-action footage with animation, the Danish film *Snedronningen* (dirs. Jacob Jørgensen and Kristof Kuncewicz, 2000) and the Hallmark TV film *Snow Queen* (2002) directed by David Wu. In the videogaming world, the tale has inspired a side story to the Japanese game, developed by Playstation, titled *Revelations: Persona* (1996). Ballet adaptations of special prominence staged in recent years include Erin Holt's *The Snow Queen — ballet redefined...* (1998), produced by the California Theatrical Youth Ballet (subsequently renamed to California Contemporary Ballet) and featuring original music composed and performed by Randall Michael Tobin, and the English National Ballet's production *The Snow Queen* with music taken from Prokofiev (2007). Furthermore, the tale has triggered various plays and musicals, while also infiltrating novels, short stories and comic books either as an overt source text or as material for oblique intertextual allusion.

In the region of anime adaptations of fairy tales, the previously cited film *Puss in Boots* directed by Yabuki (1969) enjoys special standing on home turf as a work of enduring popularity with a cross-generational fan base analogous to the one evinced in the West by Disney's *Snow White and the Seven Dwarfs* (movie; dirs. David Hand, William Cottrell, Wilfred Jackson, Larry Morey, Perce Pearce and Ben Sharpsteen, 1937) and *The Jungle Book* (movie; dir. Wolfgang Reitherman, 1967). Anime's penchant for audacious reconfigurations of its sources is manifest in the use of an original plot, triggered by the protagonist's perpetration of the most heinous crime in the feline world: the rescue of mice. While elements of the parent text are retained — e.g., the hero's posing as the Marquis of Carabas and general presentation as an endearing rogue on a madcap ride — other facets of the anime reflect an eminently indigenous sensibility. Thus, the protagonist, jocularly named Perrault, must confront a trio of ninja cats as his enemies, as well as a demon named Lucifer who possesses metamorphic powers of the kind one encounters recurrently as one of anime's most inveterate aesthetic preferences over time. Most importantly, the film bears witness to the experimental verve inherent in adaptive anime at its most accomplished — as well as a flair for eroding conventional barriers between child- and adult-oriented cinema generally — through its technical makeup. It indeed combines zestful characters and playful personality quirks familiar in Western animations targeted at kids with cinematographically sophisticated jump cuts, smooth morphs, bouncy editing and subliminal frames capable of placing the adventure on a daringly conceptual level of avant-gardish resonance.

Where anime adapted from children's books with a bildungsroman bent are concerned, a close parallel to Dezaki's *The Snow Queen* consists of Takahata's aforementioned TV series *Heidi, Girl of the Alps* (1974). In this show, as in Dezaki's, the representation of mountainous vistas, observed from a variety of angles and in contrasting seasonal and atmospheric circumstances, plays a critical aesthetic part. So does the loving depiction of both wild and domestic animals. The integration of cute juvenile physiognomies and adult looks ranging from the wisely benevolent to the arch and austere is likewise notable. As a young girl faced with challenges that repeatedly compel her to reassess not only her status in the world but also her own intrinsic identity, Heidi bears striking affinities with Gerda. Like Dezaki's *The Snow Queen*, Takahata's *Heidi, Girl of the Alps* works wonders in focusing on its protagonist's point of view as vital to the determination of the overall adventure's rhythm and mood. Both Heidi's and Gerda's realities appear filled with magic by virtue not so much of their inherent attributes as of how they are perceived by their respective heroines — i.e., through the eyes of guileless, adaptable and optimistic souls. It is in this framework that even the most prosaic details of the natural realm and city life alike acquire effervescent energy. By observing disparate situations through Heidi's and Gerda's unclouded eyes, adult viewers can enjoy these shows as experiences that far transcend the plane of infantile entertainment — as long, that is, as they are willing to enter their alternate dimensions with a commodious disposition and to look at them without the taint of generational prejudice. A further similarity between the two anime lies with their tendency to concentrate on stories that come across as disarmingly simple, without ever overexplaining them in a patronizing fashion.

A further adapted narrative redolent of Gerda's odyssey consists of another TV series briefly referred to earlier in this chapter and helmed by Takahata and Koshi: *Anne of Green Gables* (1979). Chronicling the coming-of age journey of a young orphan, the show focuses on its protagonist's impact on her community in a style that elliptically anticipates Dezaki's rendition of Gerda's invariably salutary influence on the people and places she encounters along the way. Like *The Snow Queen*, moreover, *Anne of Green Gables* makes the very most of a markedly episodic format by presenting each and every segment of the anime as an engrossing chapter unto itself, regardless of its situation within the cumulative diegesis. *The Snow Queen*'s fascination with animal actors, finally, finds an apt animated relative in Kuroda's TV series *A Dog of Flanders* (1975), also touched upon in the early stages of this discussion. In recounting the vicissitudes of a young boy named Nello and his dog Patrasche, this anime foreshadows Dezaki's powerful dramatization of the bonds tying Gerda to Amor, Olga and Bae as formative experiences which no-one who has ever experienced the peculiar bliss of living with a non-human animal could fail to recognize and treasure.

Chapter 5

Romance Meets Revolution
Romeo x Juliet

*It is nearly always the most improbable things that
really come to pass.*—E. T. A. Hoffmann

The anime series *Romeo x Juliet* (dir. Fumitoshi Oizaki, 2007) eloquently confirms Julie Sanders' assertion that "movement into a different generic mode can encourage a reading of Shakespeare from a new or revised point of view" (Sanders, p. 48). Oizaki's manipulation of Shakespearean personae simultaneously echoes Gérard Genette's assessment of the part of the adaptive process that pertains specifically to the "revaluation of character." This, the critic maintains, entails "investing him or her — by way of pragmatic or psychological transformation — with a more significant and/or more 'attractive' role in the value system of the hypertext [adaptive text] than was the case in the hypotext [source text]" (Genette, p. 343). At the same time as it boldly reimagines its source text through the infusion of epic and supernatural motifs into the archetypal drama of undying love, Oizaki's anime elliptically invites reflection on the broader phenomenon of cross-media adaptation of the Shakespearean canon. Some appropriations of the Bard's corpus have sought to honor it as the fountainhead of unsurpassed genius and others have endeavored instead to quiz its authority by exposing its ideological subtexts as instrumental in the perpetuation of conservative patriarchal values. Oizaki neither upholds nor refutes his source text's power in a clear-cut fashion. In fact, he is far more interested in pursuing the narrative ramifications — embedded, hypothetical or imaginable — of the original play as materials latent in its weave and as yet unvoiced by its previous adaptations. What concerns the director is the possibility of taking *Romeo and Juliet* as the point of departure for an exploratory journey leading out of the work's core toward alternate horizons, toward uncharted territories where it may encounter other versions of itself as its doubles, alter egos, specular images or shadows. The anime thus participates in the process of Shakespearean relocation described as follows by Daniel Fischlin and Mark Fortier: "if adaptations of Shakespeare somehow reinforce Shakespeare's position in the canon ... it is a different Shakespeare that is at work" (Fischlin and Fortier, p. 6). In this process, the Bard's oeuvre is never assumed as a stable and immutable point of reference but rather approached as the raw material for potentially endless textual metamorphoses. The anime, on this plane, mirrors the type of adaptational strategy in which, as Sanders puts it, the adaptive text uses the original as "a creative springboard for another, ... wholly different, text " so that even though its "relationship to the original remains present and relevant," its structure suggests that a "grafting has taken place of a segment ... of the original text." As this portion of the parent work is connected with an alternate "textual form," an entirely novel product comes into being (Sanders, p. 55).

As argued in depth in the ensuing pages, Oizaki's adaptation takes some daring liberties in its reconception of Shakespeare's *Romeo and Juliet* (1594– 1596). Nevertheless, it is incontrovertibly loyal to the source text in positing the conflict between love and duty as pivotal to the drama. In the original play, this tension is articulated in eminently personal terms, even though the social dimension of the ordeal is alluded to, through the presentation of the heroine as a girl who has hardly grown past childhood but is already expected by the mores of her culture to make a happy wife and mother. Oizaki's adaptation heightens the public implications of Juliet's predicament, as the duty she is enjoined to embrace transcends by far the remit of the domestic milieu by expecting her, in fact, to operate as the prime agent in a revolutionary program with momentous repercussions for a whole state and, ultimately, the human planet as a whole. In both the Shakespearean source and its anime relocation, however, duty comes starkly into conflict with love when Juliet meets Romeo — a boy whom she is, quite simply, forbidden to cherish due to the sinister family name he bears.

Shakespeare himself drew inspiration from several preexisting texts, which makes his *Romeo and Juliet* an adaptation in its own right. As Roma Gill explains, the core of the romantic tragedy as we know it "has been traced as far back as the third century A.D. [and specifically, according to a footnote, to the *Ephesiaca* of Xenophon of Ephesus], and it became popular in Europe in the fifteenth century when Italian writers began to give it details which we can now recognize in Shakespeare's play. They claim that the story was contemporary and factual — so successfully that even today tourists in Verona can be shown the balcony and tomb of Giulietta." The Bard's immediate source was the version of the story penned by Arthur Brooke in the form of a "narrative poem, *The Tragicall History of Romeus and Juliet*" (Gill, p. v). However, while Brooke delivers a cautionary moral by condemning the unfortunate lovers' behavior as lustful and selfish, Shakespeare lives up to his reputation as one of the most insightful and probing dramatists of all times by resolutely steering clear of monolithic ethical messages, choosing instead an approach that is "often amused but always sympathetic," underpinned by a unique sense of "vitality" and "precise information" about both pivotal and supporting characters (p. vi), and a flair for exhibiting the nuances of psychological development "*as it is happenin g*" (p. vii). The anime adaptation is heir to these gifts, invariably regaling the viewer's mind and senses with balanced and penetrating studies of human psychology at its most tormented and most elastic at once.

What is instantly notable about Oizaki's take on his source text is the anime's eagerness to enhance the original play's supernatural dimension in order to articulate its own independent narrative. This is not to say, however, that the series seeks to disengage itself from the grave sociopolitical issues touched upon by Shakespeare's tragedy. In fact, as the title of this chapter suggests, these are also amplified by Oizaki in the elaboration of what ultimately stands out as an ideological — no less than a romantic — drama. The maximization of the supernatural element, accordingly, asks to be understood as a means of bringing into fresh focus through defamiliarization some very pressing and very real historical vicissitudes. Thus, fantasy is emplaced as the vehicle through which the here-and-now may be not conveniently dodged but actually confronted from alternative perspectives. This idea is pithily conveyed by the character of William (or "Willy"), the Bard's intradiegetic avatar in Oizaki's adaptation: "Reality often transcends fiction. And yet, people need stories and romance and heroism to navigate reality."

Romeo x Juliet's director has helpfully explained his reasons for investing his adaptation with otherworldly overtones in an interview released at the time of the show's release. While Oizaki intended to honor the source text's underpinning "structure," thus preserving "the straightforward love story," he also sensed that "if all you're doing is a love story, it's definitely more compelling as a live-action drama than as an anime." This proposition, as documented in depth later in this chapter, is eloquently substantiated by the welter of live-action adaptations to which the Shakespearean tragedy has proved amenable over the decades. Therefore, the director and his crew were eager to draw on the distinctive properties of their chosen medium in order to infuse their adaptation with a dramatic and graphic power unaccomplishable by live-action cinema itself. It was precisely to pursue this aesthetic agenda that Oizaki resolved to make the "fantasy element" axial to his reconceptualization of the play, in the conviction that this is "the part that you can do only in anime." Such a belief results from an acute awareness, firmly grounded in plentiful hands-on experience, that in anime, "it's easy to do things that humans couldn't actually do in real life" (Oizaki). Therefore, the adaptation unfailingly capitalizes on the unique potentialities of its medium instead of slavishly striving to emulate live-action cinema by pandering to its codes and conventions — which would feasibly have been conducive to a far less satisfying adaptive experience for both the anime's creators and its viewers.

The show's fantastic atmosphere owes much to its main setting, the aerial city of Neo-Verona. This is distinguished by an architectural mélange of medieval and Renaissance motifs which includes a bewitching web of bridge-crested waterways and cobbled streets, elegant stonework and picturesque ruins, sumptuous palaces and humble plebeian dwellings, spectral cemeterial grounds and a fairytalish expanse of irises perched atop a vertiginously tall edifice, idyllic rural cottages and baleful caves housing a mysterious magical technology. The show's architectural spread is crowned by its larger-than-life skies traversed by sublime *ryuuba* ("dragonsteeds"). Central to *Romeo x Juliet*'s supernatural fabric is the "Great Tree Escalus"— the only survivor out of the twin trees upon which the floating land's very existence has thus far depended. As a preternatural agency that will foster human prosperity with its nourishing fluids and golden pomes as long as it is surrounded by benevolent energies, Escalus is doomed to "perish for want of love" under Prince Montague's pernicious influence, and eventually cause Neo-Verona to crash with devastating global consequences. The environmentalist message here entailed is discreetly yet uncompromisingly conveyed by the character of Ophelia as the action accumulates momentum. (In the source play, the similarly named Escales is the Prince of Verona and is portrayed as a character who endeavors to remain impartial in the feud between Montagues and Capulets, yet cannot be indifferent to its impact given he has relatives of his own in both factions.)

If the fantasy element is a major marker of Oizaki's imaginative take on the original, no less important, as anticipated, is *Romeo x Juliet*'s amplification of the source text's political import, whereby the anime's romantic portrayal of the bittersweet joys of first love never loses sight of the adventure's macrocosmic implications. Oizaki indeed makes the themes of despotism, revolution, anarchy and clandestine resistance axial to the story, redefining the balance of power posited by the play, where the Capulets and the Montagues are said to be "Two households, both alike in dignity," through a stark polarization of the oppressor and the victim. This topos is overtly accorded unprecedented centrality right from the start with the epic sequences, redolent of Akira Kurosawa's opus, dramatizing the truculent overthrow of the Capulets by the Montague usurper fourteen years prior to the main events chronicled in the series. Thus, *Romeo x Juliet* equips the inceptive yarn with a clearly defined villain of the piece. The magnitude of the Machiavellian usurper's evil and greed is potently conveyed not only by the retrospective dramatization of the Capulets' extermination but also by the relatively early sequences portraying the harassment of an innocent girl accused of being a descendant of the deposed dynasty and threatened with immediate execution, and the abduction of commoner maidens whose parents cannot afford to meet Prince Montague's exorbitant fiscal requirements to be traded to lecherous aristocrats. Averse to monolithic characterization, Oizaki takes care to paint the tyrant's personal background in a realistically detailed manner, presenting him as a victim of social iniquity: an illegitimate issue of the Capulet line reared in utter poverty by a lowly prostitute, Prince Montague is veritably persecuted by his hatred for those he deems responsible for his unprivileged childhood and for his mother's premature death. This information does not quite make the despot's crimes excusable but it does help us comprehend in a satisfyingly full-rounded fashion the likely causes of his ferocious detestation of Juliet's house and attendant thirst for revenge. In addition, the self-appointed autocrat has literally rewritten history by promulgating the image of the charitable Capulets as unscrupulous oppressors.

The bloody mutiny's only survivor is the overthrown ruler's daughter, Juliet Fiammata de Capulet, who is rescued by the Captain of the Capulet guards, Conrad, and brought up by a handful of loyal Capulet retainers in humble obscurity and under the protective shield of a male disguise, utterly oblivious to her real origins. It is not until Juliet reaches her sixteenth birthday that Conrad — determined to make her the leader of the extant Capulet henchmen in a glorious revolt against the illegitimate Prince Montague — finally discloses to the girl the truth about her noble lineage and about the coup responsible for her whole dynasty's brutal elimination. Set in a decrepit graveyard exuding a characteristic sense of the Romantic Sublime amid baleful shadows and thunderous skies, the revelation scene unquestionably stands out as one of the entire show's most poignant moments. Juliet is so traumatized by the revelation, which is capped by her presentation with her father's mighty sword and by her sudden recollection of the massacre, that she loses consciousness and descends into a feverish state. While an account of this scene in isolation might suggest that Juliet is just a vulnerable maiden, powerless in the face of a destiny too portentous for her to handle, nothing could be further from the truth. By the time the story reaches the graveyard sequence, the audience has already been regaled with ample evidence for Juliet's resourcefulness, courage and genuinely heroic valor.

The girl's independence of spirit is conveyed early on in the series by intimations that she resents her disguise as the boy Odin and relishes the rare opportunities she can grasp to relinquish her pseudo-self and both dress and behave like the adolescent woman she really is. This is patently borne out by the episode in which she accidentally gets to attend the "Rose Ball" hosted by Prince Montague — on which occasion she also experiences an as yet inexplicable flashback to her childhood at the Castle. Juliet is shown to derive the purest of pleasures from the feeling of a gown over her body in shots that memorably attest to her lovable personality. More crucially for the adventure as a whole, Juliet has intelligently taken advantage of her status as a crossdresser by taking on the role of a champion of justice known as the "Red Whirlwind" ("Turbine Rosso" in Neo-Verona's Italian) reminiscent of Robin Hood and the Scarlet Pimpernel, and thus endeavoring to assist her people in defiance of Prince Montague's authority. Endowed with spectacular martial talent, balletic agility and a refreshingly sharp sense of humor, the Red Whirlwind lends the show some of its most tantalizing moments. It is in this role that Juliet first encounters Romeo Candore de Montague, is rescued by the kindly youth from her pursuers and curtly neglects to thank him due to his aristocratic status. The fleeting contact they make at this juncture as their hands touch appears to have a viscerally lasting effect on the two characters' senses, succinctly presaging things to come.

Oizaki clearly departs from Shakespeare in portraying his version of Juliet as a strong and imaginative individual, whereas the original Juliet is by an large submissive and meek. With this bold shift from his source text, Oizaki tersely draws attention to the status of gender as axial to issues of identity, power and cultural interaction, emphasizing the significance of that controversial concept as a product not so much of a person's biological sex as of the web of ideological messages projected onto it by particular cultures at specific points in history. An equally intriguing redefinition of the source text consists of the characterization of the male protagonist, who tends to come across as generally more meditative and passive that his Shakespearean precursor. This is not to say, however, that Oizaki's Romeo is not capable of valiant exploits in his own right. In fact, the boy is indomitable in his efforts to resist his father's manic determination to shape him into an ideal heir to his bloodsoaked name, and audaciously flaunts his commitment to Juliet even when this leads to his imprisonment in the Gradisca mines and exposure to the subhuman brutality of their inmates' conditions. It is from these experiences, moreover, that Romeo gains unprecedented strength and the altruistic courage that enables him to transcend for good the legacy of a pampered aristocratic upbringing in the name of adult responsibility. This evolution reaches a memorable acme with the young Montague's assumption of the role of leader of the community of former hard laborers encountered at Gradisca, whom he helps establish a new and more hopeful life in an abandoned village after a momentous earthquake has enabled them to leave the accursed caves. While infusing both of his protagonists with highly original traits, Oizaki does not fail, however, to remain loyal to his source's reputation as a story practically synonymous with amorous vicissitudes. For one thing, one would have to be emotionally defunct to be left entirely cold by Oizaki's rendition of the scene that wordlessly conveys the mystery of love at first sight. The later sequence in which Romeo's *ryuuba*, Cielo, encounters a companion in the ancestral forest whence dragonsteeds originate, and Romeo makes the painful decision to relieve the animal of his royal accoutrements and set him free, succinctly consolidates the anime's heartfelt romantic sensibility.

Although Juliet stoically embraces her public role despite its dire incompatibility with her personal happiness, she remains warmly and convincingly human even as she ascends to the peak of heroic fame. The girl's innocence and vulnerability are most touchingly evoked by the installment where the Capulet rebels are ensnared by the shifty Camillo and Juliet is rescued by Tybalt, who unchivalrically states that he has only come to her assistance out of loyalty to her associate Francisco, as he personally sees her as a spoilt and useless kid. Hurt by Tybalt's words and tormented by guilt at the thought that she might have directly caused her comrades' misfortune by rushing into action with scarce forethought, Juliet wanders aimlessly around the red-light district where Tybalt has hidden her, faints in the inhospitable streets prey to exhaustion and grief and is — almost miraculously — found by Romeo's estranged mother, Lady Portia, who then proceeds to shelter the heroine in the convent where she herself has obtained refuge upon leaving the despicable Montague court. Thus, Juliet's development is portrayed as a gradual and tortuous evolution, fraught with uncertainties and fears which no degree of juvenile exuberance or romantic passion could realistically alleviate without causing the drama to degenerate into vaporous escapism.

In intensifying the story's political significance, Oizaki concurrently tends to prioritize the public dimension of Romeo and Juliet's ordeal to the purely personal drama. This is most sensationally communicated by the climax, where the anime departs to a considerable degree from the Shakespearean antecedent. In the original play, the finale emphasizes the "star-crossed" lovers' private suffering by dispassionately exposing the capricious wastefulness of fate. Romeo and Juliet's deaths do serve a public purpose insofar as they are posited as the exorbitantly steep price which the rival households must pay to achieve reconciliation. However, this conversion is deliberately made to look so unrealistic and hurried, largely through the use of flagrantly accidental mistiming, as to call its consolatory import seriously into question. The anime's ending, by contrast, unequivocally highlights the political significance of Romeo and Juliet's sacrifice by presenting it as instrumental not solely in the restoration of a just regime after over a decade of atrocious prevarication, abuse and persecution at Prince Montague's hands but also in the redemption of a blighted habitat, and hence in the salvation of the entire planet's ecosystem. Selflessly honoring the ancient bond between her dynasty and the Great Tree Escalus, and so allowing the plant's magical essence to live on within her very body, Juliet marginalizes her private dreams in the service of a purging act of self-immolation. Romeo initially tries to oppose Juliet's chosen course of action by means of both his rhetoric and his blade. These complications impart the climax with a suspensefully vibrant tempo, which Oizaki's camera flawlessly maintains until it becomes obvious that the heroine's fate is unavoidable — and indeed encrypted in the adaptation as the prerequisite of its dramatic coherence. As Romeo himself joins his beloved in the pursuit of communal redemption, Shakespeare's "death-marked" passion is gloriously elevated well beyond the level of personal tragedy as a harbinger of cosmic catharsis and regeneration.

In the dénouement, the supernatural and political dimensions join forces on an epic scale to proclaim their shared standing as the adaptation's most salient facets in its adventurous pursuit of originality. In so doing, they demonstrate that the source play, despite its stability as a landmark in the literary canon, is not a finished and self-contained product but rather a mobile, ever-evolving process capable of altering over the centuries in response to the aesthetic and ideological requirements of disparate contexts, artists and audiences in different parts of the world. The anime thus corroborates Linda Hutcheon's contention that an adaptation is above all an intertextual galaxy asking to be approached as "its own palimpsestic thing" (Hutcheon, p. 9). Instead of urging us to focus exclusively or even primarily on the extent to which *Romeo x Juliet* is loyal to its Shakespearean antecedent (or not), Oizaki encourages us to conceive of the adaptation and its source text alike as networks of discursive relationships in which both of these works and innumerable other reimaginings of the Elizabethan play fluidly participate. Moreover, in amplifying the specifically political dimension of the original drama, Oizaki augments the story's topical relevance, inviting reflection on its metaphorical connection with real contemporary events and — more broadly — with political phenomena unfolding all over the world and at all times, on both a transhistorical and a contingently situated scale. In this regard, the anime adaptation would appear to validate the proposition, advanced by Margaret Jane Kidnie in *Shakespeare and the Problem of Adaptation*, that "past histories" are not "foundational," and hence unchanging, realities insofar as "efforts to recover 'what happened' can only be pursued alongside efforts to shape 'what is happening' in terms of work recognition and the ever-shifting boundaries that separate work from adaptation" (Kidnie, p. 164). This approach entails that in evaluating an enactment of a dramatic work, one should focus not so much on "how performance departs from or otherwise adapts text" as on "the shifting criteria by which *both* texts and performances are recognized — or not — as instances of a certain work" (p. 10). Relatedly, by tackling even a corpus as canonical as Shakespeare's not as "impervious to subsequent generations of creative and interpretative enquiry" but rather as "entangled in the present," one could fruitfully effect a move away "from what one knows now" toward "what one might be able to recognize in the future as Shakespeare's works" (p. 102).

In both Shakespeare and Oizaki, the finale could be read as a dramatization of the double-suicide formula: a motif, as argued in Chapter 2 in relation to *Grave of the Fireflies* and its sources, of considerable significance in traditional Japanese culture. As R. S. White indicates, this topos has a long and artistically respectable history, being pivotal to the depiction of youthful desire not only in *Romeo and Juliet* but also in other esteemed works in various media, including "*Tristan and Isolde* and Verdi's *La Traviata*." These (and many other) classics posit "double death as the inevitable and only destination guaranteeing immortality to the state of twin narcissism" (White, p. 13). In a psychoanalytical perspective, it is possible to "'pathologise' the young protagonists and suggest that the story's tragic ending is a direct corollary of their desire and hence an outcome they choose, albeit unconsciously. In the purview of cultural materialism, by contrast, Romeo and Juliet are not seen to "seek death" but to harbor, in fact, a perfectly wholesome passion that only becomes deathly as a result of "external circumstances" that negate "the possibility of sustaining their love in life" (p. 14). In Oizaki's anime, the lovers unquestionably act of heir own free will in their climactic espousal of a fate that denies the hope of earthly fulfillment — more consciously and resignedly, it should be noted, in Juliet's case than in Romeo's. However, the show also cultivates a tantalizing mood of metaphysical ambiguity in concurrently proposing that in a pragmatic sense, Romeo and Juliet have no choice. When Ophelia first reveals to her that she alone has the power to restore Escalus' depleted vigor by acting as a "sacrificial lamb," while Neo-Verona crumbles and burns, Juliet wonders whether all of the events in her life up to this point were indeed "predestined" to build up to this grand tragic climax — from her rescue by Conrad at the time of the mutiny, through her assumption of the Red Whirlwind role, to her subsequent efforts to help her city and its oppressed citizens at any price. What makes the protagonists' climactic actions exquisitely double-edged, and hence defiant of any univocal interpretation, is that Oizaki is able to present them as a matter of choice and necessity at once.

This adaptive outlook is abetted by Oizaki's unflinching commitment to the harmonization of individual psychology and communal action, and attendant effort to reconcile humanity's atavistic (and supposedly universal) yearning for pleasure with the uncompromising forces of repression, perversion and sublimation to which human society is so often subjugated. Hence, the anime manages to maintain throughout a delicate balance between the emotional and the societal dimensions of Romeo and Juliet's ordeal, taking full cognizance of the vagaries of singular mentalities, yet intelligently assessing their claims with reference to the needs and requirements of the broader community. From an ideological point of view, this stance is fully consonant with the inveterate reverence for the values of group affiliation, guidance and loyalty that has been deeply embedded in Japanese culture for time immemorial. In engineering this nimble collusion of individual psychology and material culture, Oizaki depicts the protagonists' mutual feelings as a unique expression of a very special kind of love. This is a feeling capable of conflating the three main affects associated with that state by the anthropologist Helen Fisher in her insightful evaluation of the peculiarities of eros: that is to say, sexual desire, infatuation and steady attachment (cited in Belsey 1994, pp. 38–39).

The pictorial style deployed in the anime, with its distinctive approach to both color and light, deserves close attention insofar as it is central to the evocation of the show's magic — and hence to the consolidation of its markedly autonomous, albeit adaptive, status. Oizaki's visual register consistently echoes Renaissance Venetian painting, which is utterly consonant with the anime's location in a fictionalized version of the city of Verona, situated in the Veneto region of Northeast Italy. This aesthetic choice indicates that despite his devotion to the capture of an essentially otherworldly setting, the director nonetheless retains a firm grounding in historical circumstances, harnessing the supernatural dimension to the figurative reinforcement of the series' connection with reality and not to the fuzzy demands of escapist fancy. As the esteemed art historian E. H. Gombrich explains in his epoch-making *The Story of Art*, "Venice, whose trade linked it closely with the East, had been slower than other Italian cities in accepting the style of the Renaissance.... But when it did, the style there acquired a new gaiety, splendour and warmth which evoke, perhaps more closely than any other buildings in modern times, the grandeur of the great merchant cities of the Hellenistic period, of Alexandria or Antioch." There are few visuals produced in a post–Renaissance medium that can honestly be said to evoke more faithfully than *Romeo x Juliet*, with its cinematic adaptation of Venetian painting and architecture of the Renaissance age, the ambience described by Gombrich. This approach owes much to its director's sensitive grasp of the attitude to light and color typically evinced by Renaissance artists of a Venetian ilk. According to Gombrich, that stance emanates from an imaginative responsiveness to the physical features of the Venetian environment, and while *Romeo x Juliet* is not set in Venice but in Verona's retrofuturistic alter ego, the anime's lavish use of water as a key aspect of its mise-en-scène makes Gombrich's observations no less apposite to its setting than to Renaissance Venice itself. "The atmosphere of the lagoons," the art critic comments, which seems to blur the sharp outlines of objects and to blur their colours in a radiant light, may have taught the painters of this city to use colour in a more deliberate and observant way than any other painters in Italy had done so far" (Gombrich, p. 325).

To throw further into relief the distinctiveness of Venetian style, Gombrich contrasts it with its Florentine counterpart: "The great reformers of Florence," he states, "were less interested in colour than in drawing.... The Venetian painters, it seems, did not think of colour as an additional adornment for the picture after it had been drawn on the panel" (p. 326). In Oizaki's anime, this lesson reverberates persistently across sensational and mundane scenes alike, exuding a sense of chromatic subtlety and mellowness that reach not only the eye but the entire sensorium even before one has begun to inspect closely what the images actually represent. Oizaki's colors are not, by and large, especially bright or glossy: even the hues adopted throughout the series to symbolize the tension between the Montagues and the Capulets, blue and red, are elegantly modulated, with a preference for the cyan, periwinkle and monestial nuances, on the one hand, and the magenta, terracotta and strawberry tinges on the other. Images are often blended into a whole by the airiness and luminosity that characteristically permeate the action in both its indoor and en-plein-air sequences. The eerie light of a storm flooding the landscape, the melancholy lunar radiance penetrating a bedchamber through wrought-iron grilles, and the glorious radiance of sunlight illuminating a happy visage are among some of the effects that most resonantly attest to the adaptation's highly creative approach to light and color.

In addition, the anime's sustained efforts to harmonize its visual mood with its impressive musical accompaniment brings to mind another important facet of Venetian painting in the Renaissance era, succinctly documented as follows by John Gage's *Colour and Culture*: "In Venice, the home of *colore* [i.e., color as an artistic value independent of drawing], the virtuoso performances of painters were often compared to the skills of performing musicians" (Gage, p. 226). We are thus here reminded of the existence of intimate connections between the language of color and that of music, with words like tone, timbre, harmony, scale, rhythm and pitch (among others) featuring frequently in both discourses. Hitoshi Sakimoto's soundtrack bewitchingly complements the visuals' energy of line and chroma from start to finish, eloquently testifying to the critical importance of music in bringing out a show's dramatic essence. Oizaki himself has enthusiastically commented on the contribution made by Sakimoto's soundtrack to his own understanding of "Just how powerful music can be" in rounding off an anime's aesthetic import. "I don't think," the director has frankly noted, "I've ever felt that so keenly as on this project" (Oizaki). The soundtrack was performed in Sydney by a full orchestra, selected in the knowledge that its youthful membership would entail familiarity among the players with the medium of anime and its distinctive adaptational needs.

Oizaki's anime is most loyal to its source in the adoption of a style and register that genuinely capture the essence of Shakespearean discourse without having to resort to apish imitation. This effect is accomplished by recourse to sustained citations of actual lines from both *Romeo and Juliet* itself and other Shakespeare plays (e.g., *Othello, Richard III, A Midsummer Night's Dream, Julius Caesar* and *Hamlet*), interspersed with more elliptical hints at dramatic situations and complications associated with the Bard's oeuvre. In the English-language dub released by FUNimation, the dialogue's Shakespearean feel is heightened by the incorporation of a wider range of lines and images derived more or less explicitly from the playwright. A brilliant example of the anime's confident handling of a Shakespearean register, specifically in the Anglophone version, resides with the monologue delivered by William in the centrally positioned prologue to the fourteenth installment — a speech that openly declares its rhetorical and artistic caliber by channeling the conventions of pastiche into the expression of a grave message, all the while maintaining the sense of irony for which the Bard's opus is so justly renowned. Delivering a capsulated allegory of Juliet's predicament that yokes the source text and the anime together with prestidigitatorial dexterity, the passage is couched in the form of a full sonnet, created expressly for Oizaki's adaptation. This is a form with which Shakespeare is famously associated both within and outside the dramatic sphere, and with which *Romeo and Juliet*, in particular, bears an intimate connection due to the play's highly stylized deployment of the rhetorical conventions of amorous poetry.

In its adoption of a Shakespearean style with carefully considered regularity, the anime reminds us that an adaptation based on a play is related at once to a performance text and to a written text. Oizaki's show is not content with merely focusing on the performance dimension of the source play and hence with reworking its plot components as though they had been designed exclusively for enactment. In fact, it is also seriously concerned with its status as a written text available for reading and for motionless page-bound presentation and reception — for its significance, in other words, as a piece of nondramatic discourse. It is at this level of the adaptive process that questions of language, tone and register acquire paramount weight. In paying attention to the Shakespearean parent as *both* a performance text *and* a written text, Oizaki's anime obliquely proposes that a dramatic work can never be conclusively regarded as a solid entity — a substratum in relation to which successive staged enactments and printed editions can be measured as more or less faithful or innovative derivations. It is actually a concept that only comes to fruition *as a result* of its translation into either a particular enactment or a particular edition: prior to that point, it only holds a composite potential status as either, both and neither of the two colluding parties. This move toward the hybrid recalls the quintessentially Japanese aesthetic proclivity for daring amalgamations of opposites — e.g., stability and unrest — as highlighted in the preface to this study.

    A prime indicator of the adaptation's imaginative treatment of the parent materials resides with its utilization of characters named after Shakespearean personae featuring in either *Romeo and Juliet* or other plays from disparate phases of the dramatist's career. The latter are drawn from all of the categories into which Shakespeare's corpus is conventionally subdivided. At times, the anime's characters echo quite blatantly their literary namesakes in their roles and mentalities, while at others they share no more than their appellations with the Shakespearean precursors. The Great Tree's guardian, Ophelia, exemplifies the latter typology insofar as this character does not obviously partake of any of the traits famously associated with the hapless maiden from *Hamlet*—except, arguably, a penchant for allusively dreamy language punctuated by phrases from *Hamlet*: e.g., "perchance to dream" and "all the rest is silence." Conrad falls into the same category, his namesake being a villain from *Much Ado About Nothing*. So do Juliet's closest comrades and mentors: Francisco, feasibly designated after ancillary personae from *Hamlet* and *The Tempest*, and Curio, who shares his denomination with one of Duke Orsino's attendants in *Twelfth Night*. We also meet a Petruchio (in Shakespeare, the male protagonist in *The Taming of the Shrew*) in the person of the unfortunate boy befriended by Romeo in the abysmal underworld of the Gradisca mines, and a Titus (the eponymous hero in Shakespeare's *Titus Andronicus*) in the person of Mercutio's father, a debauched but peculiarly shrewd and insightful member of the Montague court. Antonio, Conrad's grandson, shares his denomination with various Shakespearean characters, including the male lead from *The Merchant of Venice*. In some especially tantalizing cases, Oizaki's personae do not fulfill functions that can be regarded as literally faithful to the ones served by their co-designated ancestors but rather evince latent or even cryptic affinities with the Bard's own cast which it is up to the viewer to detect and interpret. Romeo's mother, Lady Portia, derives her name from the heroine of *The Merchant of Venice*, with whom she also shares an unwavering dedication to justice, and from the icon of virtuous womanly strength immortalized in *Julius Caesar*. The Neo-Verona Tyrant's given name, Leontes, is most felicitously chosen when one recalls the hubristic folly of his Shakespearean namesake from *The Winter's Tale*. This same play supplies Oizaki with the name of Hermione, Romeo's enforced betrothed, that of Camillo, Conrad's devious friend, and that of Emilia, cast by the anime as an actress enamored of Odin. (Please note that Oizaki is intentionally flouting the convention, pivotal to Elizabethan drama, that barred women access to the stage and required boys to play female roles instead.)

The name of Ariel — the charismatic leader of the Farnese family in the anime — is drawn from *The Tempest*: the Shakespearean sprite's magical powers are indeed echoed by Oizaki's Ariel in her providential role as something of an arch fairy godmother when it comes to the protection of Juliet and her beleaguered followers. Another oblique correspondence worthy of consideration can be found in the character of Cordelia, Juliet's confidant, maid and elder-sister surrogate in the adaptation, who shares with *King Lear*'s youngest daughter an affectionate and unfailingly loyal disposition. *King Lear* also provides the designation of Regan for the endearingly tomboyish granddaughter of Ariel's majordomo, Balthazar, whose own name is derived from that of a manservant in *Romeo and Juliet* itself. A few more personae with direct counterparts in the original play deserve notice in the present context. One of them is Mercutio, a character cast by Shakespeare in the role of an incandescent youth renowned for his sharp tongue and unforgivingly caustic sense of humor whom Oizaki reconfigures as a comparably irreverent and astute free spirit with an additional dark twist: a burning desire to usurp Romeo's place as Prince Montague's heir. Another one is Tybalt, Juliet's maternal cousin in the original play and Romeo's half-brother (i.e., Prince Montague's illegitimate son) in the anime.

There is a sense in which Tybalt can be thought of as the tyrant's alter ego insofar as he is an illegitimate outcome of the Montague line's selfish lecherousness in much the same way as Prince Montague is a product of a Capulet nobleman's exploitation of a vulnerable female. Tybalt and the despot thus stand as specular images of each other, united by a blistering and vindictive hatred for anyone and anything connected with the house which each of them deems responsible for his misfortune. This direct correspondence between the two characters is vividly conveyed by the installment in which Tybalt reveals to Juliet the truth about his own and Prince Montague's parentage. His speech is here vibrantly intercut with a sequence where Prince Montague engages in a fierce duel with Titus, whom he resents for being intimately acquainted with his murky past even though the older man has assiduously covered up the impostor's crimes. The duel, in turn, is punctuated by flashbacks to Prince Montague's deprived upbringing and burgeoning hatred for the Capulets. Another notable figure still is Benvolio, a character cast by Shakespeare as Romeo's cousin and recast by Oizaki as the male lead's best friend. In both instances, the character functions as the voice of reason in seeking to temper Romeo's more impetuous disposition. One of the most unforgettable characters of Oizaki's own conception is that of Lancelot, the doctor who selflessly strives to alleviate the suffering of the indigent and the abused with the help of supplies provided by the Red Whirlwind, whom he patches up after each fight to the best of his competence. Lancelot immolates himself by posing as the outlaw to save the lives of many innocent citizens accused of being the notorious figure who face execution. While the scene in which the physician heroically embraces the fire bound to consign him to the most agonizing of deaths stands out as one of the entire anime's most pathos-fraught moments, equally memorable — albeit far less spectacular — is the scene in which Lancelot's surviving spouse bids Juliet farewell before leaving Neo-Verona with her two little daughters. Alluding to her knowledge of the heroine's secret, the lady unreservedly exonerates Juliet from any sense of responsibility she might harbor for her husband's horrific end. It is in moments such as this that Oizaki's flair for imbuing his adaptation with autonomous energy gloriously asserts itself.

A further character of Oizaki's ideation here deserving of notice is Benvolio's father Vittorio, Neo-Verona's mayor and the leader of the House of Frescobaldi. Seeking to counteract Prince Montague's totalitarian policies by preaching moderation and a humane approach to law-enforcement, Vittorio is stripped of his title and possessions, sent into exile and threatened with assassination, and eventually sheltered in secret plebeian quarters by his old friend Conrad. The character is very effective in helping Oizaki engage with the story's political dimension in ways that transcend the hero-versus-villain formula and allow, in fact, for mature reflection on the forever unresolved tension between justice and order. An honest politician like Vittorio tirelessly advocates the need to reconcile the two in the service of what he envisions as the only authentically equanimous society one could ever aspire to achieve. Although the blind forces engulfing Neo-Verona at an ever increasing pace in the main body of the adventure mock those hopes as vapidly utopian, the finale does promise the prospect of a world in which even aspirations as seemingly idealistic as Vittorio's might one day reach fruition. Oizaki's handling of the personalities and names inspired by disparate portions of Shakespeare's corpus — and not, univocally, by *Romeo and Juliet* alone — exposes the limitations of theoretical models based on the premise that the distinction between a source and its reconceptualization is an unproblematic given. In fact, that strategy serves to show that an adaptation does not have to draw upon a single recognizable precedent but is in fact capable of bringing into play multiple sources and thus intimating that if an adaptation is somehow dependent on a prior work, that work is, in turn, also dynamically implicated with other works with which it may come into collusion at the adaptation's own behest.

One of Oizaki's most brilliantly inspired adaptive flourishes lies with the incorporation of the Bard himself into the cast as the character of William —

or rather "Willy," as several of his closest friends tend to address him, Juliet included when she dons the Odin mask. The family name "Shakespeare" is not explicitly used by Oizaki but William at one point boasts his ability to protect Juliet and her companions from the Montague guards on the grounds that no soldier would ever dare "shake his spear" at him. (The sexual innuendo is precisely of the kind Elizabethan and Jacobean audiences would have relished.) Alternately evincing zany extravagance and meditative gravity, melodramatic self-indulgence and pure genius, Oizaki's William engineers an alchemical fusion of reality and fantasy throughout, unobtrusively imparting the adventure with a cohesive force. He accomplishes this dramatic feat by suggesting direct intertextual correlations between his own plots and Juliet's life, often interspersing his own everyday colloquial register with lines from the actual Shakespeare (assuming such a creature ever existed outside the canonical imagination). *As You Like It*, for example, offers a perfect analogy with the status of Oizaki's heroine as a crossdresser. William also acts as a visible bridge between fantasy and reality by occupying the dwelling where Juliet and her associates find shelter from Montague's implacable persecution: an edifice owned by his own powerful mother Ariel. This, it should be noted, functions as an ideal shield for the Capulet insurgents due to its superficial appearance as a popular playhouse which any self-righteous member of the upper classes would unproblematically shun. While for William himself the house is a nest wherein his imagination can be given free rein and all manner of fantasy worlds can materialize, for the Capulets it operates, in its illusory safety, as a constant reminder of their vulnerability in the outside world as a sinister political reality.

In unleashing the full powers of fantasy, yet persistently commenting in an elliptical vein on the rebels' real predicament, William provides a poignant narrative link between the two dimensions. Whenever William hints at the existence of a parallel between his yarns and Juliet's actual experiences, he articulates those correspondences with such ironical panache that it not always incontrovertibly clear whether William's plays are supposed to stand as reflections of or rather templates for the girl's actions. A paradigmatic illustration is supplied by the sequence in which William admits to having been aware for a long time of Juliet's real identity and studied her ordeal in search of a plot bound to achieve immortality. His "quill" has thus been "graced" at last with "the love story that has so long eluded" him. William encourages Juliet to "surrender" to her emotions so that he "may cut" her story "into little stars and adorn the heavens for time eternal." In a sense, this is precisely what the historical Shakespeare can be said to have accomplished with his *Romeo and Juliet*—as borne out not only by the tragedy's enduring hold as a work in its own right but also by the countless adaptations it has so eclectically spawned.

Oizaki's Juliet, however, retains on this occasion the independence of mind that has distinguished her from the start from her Elizabethan precedent and simply refuses to embrace the passive status of a dramatic stereotype: "Forgive me, Willy," she tersely announces. "I cannot play your hero." The subtlety and humor with which Oizaki ideates the dramatist's persona throughout the show find commendable confirmation in the anime's apocalyptic climax: with Neo-Verona rapidly disintegrating around him, William laments that if the world were to come to an end, there would no longer be any need for stories — the prospect he fears is clearly not the extinction of humanity but rather the demise of narrative creativity.

Most importantly, through the character of William, Oizaki is in a position to enthrone language itself as a major character throughout the anime. This topos reaches an exhilarating apotheosis with the episode in which Juliet and her companions rehearse and perform a play written by William — and crowned by an entirely unforeseeable extempore climax by Juliet herself in her Red Whirlwind persona — in order to mobilize public support in Mantua and thence help it spread to Neo-Verona. William simply glories in this atmosphere of fervent creativeness, in which even the surly Curio is willing to draw fliers and posters to advertise the play and the athletic Casanova Francisco is quite prepared to lend a hand at costume-making, while Antonio discovers unsuspected acting talent in performance with his new friend Regan. At one point, proudly riding a stick horse while stentorianly offering his "kingdom" in exchange for a "horse," William avers that his genius benefits considerably from the country air.

Language's privileged status is persuasively corroborated by the vital significance attached to names and their connection with both personal and collective identities. This theme is particularly prominent in Oizaki's rendition of his source's most famous portion, the balcony scene. *Romeo x Juliet* repositions this moment radically but retains the original's emphasis on the uneasy relationship between individual desires and the overarching system of language by which those are framed, limited and indeed *spoken*. Jacques Derrida's discussion of the play deserves attention, in this matter. As Derek Attridge points out, in the analysis of the balcony scene conducted therein, Derrida emphasizes "the force of *contretemps* [countertime] both in the play and the institutional and intellectual context in which, and by means of which, we experience it" (in Derrida 1992, p. 414). The focus is on issues of names and naming: "The names of Romeo and Juliet, Montague and Capulet, produce both the desire that drives the events of the play and the tragic mischances that thwart it. [Please note that *contretemps* also translates as 'mishap.'] ... Love and hate are to be understood neither as arbitrary individual emotions nor as determined cultural products, but as powerful effects of chance built into the network of names and dates that make relationships possible and impossible" (p. 415). Derrida himself ponders the tragic kernel of the play in terms of the stubborn inextricability of names from their bearers, on the one hand, and in those of a no less insistent disjuncture between the sanctioned meaning of a name and the individual's fruitless yearning to oppose it on the other. "Romeo and Juliet," the deconstructive philosopher contends, "love each other across their name, despite their name, they die on account of their name, they live on in their name ... Romeo and Juliet bear these names. They bear them, support them even if they do not wish to assume them. From this name which separates them but which will at the same time have heightened their desire with all its aphoristic force, they would like to separate themselves. But the most vibrant declaration of their love still calls for the name that it denounces" (Derrida 1992, p. 423).

The most uncompromising indictment of the tyranny of names — and, by implication, of language at large — lies with Juliet's address of her illicit nocturnal suitor, which Derrida provocatively rephrases as follows: "Not only does this name say nothing about you as a totality but it doesn't say anything, it doesn't even name a part of you, neither your hand, nor your foot, neither your arm, nor your face, nothing that is human!... A proper name does not mean anything which is human, which belongs to a human body, a human spirit, an essence of man" (p. 430). Oizaki's adaptation of the relevant scene poignantly brings out the lacerating drama of language, reminding us in a terse and unsentimental fashion (i.e., aphoristically indeed) that words are never tied to meanings in unbiased, univocal or even logical ways. Language, therefore, cannot be used objectively — let alone, as Romeo and Juliet's tragedy emphasizes, disinterestedly. Words are intrinsically flawed, precariously situated over the chasm of incomprehension and, in the direst scenarios, corrupted by ideological constraints or — as the lovers' ordeal shows — even perverted so iniquitously as to amount to death sentences. If words can never be unproblematically presumed to mean what they say or say what they mean, they can nevertheless be adopted, plausibly by virtue of their intrinsic emptiness, to carry burdensome messages of life-shattering magnitude.

The issue of naming in *Romeo x Juliet* will shortly be returned to. It is first worth noting, on a more jocular note, that the balcony scene has also enjoyed a brief yet memorable adaptation in *Tsuyokiss — CoolxSweet* (TV series, dir. Shinichiro Kimura, 2006), an anime that often indulges in self-reflexive gestures commenting on dramatic and cinematic artistry with a focus on the process of production as an eminently material reality. In its take on the famous scene, Kimura's show confirms anime's attraction not only to the general import of the quintessential romantic tragedy of all times but also, more specifically, to its arguably most iconic and globally renowned segment. In the scene in question, the heroine, Sunao, strives to prove her thespian caliber to the annoyingly supercilious president of her school's student council so as to obtain permission to form a drama club. In enacting the famous piece, Sunao plays the roles of both Juliet and Romeo by nimbly switching places across the stage and hence seeming to influence the mood and style of the setting itself with each shift of position. A concisely impactful change of costume, achieved by simply wearing a dark cape-like curtain over Juliet's frilly accoutrements works marvels in imparting the scene with a distinctive atmosphere — and thus in imbuing Kimura's adaptive flourish with both drama and charm. In addition, the explicit and deliberate foregrounding of theatrical artificiality inherent in the scene emanates a genuinely Brechtian feel while also conveying an authentic sense of enthusiasm about the joys and hazards of performance.

Returning to the issue of language in *Romeo x Juliet*, Catherine Belsey's remarks concerning the relationship between love and language are especially deserving of attention. The critic maintains that if love is to be understood not as an entirely personal and isolated experience but rather as a communal reality, then it is far more likely to be an offshoot of an officially sanctioned and recognized discourse than of psychological and affective agencies. Belsey develops Derrida's argument regarding the instability of language and the related fallacy inherent in the assumption that words and their users can adequately express their meanings, by emphasizing that desire always exceeds and surpasses the language deployed to voice it. In defying the power of words, desire ostensibly challenges the distinction between mind and body, abstract symbols and material reality. Yet, it can do no more than challenge it: it cannot actually bypass or defeat it for good. In longing to divest themselves of the names that culturally define them, the lovers seek to give free rein to their "desiring bodies as pure sensation ... separable from the word that names it." Nevertheless, such "unnamed bodies ... are only imaginary. The human body is already inscribed: it has no existence as pure organism, independent of the symbolic order" of language, its signs, its codes and, ultimately, its love-stifling laws (Belsey 2001, p. 52).

References to the arbitrariness and injustice of naming feature at various points in the anime prior to the balcony scene. Juliet unceremoniously professes her resentment against her name in the scene where Conrad rebukes her for donning the Red Whirlwind costume and acting rashly to rescue Lancelot from the Montague dungeons when, the old man avers, she should be placing her title and the political duty that goes with it above all else. What fuels the heroine's chagrin, at this juncture, is the fact that she has only just found out that her beloved is Prince Montague's son — an unpalatable truth accidentally disclosed by the doctor at the close of the salvage mission in which Romeo has come to Juliet and Lancelot's assistance with spectacular results. A touching allusion to the tyrannical authority of names comes later with the scene in which Cordelia advises Juliet to try her hand at the mysterious art of needlework not by attempting to sew a whole shirt, as the girl wishes to do to replace the garment she has inadvertently caused Romeo to lose in fire, but rather by embroidering a handkerchief, adding that Juliet can put the cherished one's "name" on it. When the girl instinctively inquires "His *full* name?" her confidant, oblivious to the complexity of her predicament, innocently remarks: "I would hope you'd know that much about him now." What Cordelia cannot fathom, alas, is the dire extent to which Juliet herself would like *not* to partake of that knowledge.

A supple adaptation of a famous line from the source play features in the scene where Juliet, in her Odin mask, pays a visit to her parents' violated tomb at night and, picking up the flower that ironically binds her to both the Capulet line and Romeo throughout the anime, muses: "An iris by any other name would smell as sweet." The apotheosis of the series' engagement with the thorny issue of naming occurs in the sequence where Romeo and Odin are cruising the Neo-Verona skies aboard the loyal Cielo. When the boy introduces himself as "Romeo," his companion asks: "Romeo, *what*?" and elicits the following response: "I'd rather not have any other name. Let me just be Romeo, at least for a while." The genuinely heart-wrenching moment, in this exchange, is the aside recording Juliet's inner thoughts that immediately precedes Romeo's reply: "You fool," she chides herself. "Why bother asking? Do you expect him to claim some other family as his own?" The dialogue reaches its culmination with a succinct encapsulation of Romeo and Juliet's semiotic tragedy:

> ODIN/JULIET: Are you saying that you refuse your name?
> ROMEO: If I could ...

Even when the relationship between names and identities is couched in loving terms, it is hard not to sense its underlying arbitrariness. This is demonstrated by Romeo's early allusion to the concept of the name as a personal possession — a bizarre assumption indeed. Thus, when Juliet asks him why he wishes to know her name, he ripostes: "Simply because it is yours."

Any genuine *Romeo x Juliet* aficionados will undoubtedly rejoice in the invaluable pictorial companion to the anime, the art volume *Romeo x Juliet Destiny of Love Visual Fan Book*. In this text, the concurrently warm and robust nature of the show's artwork comes gloriously to the fore. In allowing us to focus closely on multifarious facets of the aesthetic vision sustaining the anime's characterization, dramatic composition and worldbuilding mission, the book also encourages us to reflect on some key aspects of its thematic take on the Shakespearean original. The deployment of color palettes that serve to individuate both single actors and whole factions and social groupings in an emblematic vein contributes to the richness of the images throughout without pandering to blatantly formulaic chromatic coding. In fact, color is used as a stylistic leading thread capable of imparting the volume in its entirety with admirable artistic coherence as an artifact of independent value. The companion is most helpful in highlighting the sheer magic of character designer and chief animation director Daiki Harada's inceptive visuals, their ability to capture the actors' personalities with a deft balance of naturalism and stylization, and their attention to subtle emotional tinges that render Oizaki's whole cast so prismatically diversified. The graphics indeed endeavor to foreground the main personae's multifacetedness, contrasting divergent aspects of their mentalities and roles at different stages in the action, thereby implying that human identities are always context-bound and hence predicated upon contingent social, familial and even metaphysical imperatives. Identity, it is thus obliquely proposed, can never be approached as a universal or transhistorical reality either at the level of the psychic apparatus or at that of materially encoded selfhood. Just as love, in the logic of both the source text and its anime adaptation, is inexorably performed within cultural boundaries, so the various characters' identities inevitably take shape vis-à-vis complex networks of intersubjectivity.

The character sheets devoted to Juliet are a prime example of Harada's penchant for multiplicity in the rendition of both physiognomy and psychology, studiously conveying the heroine's transitions across the roles of Odin, the Red Whirlwind and the adolescent girl as well as, within the Juliet persona as such, the oscillation between the bashful maiden in the throes of a forbidden passion and the duty-bound Capulet heir. The pages dedicated to Curio and Francisco are notable in their portrayal of the former's proverbial toughness and of the latter's suave manners while caring to draw attention to Curio's underlying gentleness and to Francisco's cold-blooded resolve. Analogously, Hermione's docility is highlighted without, however, obfuscating her lingering frustration and occasional concession to undiluted ire. The coexistence of selfless loyalty and pure good humor at the core of Cordelia's personality is simultaneously conveyed, as are Mercutio's duplicity and Tybalt's nightmarishly contorted psyche in the face of seemingly irreconcilable obligations. As for Oizaki's commitment to meticulous worldbuilding, the images isolating the most diminutive aspects of each actor's distinctive garments and accessories are no less telling, though obviously less theatrical, than those devoted to different types of dragonsteeds (and their respective accoutrements) or those focusing on both recurrent and sporadic settings in the format of miniaturized tableaux. Thus, even a single page of frames depicting the anime's natural and architectural locations is sufficient to regale the eye with a powerful impression of the series' environmental diversity and to enable imaginative juxtapositions in the viewer's mind. Therefore, the artbook fully substantiates Oizaki's enlisting of Harada and his associates as instrumental in the evocation of an alternate universe which, ironically, gains concreteness and credibility from its speculative nature and wholly hypothetical underpinnings more than from any degree of realism imparted upon its forms. Commenting specifically on Harada's accomplishment, Oizaki has drawn attention to the artist's unmatched flair for communicating the story's "human drama" thanks to an apparently innate ability to "breathe life into his drawings," make the characters palpably alive by conjuring up "the warmth of their skin" and hence enable them to "seem ready to leap off the page" (Oizaki).

Romeo and Juliet is one of the Bard's works to have been most frequently adapted all over the globe to cinematic form. The earliest — and vastly popular — adaptations can be witnessed in the province of silent film, which might seem ironical considering that many of us have been trained to associate Shakespeare's genius principally with rhetorical and dialogical powers. What is most intriguing about silent versions of *Romeo and Juliet* is that, as White points out, on numerous occasions they did not handle the tragedy deferentially but rather "as a burlesque apparently unworthy of the seriousness accorded to the other tragedies" (White, p. 20). The first widely acclaimed adaptation of *Romeo and Juliet* for the screen was helmed by George Cukor in 1936 and cast in the key roles Trevor Howard and Norma Shearer. Being already in their late thirties at the time, these actors might seem an odd choice as the champions of youthful love but their immense popularity would no doubt have secured positive responses from older audiences familiar with their talent. Producer Irving Thalberg was especially keen to convey the authenticity of the film's cultural context, tirelessly instructing the artists and researchers in the crew to derive aesthetic inspiration from the city of Verona itself and from the works of painters such as Giovanni Bellini, Sandro Botticelli, Benozzo Gozzoli and Vittore Carpaccio. In this regard, the film bears affinities with Oizaki's own relocation of the Shakespearean drama as a likewise impeccably documented visual text.

A highly imaginative intervention in this adaptive history consists of Renato Castellani's 1954 film, which was shot entirely on location in Italy and features costumes designed by Leonor Fini inspired directly by the works of illustrious Italian painters of the Renaissance. According to Solimano, the most notable examples are Piero della Francesca's fresco representing King Solomon and the Queen of Sheba, to which the film's portrayal of Juliet is explicitly indebted, Andrea Mantegna's series of frescoes for the Gonzaga Wedding Chamber, particularly in the representation of the Court of Mantua, and Vittore Carpaccio's *Vision of St. Augustine* for the representation of Friar Lawrence's monastic cell. Castellani's movie, moreover, echoes the oeuvre of Domenico Ghirlandaio in its approach to perspective and framing (Soliman). Castellani's adaptation sets an immediate precedent for Franco Zeffirelli's own screen version of *Romeo and Juliet* (1968). This makes sustained reference to several of the most pressing issues thrown into relief by the period in which it was released, making the action pivot on the interpenetration of dynastic conflicts with generational tensions marring all relationships between the young and their often corrupt elders. One of the most thought-provoking adaptations of recent decades is indubitably Baz Luhrmann's 1996 film. In this version, according to White, the preoccupation with social issues progressively evinced by some of the more inspired adaptations of *Romeo and Juliet* since the 1960s takes a new turn in order to highlight the "nihilism of the senses" bred by "profiteering multinational corporations, ... seedy urban decay ... and the frustrations of a neglected generation" victimized by "the insatiable greed of the news moguls who exploit 'human interest' stories such as suicide — their narrative is framed in a typically disposable television news story" (White, p. 23). According to Gill, Luhrmann's production can also be regarded as an innovative moment in the field of Shakespeare adaptations insofar as it "illuminated some tired metaphors with daring visual puns, and demonstrated that there is nothing sacred about the iambic pentameter when it is spoken quite naturally in 'Verona Beach' (California), where the fighting is with 'Sword 9mm' guns, Captain Prince patrols his territory in a helicopter, and Romeo courts Juliet while swimming in her father's pool" (Gill, p. viii).

In looking at previous adaptations of *Romeo and Juliet*, a primary instance of imaginative reconceptualization is supplied by the film *West Side Story* (dirs. Jerome Robbins and Robert Wise, 1961), itself an adaptation of a 1957 Broadway musical with music by Leonard Bernstein and lyrics by Stephen Sondheim. The theme of dynastic rivalry is radically relocated and recontextualized as a feud involving two gangs in a 1950s New York plagued by racial conflict. The Capulets, accordingly, are recast as a Puerto Rican group dubbed the "Sharks," whereas the Montagues are white Americans of Anglo-Saxon provenance known as the "Jets." The themes of youth anarchy, urban warfare and parental failure gain great prominence in this adaptation. Racial conflict is also central to Charles Kanganis' hip-hop imbued film *Rome and Jewel* (2006), where the Veronese couple is reimagined as consisting of the African-American son of a Compton minister and the Caucasian daughter of the mayor of Los Angeles. *Shakespeare in Love* (movie; dir. John Madden, 1998) is also notable in this context due to its insertion of Shakespeare's own (fictionalized) life into the cinematic dimension. Madden's dramatization of the playwright Will Shakespeare's relationship with his top actor Thomas Kent disguised as Viola de Lesseps parallels Oizaki's use of the persona of Willy in *Romeo x Juliet*. Among some of the more radical adaptations rank Peter Ustinoff's Cold-War take on the play, retitled *Romanoff and Juliet* (1961), and the martial-arts appropriation *Romeo Must Die* (movie; dir. Andrzej Bartkowiak, 2000). In the specific domain of animated cinema, notable instances are *Romie-0 and Julie-8* (1996), a made-for-TV movie helmed by Clive A. Smith in which the protagonists are portrayed as robots, and Phil Nibbelink's *Romeo and Juliet: Sealed with a Kiss* (2006), where the lovers are cute seals rewarded with a child-friendly happy ending. Additionally, filmic adaptations of *Romeo and Juliet* include pornographic versions of the basic story, such as the Swedish movie *The Sex Lives of Romeo and Juliet* (dir. Peter Perry, Jr., 1969), and the "trash" or "grunge" appropriation *Tromeo and Juliet* (movie; dir. Loyd Kaufman, 1996).

Regardless of the extent to which individual adaptations of Shakespeare's tragedy, Oizaki's included, depart from the source, they all point to the creative powers of the art of adaptation per se by varyingly demonstrating that directors and actors collaborate actively with the original play. Relatedly, in taking cognizance of the vast differences in outlook and style exhibited by separate adaptations, viewers might fruitfully take greater critical ownership of the source text while also learning to be more questioning of the media through which its adaptations are divulged. Oizaki's own anime participates in these interrogative processes with arguably unparalleled fervor, thus bearing full witness to Pierre Macherey's description of the imaginative potentialities inherent in the adaptive mode: "Man can create only in continuity, by making the potential actual; he is excluded, by his nature, from originality and innovation. But this difference is an adaptation" (Macherey, p. 230).

If cinematic adaptations of *Romeo and Juliet* are so numerous as to defy comprehensive documentation in the present context, it must also be noted that the original play has served as the source of inspiration for countless paintings over the centuries. Oizaki's *Romeo x Juliet* does not overtly, let alone univocally, adopt the style prevalent in any one isolatable work of art. Yet, it does exhibit some intriguing points of contact with diverse pictorial relocations of the Shakespearean tragedy. A relatively early pictorial adaptation of *Romeo and Juliet* here worthy of consideration is Henry William Bunbury's *Romeo and Juliet with Friar Lawrence* (1792–1796), a narrative painting that emphasizes Juliet's virginal reticence and hence her reluctance to give in to the call of desire. Although, as observed, Oizaki's heroine is a far more active persona than Shakespeare's own Juliet, she does evince a similar stance in the anime's climax when she resists Romeo's entreaties in the knowledge that her personal yearnings and her public duty are hopelessly irreconcilable. An intriguing affinity can also be detected between the moonlit scene set by Oizaki in Juliet's humble bedchamber, portraying her disconsolateness in the wake of the discovery of Romeo's family name and Philip H. Calderon's *Juliet* (1888), where almost identical color and lighting effects are deployed to convey a germane atmosphere. With Ford Madox Brown's *Romeo and Juliet* (1870), Oizaki's anime shares a passion for Mediterranean settings (especially at the architectural level), as well as for warm palettes of the kind associated by the series with Juliet and the Capulet line throughout its unfolding. Concomitantly, the show echoes Sir Francis Dicksee's *Romeo and Juliet* (1884) in its more fairytalish moments of innocent romance.

The adaptive potentialities entailed by the finale of the original play, emphasized by numerous visual adaptations and obviously significant to Oizaki's own enterprise, are dramatically captured in Frederic Lord Leighton's *The Reconciliation of the Montagues and Capulets Over the Dead Bodies of Romeo and Juliet* (1853–1855). The sense of aerial suspension so pivotal to the Neo-Veronese ambience portrayed by Oizaki's anime is also the most salient feature of Marc Chagall's *Romeo and Juliet* (1964), where the lovers — in a style instantly redolent of the artist's cachet — float through space in a deceptively tranquil and ethereal environment, in fact coursed by violence and discord. In the realm of contemporary art, *Romeo x Juliet* finds a close correlative in Dorina Costras' *Romeo and Juliet*, a painting that echoes the anime in its emphasis on the centrality of masks to the construction and maintenance of public identities. Another notable instance is Todd Peterson's *Romeo and Juliet*, where prominence is given — as is repeatedly the case in Oizaki's series — to an oneiric dimension in which even the sweetest of dreams is capable of degenerating into a baleful nightmare. Finally, Oizaki's heroine recalls quite vividly — though, one assumes, fortuitously — John William Waterhouse's *Juliet* (1898), another persona likewise marked by a stance so reserved as to verge on timidity blended dynamically with a sense of inquisitive intelligence and independence of mind.

Romeo and Juliet's standing as one of the most often adapted of Shakespeare's works may seem somewhat ironical when set against the tendency, pervasive among mainstream critics and commentators of the Bard's corpus, to regard the play as the Cinderella of the tragedies. This proclivity has insistently led to *Romeo and Juliet*'s relative marginalization in favor of the so-called mature tragedies (especially *Hamlet, Macbeth, Othello* and *King Lear*) as dramatizations of the fall of a noble soul in Shakespeare's distinctly modern adaptation of the classical template mapped on concepts of *hamartia, hubris* and *nemesis*. The play itself has fomented such critical attitudes due to Shakespeare's own parodic employment of its tragic core in "Pyramus and Thisbe," the play-within-a-play grotesquely performed by the "rude mechanicals" in *A Midsummer Night's Dream*. It is worth noting, on this point, that Lindsay

Kemp's 1979 adaptation of *A Midsummer Night's Dream* in pantomime form actually replaces "Pyramus and Thisbe" with snippets of *Romeo and Juliet*, featuring a farcical version of the famous balcony scene, sardonically debunked through the use of actors perched on stilts and squeaky voices. However, *Romeo and Juliet* undeniably carries serious ideological and psychological implications, as the foregoing pages have sought to show with specific reference to Oizaki's extrapolation and intensification of the original play's macrocosmic import in his anime.

The source text's richness may well be conveyed more effectively by its adaptational reconceptualizations than by tiresome attempts to stage and restage ad infinitum some putatively authentic Shakespearean text unsullied by history and circumstances, which ultimately only serve to deliver uninspiring spectacle — in other words, something inauthentic if measured by the standards of Shakespeare's proverbial vitality and zestful discourse. Indeed, by reimagining the source text in relation to variable and tangible cultural contexts rather than to some dusty archeological vestige safely snuggled in the concept of literary tradition, adaptive performances show us that no work is genuinely alive unless it is amenable to pluralizing rewriting by different generations and for different reasons and purposes. Oizaki's series validates this hypothesis not solely by radically reconfiguring *Romeo and Juliet* but also — indeed, more significantly — by yielding a convincing portrait of the original play's more poignant subtexts. It does so most memorably, paradoxical though this may sound, when it departs most starkly from the parent yarn. This is because its leading goal does not consist of seizing the essence of *Romeo and Juliet* per se (whatever this might be) but rather the play's transhistorical relevance and this relevance, ironically, can only be credibly demonstrated by giving it contingent historical (or mock-historical) grounding. Thus, Neo-Verona and the dynastic lore revolving around the Great Tree could be viewed primarily as tropes through which Oizaki anchors a floating fantasy to a speculative reality, and thus alludes to the original text's ability to speak to the specific audiences of disparate epochs.

Oizaki's adaptation concomitantly redefines, in light of both the specific capacities of his medium and his fresh take on the plot, an important eros-related aspect of the original play which Lloyd Davis has pithily described as the "notion of desire as lost presence" (Davis, p. 38). Whereas Shakespeare's tragedy conclusively consigns desires to this melancholy state, Oizaki's adaptation, as suggested, offers an ambiguous finale in which desire might reach at least partial fulfillment. However, the anime is faithful to its source text's depiction of love as a state which no individual can unequivocally appropriate as a personal possession or prerogative insofar as it is always bound "to slip back into constraining and distorting social forms." This is foreshadowed, in both the original play and the anime, by the context of Romeo and Juliet's first encounter: "an elaborate ritual of masks and misrecognition" (p. 38). In its dramatization of Romeo and Juliet's passion, Oizaki's series also replicates the inceptive tragedy in its structural penchant for repetitive patterning. In the Bard's own text, this preference is borne out by the orchestration of the love yarn in relation, as Davis notes, to "Four meetings and kisses shared by Romeo and Juliet ... in counterpoint to four violent or potentially violent eruptions" (p. 41). Oizaki's anime likewise alternates between amorous lyricism and martial turbulence by employing seven key events, pivoting throughout on the protagonists' romance as its diegetic backbone. These correspond to Romeo and Juliet's first meeting while the heroine is disguised as the Red Whirlwind and Montague's son rescues her from the pursuing guards, their epiphanic experience of love at first sight at the Rose Ball, the rescue of Lancelot from the dungeon where Juliet is again donning her outlaw mask and Romeo gets her and the doctor out of trouble, the sequence where the couple shelters from the rain in a lakeside cottage and Romeo discovers that Odin and Juliet are one and the same person, the exchange of vows in the abandoned country church, the reunion in the derelict village which Romeo is seeking to resuscitate with the freed Gradisca prisoners, and the lovers' climactic encounter at the time of Romeo's return to Neo-Verona just as the Capulet insurgents are gaining control of the capital.

With its own treatment of repetition as a structural mainstay, the show pays homage to Shakespeare's own rendition of the unresolved conflict between a fantasy of transcendence and a reality of time-bound obligations. Much as the lovers may strive for a dream that could surpass both temporal and spatial boundaries, their destiny brutally decrees, according to Davis, that the connections between "past and present, social and personal, cannot be transcended." Oizaki's intensification of his source's political dimension foregrounds this perspective with undeniable poignancy, simultaneously reinforcing the original text's rhythmic oscillation between moments of "passion, when time seems to stand still" and dream-shattering "returns to the ongoing rush of events" (p. 32). If Romeo and Juliet's love defies the constraints of clocktime in favor of a timeless flow of affects and projections, the strictures of social calendars, historical landmarks and pressing dates haul them back to a rigidly defined pattern of temporality and attendant responsibilities. The insistent references, peppered throughout the anime, to the events held to have taken place fourteen years prior to the present-day adventure powerfully serve to index public time against the lovers' yearning for suspension or dissolution in a somehow atemporal forever. The repetitive scheme is strengthened by the show's alternation between hyperkinesis and reflective stasis, marked by a tendency to intersperse and juxtapose the more dynamic sequences with pauses for meditation and reassessment. Thus, the dramatic revelation of the heroine's real identity in the graveyard scene is followed by the moment of petrified paralysis in which she faces the immensity of the task ahead. Later, her resolve to take up the legacy borne by her father's sword is superseded by a likewise stalling reluctance to act due to her knowledge of Romeo's parentage. The intense sequence in which the Capulet rebels are besieged and attacked by the Montague guards as a result of Camillo's betrayal is then counterpointed by Juliet's disabling shock as she confronts at first hand the reality of bloodshed. The lovers' brief rural idyll later nests itself precariously between episodes of frantic action, as does the temporary retreat by the heroine and her companions to the haven of Lady Farnese's Mantua estate. This pattern serves to highlight, to cite Davis' comments on the original play, how "The lovers create new images of individuality and of togetherness.... Yet their efforts remain circumscribed by social forces" (p. 37).

The Shakespeare play's seemingly infinite amenability to adaptation is, according to Davis, a possibility which *Romeo and Juliet*'s own finale overtly decrees. According to the critic, "The play affirms precedents and conditions for its own reproduction as if anticipating future responses. Before ending, it even shows these possibilities being realised. The grieving fathers decide to build statues of the lovers, and the prince's final lines look forward to 'more talk of these sad things'" (p. 40). According to Dympna Callaghan, moreover, at the same time as it "perpetuates an already well-known tale," *Romeo and Juliet* also delivers an open-ended resolution that entails "the possibility of almost endless retellings of the story — displacing the lovers' desire into a perpetual narrative of love" (Callaghan, p. 61). The interpretation of *Romeo and Juliet* as a play whose closure alludes to options for textual regeneration and relocation is also implied by Julia Kristeva's psychoanalytical reading of its treatment of the love-death dyad, particularly in the finale. "Even though the death of the Verona lovers is beyond remedy," Kristeva maintains, "one has the feeling that it is only sleep.... The sleep of lovers ... refills a stock of imaginative energy that is ready, at the wakening, for new expenditures, new caresses, under the sway of the senses." Thus, the situation captured at the close of *Romeo and Juliet* can be said to "provide us with a certain amorous, imaginary stock for our erotic and social dramas" (Kristeva, p. 82). In Kristeva's assessment, Romeo and Juliet would appear to have entered a temporary condition of dormancy and to be awaiting resuscitation, metaphorically speaking. No force could more dependably undertake such a task than textuality — a sphere of human activity that is famed to lack any clear origin and any obvious destination and therefore to be, by implication, limitless. The ending of Oizaki's adaptation is also amenable to Kristeva's reading of the original play's finale, at the same time as it lends the source an inspired twist by plausibly taking Romeo and Juliet into a parallel dimension. Thus, the anime does not merely revive the Shakespearean lovers: it actually engineers their transposition to profoundly Other imaginary worlds — first, that of Neo-Verona and then that of the realm they are ushered into by their redemptive actions: alternate realities whence yet more textual journeys might conceivably ensue. In these conjectural experiments, one glimpses the possibility of a love founded on respect, mutuality and equality that may elude exile to a tragic neverland, achieve fulfillment and, more importantly still, go on operating as a source of inspiration from a world that is beyond our own world and yet dialectically conjoined with it.

Chapter 6

A Magical Murder Enigma
Umineko no Naku Koro ni

> *The only words that ever satisfied me as describing Nature are the terms used in fairy books, charm, spell, enchantment. They express the arbitrariness of the fact and its mystery.*
> — Gilbert Keith Chesterton

Umineko no Naku Koro ni ("When Seagulls Cry") first came into existence in 2007 as a visual novel created by the *doujin* group 07th Expansion. The initial game has since spawned an entire series comprising six story arcs: *Legend of the Golden Witch* (2007), *Turn of the Golden Witch* (2007), *Banquet of the Golden Witch* (2008), *Alliance of the Golden Witch* (2008), *End of the Golden Witch* (2009) and *Dawn of the Golden Witch* (2009). In order to appreciate *Umineko no Naku Koro ni*'s textual constitution, it is vital to consider the principal features of its medium as both a ludic and a narrative construct. The phrase visual novel typically designates a videogaming package of an emphatically interactive and immersive character, which shuns the notion of authorial mastery and enlists instead the player's own creativity as instrumental in the production of the narrative weave. The player is indeed responsible for narrativizing the game insofar as the game itself does not yield a story as such but rather the raw materials (dramatis personae, situations and settings) from which a narrative might be concocted, and a purely virtual reality might thereby achieve contingent realization. Visual novels capitalize on parallel, multiperspectival, crisscrossing and intertwining story arcs, and their conclusions alter according to the specific choices made by players at critical "decision points." Players may gradually sample all of a game's potential outcomes by exploring alternative possibilities through multiple replay. Structurally, visual novels rely on extensive textual passages capturing the characters' dialogues and internal monologues, accompanied by frames featuring character sprites meant to connote the sources of particular utterances and by intensely atmospheric backgrounds. Characterization is indubitably one of the game's key priorities, bearing witness to psychological complexity, a serious concern with contemporary cultural anxieties and a hearty appetite for convoluted relationships. *Umineko no Naku Koro ni* constitutes a particular kind of visual novel normally described as "sound novel," in keeping with 07th Expansion's distinctive aesthetic proclivities. In this kind of game, sound operates as a pivotal expressive vehicle and considerable prominence is accordingly attributed to acoustic effects, dialogue and music. *Umineko no Naku Koro ni*'s graphic style, relatedly, is terse and carefully stripped of redundant ornamentation, in favor of dramatic color contrasts and line patterns capable of evoking chromatic and geometric harmonies that aptly replicate the game's aural leanings.

At base, the series chronicles the adventures of a group of eighteen characters trapped by a typhoon on a remote island, Rokkenjima, over two days (i.e., 4 and 5 October 1986) as they become embroiled in a chain of bizarre murders. The aim of the game is to ascertain whether the crimes emanate from human or supernatural agencies while striving to ideate an outcome guaranteeing all of the main personae's survival. The first four *Umineko no Naku Koro ni* games serve to familiarize players with the story's setting and bizarre circumstances, while the last two games, known as *Umineko no Naku Koro ni Chiru* ("When Seagulls Cry Breakdown") dig into the nub of the axial conundrum, supplying fractional solutions to the questions raised in the previous games but also moving the action into fresh territory. The cast includes the ailing head of the affluent Ushiromiya family, Kinzo, three of his family members stationed on the island alongside his personal doctor and five of his servants, and eight additional family members visiting Rokkenjima to discuss the distribution of Kinzo's inheritance after his forthcoming demise. Pivotal to the game's progression are the exploits revolving around the character of Battler Ushiromiya, a hitherto estranged member of the prosperous dynasty, and his investigation into the legend claiming that as a young man, Kinzo received a handsome amount of gold from the Golden Witch Beatrice, whose charismatic portrait hangs in the hall of the island mansion. (The edifice itself, incidentally, offers a faithful adaptation of the palace in the Kyuu Furukawa Gardens in Kita, Tokyo.)

The cryptic epitaph inscribed on a stone block beneath the painting intimates that unless its meaning is disclosed, more and more people will come to nefarious ends until Beatrice herself is eventually resurrected. Battler and Beatrice are caught together in their own bizarre game as they inspect the events taking place on the island from the bird's-eye perspective provided by their teleportation to the alternate universe of "Purgatorio" (courtesy, putatively, of Beatrice's preternatural skills). The relationship between the two characters gains tremendous dialectical tension from their conflicting world views: while the Golden Witch seems only too keen on demonstrating the ascendancy of magical factors in the lethal charade they are witnessing, Battler has no time for anything other than hard-nosed factuality. The player is assisted by "Tips," systematically updated as the story progresses, providing additional information about the actors and plot which may or may not be helpful in unraveling the mystery. Further clues are supplied, at different stages, by features tagged "red truth" (a statement claiming to be true and challenging the player to formulate hypotheses regarding the culprit or culprits), "blue truth" (a statement presenting theories that might become true unless they are contradicted by the red truth), and "gold truth" (a statement that is only available to the Game Master — or Game Manager [GM] — that may or may not override the red truth). The levels of truth attendant upon each turn of the game and related efforts to unravel the central puzzle are therefore not only multifarious but also, at least potentially, incompatible and often rescindable. This ruse works very effectively in encouraging players to bring to fruition the game's speculative narrative by recourse to their own hermeneutic capabilities.

Moving on to consider the original visual novel's anime adaptation *Umineko no Naku Koro ni*, a TV series encompassing the first four arcs of the game and helmed by Chiaki Kon (2009), an important difference must first of all be noted. The source game can afford to leave its multiforking threads pretty much open, on the assumption that it is ultimately up to the player to actualize their otherwise purely potential and hypothetical status as narrative leads. Due to its fundamentally episodic and finite format, the anime has no choice but to braid its plot strands more firmly together — albeit by no means with unequivocal finality — and hence provide at least partial resolutions. The show's dramatic constellation does, however, bear witness to Kon's endeavor to produce an animational equivalent of 07th Expansion's ramifying ludic structure. To allow this aspect of the series incrementally to manifest itself, it is necessary not to examine it exclusively in terms of either its overall parable (in search for content-oriented answers to its riddles) or its individual installments (in the interests of formalist analysis). In fact, it is both more apposite and more rewarding to approach it on the basis of clusters of episodes wherein plural narrative possibilities converge, collide or collude, and finally deliver provisional resolutions to the characters' and the audience's quest for meaning and shape in the face of a seemingly inchoate tangle of murky enigmas. Visual novels, as argued, do not constitute autonomous narratives in themselves, yet host all the basic elements of an imaginable or plausible story. These materials rise to the status of actual narratives as the game enlists its players' story-making proclivities, encouraging them to constellate the available materials into a cohesive semiotic ensemble. Emulating the task undertaken by the visual novel's players, Kon's anime seeks to muster its source game's disparate components into a harmonious cinematic event. This analogy situates the series' director and designers on the plane of imaginatively involved players unto themselves. Viewers of the anime adaptation further contribute to the story-making process as they distil the yarn proffered by the show in consonance with their aesthetic preferences and interpretative skills.

Approaching Kon's *Umineko no Naku Koro ni* in terms of its episode clusters rather than in those of discrete dramatic units can help us engage in the narrativizing act with sharpened sensitivity to the anime's overarching structural orchestration and, by extension, abet our understanding of its adaptive intervention as a narrativizing act in its own right. The anime pays frequent homage to its parent genre by commenting self-reflexively on its events and formal attributes. Thus, the characters themselves reflect on the crimes of which they have been either the witnesses or the victims as though those lurid occurrences had resulted purely from the decisions performed by the player (or players) of a visual novel. Beatrice herself, moreover, is described as the "host" of the "game," while her rival witch Bernkastel emphasizes the nature of the Golden Witch's magic game as "endless," thus elliptically pointing to the infinite replayability of the game whence the show derives its central plot and personae. Bernkastel also involves the audience directly into the adventure, alluding to our status as potential players of both the source game and the game of cat-and-mouse initiated by Beatrice, by stating that just as she expects her competitor to pull off an interesting performance so as to avert her boredom, she also expects us to contribute actively to her entertainment.

Umineko no Naku Koro ni sets out as a dramatic chronicle of the fears, obsessions and disputes plaguing a quintessentially dysfunctional family, garnished with elements of the macabre and the occult. This mix allows for considerable generic flexibility: a trait of the anime which the director seeks to maintain throughout his adaptation. However, in order to grasp the nature and amplitude of Kon's reconceptualization of 07th Expansion's parent materials, it is desirable to assess specifically the drama's connections with the broader traditions of mystery, detective and crime fiction. As G. J. Demko maintains, "The mystery genre has been, and is, enormously popular in Japan.... Crime stories had a rather early start in Japan as evidenced by the publication of a collection of criminal cases by Saikaku Ihara in 1689." However, *Umineko no Naku Koro ni* does not simply confirm the popularity of the genre on home turf in generalized terms by underscoring its imaginative infiltration of the videogaming industry. In fact, it also reflects a distinctive aesthetic preference in the Japanese handling of fictive mystery. This, Demko explains, consists of a somewhat "old fashioned tendency to emphasize the puzzle-solving dimension of the genre. Given the absence of guns, murders are often rather messy and/or very imaginatively performed — methods may vary from axes to sound." Yet, *Umineko no Naku Koro ni* boldly challenges another cultural dominant: the tendency to couch most mystery plots as "police procedurals," with a resulting "dearth of flashy and flamboyant private eyes" (Demko). Kon's anime does feature what could be loosely described as private eyes in the characters of Beatrice and Battler as they observe the events taking place on Rokkenjima and strive to decipher their origins and meaning. Yet, the drama's overall emphasis is laid on the programmatic, step-by-step methods through which Beatrice seeks to persuade Battler to accept the transcendental authority of the otherworldly and Battler, conversely, endeavors to relegate all things magical, witchly and esoteric to the province of old wives' tales. Concurrently, the series evinces a sustained tendency to interweave several of the classic elements typical of the mystery, detective and crime genres with diverse facets of other prolific traditions veering toward the supernatural and the Gothic.

According to Maurizio Ascari, in the early stages of its evolution, detective fiction sought to supersede existing forms thriving on irrational and inexplicable phenomena by means of "riddles and enigmas which respectably set the mind to work with crystal-clear lucidity. Death and crime ... were exorcised by the focus on the enquiry, an incontrovertible proof of the enlightened human potential for good" (Ascari, p. 1). *Umineko no Naku Koro ni* adopts a tongue-in-cheek stance toward this critical outlook, positing its intradiegetic detectives, Battler and Beatrice, as fairly rational observers of events, physically detached for a significant portion of the action from the crime scene itself as though to underscore their transcendental omniscience. Yet, the anime's dialectical structure assiduously emphasizes the nature of Battler and Beatrice's interaction as a strenuous struggle of wills precluding any chance of their harboring the kind of logical and level-headed objectivity expected of the detective type portrayed by Ascari. Each of the anime's potential detectives, in other words, has far too much of an axe to grind to be capable of genuinely dispassionate detection. In the process, the anime's in-text investigators guide the spectator's own perceptions and cumulative hermeneutic project in much the same way as directors can be expected to do, echoing Paul Auster's hypothesis that detectives and authors carry out analogous tasks: "The detective is the one who looks, who listens, who moves through this morass of objects and events in search of the thought, the idea that will pull all of these things together and make sense of them. In effect, the writer and the detective are interchangeable. The reader sees the world through the detective's eyes, experiencing the proliferation of its details as if for the first time" (Auster, p. 15). Equally apposite, however, is the equation of readers themselves to detectives — an idea adumbrated by Sherlock Holmes when he implicitly compares his activity to that of Watson's audience by stating: "for I hold in this hand several threads of one of the strangest cases which ever perplexed a man's brain, and yet lack the one or two which are needful to complete my theory" (Doyle, pp. 139–140).

Moreover, the show repeatedly points to the inextricability of the detective mode from the irrational, the supernatural and the magical. In the process, it deploys the art of adaptation to celebrate generic fluidity and implicitly propose that the ultimate appeal of both investigation and revelation lies in the interstices between genres rather than in any one clearly defined form. This epistemological tension is ushered in by Kon's series right from the start of its first arc with an incident revolving around the character of Maria, who claims to have been presented with an umbrella by the mysterious Beatrice. While Battler, ever faithful to his resolutely pragmatic world view, disputes Beatrice's very existence, it soon becomes clear that none of the original eighteen residents has given Maria the umbrella and this seriously poses the possibility of an unknown nineteenth presence among them. The coexistence of contrasting generic allegiances at the heart of the anime is later confirmed as six characters (namely, Krauss, Rudolf, Rosa, Kyrie, Shannon and Gohda) are found ferociously murdered inside an outdoor storehouse in a style consonant with the type of plot one would expect to encounter in a classic of the Golden Age of detective fiction, such as an Agatha Christie story. However, the primacy of this generic mold is challenged by the incorporation of dramatic elements typical of the supernatural thriller and the sensation yarn. This is most explicitly borne out by the prominence accorded by the drama to a cryptic emblem drawn on the shed, alluding to the brutal crime's preternatural connotations. Reminiscent of a magician's circle of the type associated with Satanic rituals, the symbol is later revealed by Maria — whose expertise in esoteric matters, underpinned by vast textual erudition, far surpasses her age group's average competences — to be "the seventh magical circle of the Sun." (Later in the series, Maria will also elucidate the origins of other peculiar symbols with reference to astrology and the Psalms.) A classic detection game is subsequently supplied by the sequences in which Battler and his relatives formulate the hypothesis that one of the eighteen residents is pretending to be Beatrice in an effort to lay his or her greedy paws on Kinzo's assets, and set their eyes on various suspects by turns.

An ominous legacy darkens their speculations: the contract binding Kinzo and Beatrice, and responsible for the old man's acquisition of fabulous wealth, stipulates that the moment the head of the Ushiromiya family calls off the deal, the witch will be automatically entitled not only to reappropriate the original gold itself but also to seize all of the assets accrued by the clan over the years of Kinzo's prosperity. Since the family members know full well that they, too, are just the breathing components of the old man's investment portfolio, so to speak, they are also aware that in principle, Beatrice can claim their lives as part of the property she feels entitled to unless they unravel the epitaph and discover the location of her treasure. The shadows thicken around the cast's hazy suspicions as Kinzo is later said to have practiced black magic in a desperate attempt to revive his beloved Beatrice after her demise as a human and to have used innocent children as experimental subjects in the course of diabolical rituals. Kon also inserts into his adaptive tapestry as an inspired luxury thread the suspicion that the so-called real world harbors no magic per se but Beatrice, as long as she can shift reality's parameters and replace the everyday world with a virtual realm of her own conception, is capable not only of appearing to be real in a palpably embodied sense but also of wielding uniquely powerful magic. All this depends on other people's acknowledgment and eventual acceptance of her existence as a supernatural agent. Such a portentous ruse makes the Golden Witch a very skilled illusionist. According to local lore, her abilities are indeed of a kind not to be trifled with — as attested to by the time-honored legend maintaining that Rokkenjima was once notorious for its knack of attracting evil spirits, putatively summoned by Beatrice herself and held to have occasioned many a dire shipwreck. Once again, the anime's generic affiliations to the rational side of the detective mode are thus partially undermined by the infusion into the action of both discrete allusions to otherworldly phenomena and blatant manifestations of the workings of potentially pernicious superhuman energies. The use as a graphic refrain of a gleaming golden butterfly, held to represent the visible avatar of the otherwise bodiless Beatrice and mirroring her title as Golden Witch, economically enriches the show's magical mood.

These unsettling signals balefully escalate as two more residents, Eva and Hideyoshi, meet a dismal end, the character of Kanon is lethally wounded in the course of his investigation of the boiler room, and Kinzo's own body is discovered in a partly incinerated state. Following the receipt of an enigmatic missive from Beatrice (one of many items of epistolary evidence of the Golden Witch's existence in the series), the three characters singled out as plausibly responsible for its planting — Genji, Nanjo, and Kumasawa — are also found murdered. The person responsible for their accusation, Kinzo's daughter-in-law Haruhi, takes great pride in her position as the standing head of the now decimated Ushiromiya family but does not stand a chance to bask in her glory for too long: only moments after the previous victims have met their dismal end, Haruhi herself commits an inexplicable suicide while attempting to shoot one of Beatrice's glowing incarnations. As many of the guests are killed, the epiphanic appearance of swarms of golden butterflies counterpoints the gruesome events, operating as potent reminders of the ubiquitous incidence of Beatrice's preternatural agency. The central, yet subtly modulated, role played by powers operating in defiance of both reason and logic up to this point is blatantly brought to the fore as the survivors — or ostensible survivors, as the case may be — find themselves in an alternate space in the company of erstwhile victims restored to a perfectly healthy state and facetious mood. Everyone believes that the villain of the piece is a witch except Battler, who adamantly avers that all of the events they have experienced could have been engineered by human agents. At this point, Beatrice herself defies Battler to demonstrate conclusively that the crimes were not triggered by magic. These examples, drawn from the anime's first arc, bear witness to the series' consistent amalgamation of tropes typical of detective fiction in various familiar expressions of the form, commonly found in both Japan and the West, with motifs emanating from traditions in which the priorities of cold-headed analysis and deduction hold no unproblematic sway.

In the show's second arc, the multi-murder format is again proposed as the Ushiromiya clan is once more seen to congregate for their annual conference and many of the situations dramatized in the previous arc repropose themselves with more or less significant variations, while a chain of grim killings methodically traverses the screen amid assorted family debates, squabbles and disputes of alternately rational or capricious import. The anime thus continues, at one level, to pay homage to established generic models. Yet, the supernatural component is enthroned, at another level, as an even more dominant actor in this segment as Beatrice manifests herself in human form from an early stage in the action. The supernatural's ascendancy is even more trenchantly proclaimed with the relocation of Beatrice and Battler to a parallel dimension, where their magic-versus logic game is staged. In the anime, this is simply, yet effectively, rendered by arresting the dynamic flow of certain key scenes displaying the Rokkenjima characters, as they actually live through their hideous ordeals and reason out their meaning, locked in frozen black-and-white screen shots, with Battler and Beatrice in full color and with regular powers of motion acting around them or in their midst. In this alternate dimension, the anime also plays with its own version of the red and blue truths described earlier through captions spiraling, curling, uncoiling or scrolling horizontally, vertically and diagonally through the screen.

Umineko no Naku Koro ni's appetite for irrational and inscrutable forces is further consolidated in the following arc, where additional magic presences — veritably formidable on both the dynamic and the graphic planes — come into play, including the Seven Sisters of Purgatory, Lucifer, Leviathan and Belphegor. Supernatural battles, seemingly miraculous occurrences and bizarre resurrections garnish this gourmet platter with no dearth of zesty ingredients. With the fourth segment, Kon's series provides additional evidence of its genre-straddling proclivities while engaging its audience more intimately with a poignant transgenerational drama. This far exceeds, in both its dramatic pathos and its stylistic sophistication, the formulaic strictures of the bickering family plot whence so many classic detective stories derive their narrative premises. The familiar formulae of mystery, detective and crime fiction continue playing a part in this segment: most prominent among them is the "closed room" motif seen to hold privileged dramatic weight throughout the show. At one point, the anime also invokes the topos of the spatial doppelganger, inserting into its heady mix the suggestion that Rokkenjima accommodates the spectral reality of a second harbor and a second mansion, known only to a few residents, alongside those commonly recognized. The mansion, named "Kuwadorian," is said to have been occupied by the Golden Witch among "miscellaneous gods" until her presumed departure in the year 1968. Thus, *Umineko no Naku Koro ni* remains loyally devoted to its parent genres right through to the end with the deployment of established tropes. However, the codes and conventions of classic murder-laced storytelling recede to the periphery toward the end of the show to allow the magical strand to gain unprecedented metaphysical poignancy. The game in which Battler and Beatrice have been locked from a relatively early stage in the diegesis accordingly acquires fresh resonance as an emotional tug of war in which the key actors are ultimately enjoined to defend not merely some dogmatic matter of principle but both their own and each other's spiritual and ethical integrity and commitment to the truth — whatever this may be, regardless of how unsavory it may prove and, of course, assuming it truly exists.

The written word is accorded a special position over the anime's four arcs, as attested to by the pivotal epitaph accompanying Beatrice's portrait and other cryptic messages sprinkled throughout the adventure — e.g., the aforementioned storehouse emblem, as well as various bloody patterns traced on the mansion's internal doors, diagrams in books and inscriptions on charms inspired by Biblical lore and the Zodiac, and numerous letters ostensibly penned by Beatrice herself and evincing a knack of appearing out of the blue in the characters' midst without any trace of their deliverer or delivery method. As Patricia Merivale and Susan Elizabeth Sweeney point out, "In many metaphysical detective stories, letters, words, and documents no longer reliably denote the objects that they are meant to represent; instead, these texts become impenetrable objects in their own right. Such a world, made up of such nameless, interchangeable 'things,' cries out for the ordered interpretation that it simultaneously declares to be impossible" (Merivale and Sweeney, pp. 9–10). It could indeed be argued that in *Umineko no Naku Koro ni*, the hermetic text stands out as a character of autonomous standing endowed with palpable presence and resolutely unwilling to bow to the conventional assumption that a text should function as a visible bridge to an objective meaning. In so doing, it makes both characters and viewers long all the more ardently for conclusive answers even as it tenaciously reminds them that such a reward is incompatible with the series' entire world and raison d'être. This situation recalls the semiotic drama staged by Edgar Allan Poe in "the Purloined Letter," where the titular missive carries momentous significance for all of the pivotal personae without its contents ever being disclosed — or unproblematically shown even to exist for that matter. In severing meaning from content, both the anime's elusive texts and Poe's letter urge us to ponder the nature of the linguistic sign as an arbitrary pseudo-reality at liberty to mean much without actually saying anything (or, conversely, seeming to utter much without holding any genuine meaning). It is here also noteworthy that Kon's anime also shares with Poe's fiction the proposition that puzzles are best solved by identifying with the criminal party's mentality and thus extrapolating his or her modus operandi. The investigative strategy promoted by Poe, and mirrored by his own structural preferences, is therefore based on the doubling of one's antagonists' thought processes to turn their methods against them and thus catch them in their own nets. Battler adopts an analogous approach, which he has learnt from his mother, with the art of "flipping the chessboard" as a means of placing himself in the "opponent's shoes" to unravel enigmas of all kinds — from the most prosaic to the most momentous.

Most of the illustrative examples supplied in the preceding paragraphs have been intentionally drawn from the series' inceptive segment so as to provide a cogent impression of the plot's murder enigma skeleton. In addition, all references to specific events have been deliberately kept to the bare bones due to *Umineko no Naku Koro ni*'s distinctive thematics and formal handling of its puzzle-posing and puzzle-solving components. In anticipating the eponymous hero's successful accomplishment of his intricate revenge scheme in *Gankutsuou: The Count of Monte Cristo*, presaging Gerda and Kay's eventual reunion in *The Snow Queen*, making explicit reference to the lovers' heroic sacrifice in *Romeo x Juliet* or dwelling on salient details of the protagonist's vicissitudes in *The Tale of Genji*, one does not risk dispensing undesirable spoilers. Indeed, the series in which those occurrences are located do not appear to treasure secrecy as one of their major assets and are, in fact, often quite profligate in the provision of anticipatory and revelatory clues. Matters are radically different when it comes to Kon's anime, a densely layered accretion of hermetic strata imbued with frequent concessions to the whodunit mode. Although the series here examined, as noted, encompasses only the first four arcs of the parent game series and its mysteries hence remain somewhat unveiled at the end, much is disclosed along the way and the prodigal inclusion of detailed illustrations in this text would inevitably impair the prospective viewer's chances of pristine enjoyment. In this instance, the discussion therefore requires judicious avoidance of specific plot developments, in favor of a relatively content-free analysis of the conceptual features — and related theoretical implications — of Kon's adaptive enterprise.

Returning to the anime's generic alliances, it would not be preposterous to suggest that *Umineko no Naku Koro ni* encapsulates the very essence of the Gothic as "a cultural discourse that utilizes images of disorder, obsession, psychological disarray and physical distortion for the purposes of both entertainment and ideological speculation," typically evincing an almost obsessive fascination with "tropes of mental, bodily and ethical disintegration" (Cavallaro, p. vii). The anime's connection with the Gothic tradition is explicitly announced by Kon's deployment of its most distinctive themes, and especially the passion for spooky mansions and villainous families cursed by rapaciousness and a manic thirst for revenge. Any agency capable of resolving the conflicts to which those depraved instincts ineluctably give rise is perceived as a source not of benevolent justice but of awe-inspiring terror of sublime proportions — a dread so deep and amorphous as to often drag its victims into the abyss of delusional self-persecution, self-destructiveness and, ultimately, even downright lunacy. The affective disturbances and ghastly psychosomatic repercussions which these predicaments spawn at several key junctures in Kon's series point precisely to its embroilment in a Gothic world of ontological uncertainty wherein discovery may only be attained by inscrutable forces or the random peregrinations of blind chance. Therefore, while several possible answers to the story's enigmas are provided, none of them carries the conclusiveness, let alone the judicial authority, of the type of resolution crowning a narrative guided by a luminous trust in the secular power of rationality.

Umineko no Naku Koro ni's simultaneous entanglement with disparate discourses connotes to an experimentative drive that refrains Kon from deriving self-congratulatory satisfaction from the cheap pleasure of straightforward conclusions. The frisson yielded by the playful blend of diverse ingredients far exceeds in value the reward of neat answers. In this respect, the series would seem to validate Julian Symons' proposition regarding the essence of detective fiction: "The detective story pure and complex, the book that has no interest whatever except the solution of a puzzle, does not exist, and if it did exist would be unreadable. The truth is that the detective story, along with the police story, the spy story and the thriller ... makes up part of the hybrid creature we call sensational literature" (Symons, p. 15). In other words, it partakes of a form eager to put to maximum advantage the dramatic strengths not only of supernatural phenomena but also of grisly crimes, socially transgressive behavior and perverse passions with a general preference for flamboyantly melodramatic gestures — a propensity which *Umineko no Naku Koro ni* incrementally emplaces as one of its governing aesthetic dictates.

While the generic factors delineated above undoubtedly play an important part in the shaping of the anime's autonomous identity as an adaptive, yet imaginative, work, more vital still is its guiding dramatic principle. This could be boldly defined as the quintessential quest spirit — an atavistic storytelling device embedded in human history for time immemorial which mystery, detective and crime fiction evidently share with several both related and quite independent genres and media. What is most distinctive about the show's handling of the quest spirit is a tripartite organization whereby that motif acquires both momentum and complexity as the action progresses. Thus, we are initially presented with a quest situation revolving around singular individuals and their personal perceptions and thoughts in what could be described as an inherently monological structure. With the transition to the episodes in which Battler and Beatrice strive to prove to each other the superiority of either the pragmatic or the magical perspective, we enter a dramatic situation redolent of Anatol Rapoport's concept of the "two-person" game and hence an eminently dialogical structure. As the action sequences grow increasingly acrimonious and brutal, and larger casts of human — or seemingly human — opponents come into play, while overtly otherworldly agents join their ranks, the quest spirit becomes framed into something of a tournament format ushering in a polylogical structure. With the final shift of focus back to Battler and Beatrice's contest, the earlier modalities are revisited and adapted, as the drama regains a dialogical emphasis, yet also draws attention to the monological dimension by underscoring the intractable inevitability of human isolation and loneliness.

Battler and Beatrice's teleportation to an alternate reality does not simply constitute a tantalizing dramatic strategy per se: in fact, it also abets the anime's genre-crossing tendencies by juxtaposing and gradually integrating the realms of mystery and detective narrative as defined by Carl D. Malmgren. "Mystery fiction," the critic maintains, "presupposes a centered world; detective fiction, a decentered world. By 'centered' we mean a world which has a center, an anchor, a ground; ... In mystery fiction, there is usually one significant scene of the crime (estate, village, railway car); the investigator examines this scene, trying to link its signs (clues) to their root causes. In detective fiction, the investigator invariably traverses a decentered world comprising a variety of physical spaces; he interviews clients, tails suspects, stakes out residences, and so on" (Malmgren, p. 13). Malmgren is clearly using the concept of mystery fiction as the equivalent of what Ascari designates as detective fiction to describe a safe and knowable world, using the idea of detective fiction itself to designate a contrastive destabilizing discourse. This terminological divergence bears witness, in nuce, to the general lack of agreement among theorists and commentators regarding the exact constitution of the various categories gravitating, like flustered satellites, around the composite planet of mystery, detective and crime fiction. In one available — and quite popular — perspective, it is possible to view crime fiction as the broad genre of which detective fiction, the whodunit, the thriller, hardboiled fiction and courtroom drama (among others) represent the subgeneric offspring. Mystery fiction, in this purview, is commonly held to represent the branch of detective fiction in which an investigator deals with a crime and, ideally, solves it. This type of story is supposed to emphasize the puzzle component with partial or total disregard for contingent social and historical circumstances, in contrast with the hardboiled typology, where a preference for action and dispassionate realism is held to dominate the scene. It is, however, also plausible to approach mystery, detective and crime fiction as relatively autonomous genres, marginally overlapping but nonetheless retaining certain distinctive markers of their own as cultural products sui generis. A hybrid construct like *Umineko no Naku Koro ni* makes such a prospect seem not merely appropriate but almost inevitable since it is hard to see how one could even begin to do justice to the drama's multiforking constellation without devoting equal and unbiased attention to all of its plural generic sources.

With the introduction of a parallel world into the story, *Umineko no Naku Koro ni* disrupts the potential centeredness of the mystery plot woven around the mansion on Rokkenjima by subjecting it to the dramatic demands of the detective plot spun by Beatrice and Battler in their transmundane setting, and thus exploding an initially unitary locale into a virtually boundless spatial sprawl. The sense of order, stability and immutability associated with the mystery setting — and the intersubjective relationships unfolding within it — is characteristically reinforced by a foundational trust in the possibility of "a rational world grounded in laws of cause and effect, where people behave in certain ways in order to achieve certain ends" and where the detective is in a position to assume a clear sense of "planning and intentionality" (p. 14). George Grella corroborates this proposition by arguing that the mystery narrative is sustained by a belief in a "benevolent and knowable universe" (Grella, p. 101). *Umineko no Naku Koro ni* subverts the mystery yarn's atmosphere of permanence and balance by intertwining it with a detective yarn that is, by contrast, unstable, disorderly, aleatory and at all times prey to the vagaries of contingency and fortuity — a world in which the methodical orchestration of Battler and Beatrice's philosophical debate is powerless to either preempt or control the onslaughts of violence and chaos.

According to Tzvetan Todorov, the mystery narrative typically evinces a double-narrative structure based on the coexistence of two parallel strands: "the story of the crime," which narrates "'what really happened,'" and the "the story of the investigation," which elucidates "'how the reader (or the narrator) has come to know about it.'" In Russian Formalist parlance, the first strand corresponds to "the *fable* (story)" as a record of what happens "in life" and the second to "the *subject* (plot)" as "the way the author presents it to us" (Todorov, p. 45). As the story of the investigation seeks to piece together incrementally over a more or less protracted period of time disparate facets of the story of the crime, an important corollary of Todorov's argument is the idea that the mystery story is oriented toward the past as a defining aspect of its generic identity, not just a convenient temporal and spatial setting for its investigative drama. This is indubitably an aspect of the mystery modality to which Kon's show adheres with overall fidelity. Yet, *Umineko no Naku Koro ni*'s preoccupation with the past is drastically unorthodox in comparison with standard generic expectations associated with the mystery story insofar as it is not transparently conducive to the reestablishment of a temporarily disturbed atmosphere of order and harmony. In fact, as each successive layer of each character's convoluted past is explained, its penetration does not give access to a solid substratum of truth beyond which no further delving is feasible but a proliferation of additional tiers of unforeseeable toughness and thickness. Much as the actors might endeavor to emulate Todorov's formalist model, a seemingly unpluggable gap goes on separating the drama of what actually came to pass and the drama of how they have become (dimly and haphazardly) acquainted with it. Neither the underlying facts nor the characters' knowledge thereof has a chance of remaining uniform and dependable without further discovery threatening to dislodge the entire edifice of both their certainties and their speculations.

Despite *Umineko no Naku Koro ni*'s tendency to undermine some of the ideological mainstays of mystery fiction, it is vital also to appreciate the existence of potent parallels between Kon's series and that tradition. Especially prominent, in this regard, is the idea that the universe is governed by inherently unfathomable laws which may or may not emanate from a conscious agency and which, even if it could somehow be demonstrated that they were, would not automatically prove anything other than inimical to the advancement of human happiness. In many mystery narratives, this notion is mollified by an ingenuous trust in the existence of a providential "Superorder" (Malmgren, p. 35) capable of guaranteeing the endurance of justice and truth in the face of the direst criminal violations of the status quo. *Umineko no Naku Koro ni* does not offer any such obviously comforting route for the putatively providential forces which appear to play a part in its tortuous trajectory do not promise absolution except in exchange for hideous "sacrifices." In engineering the sustained interplay of the mystery element and the decentered thrust of detective fiction, *Umineko no Naku Koro ni* offers an imaginative reconfiguration of the murder mystery yarn that tersely transcends the boundaries of adaptation as no more than a derivative venture. Its multibranching structure and penchant for the recapitulation of analogous chains of events in variable dramatic constellations and from changing perspectives maximize to undeniable effect the principle of decenteredness.

In this respect, an ideal description of Kon's anime is offered, elliptically, by Dennis Porter's assessment of the "hardboiled detective novel" as a genre informed by "the metaphor of the spreading stain" since the "initial crime often turns out to be a relatively superficial symptom of an evil whose magnitude and ubiquity are only progressively disclosed during the course of the investigation" (Porter, p. 40). As Malmgren comments, "the contagion of crime eventually affects most of the characters, including the detective. Indeed, at times the detective is the catalyst who precipitates the violent chain of events" (Malmgren, p. 73). *Umineko no Naku Koro ni* dramatizes a comparable state of affairs not only by capitalizing on the sheer diffusion of criminal activity over its fabric but also by using the structural principle of multiperspectival reiteration to intimate that any one crime holds a self-reproductive power that enables it to repropose itself time and again with subtle variations. At the same time, it portrays Battler and Beatrice themselves, in their capacity as figurative detectives, as intimately implicated in the crimes they strive to investigate and ultimately responsible for initiating and accelerating — in an ostensibly aberrant logic reminiscent of the lessons of chaos theory — many of the action's increasingly mind-bending and brutal complications. By literally separating Battler and Beatrice from the crime scene through its idiosyncratic approach to dramatic topology, Kon also opens up metafictional opportunities for its anime: insofar as Battler and Beatrice's status as in-text detectives is explicitly foregrounded by their spatial removal, we are invited to reflect consciously on the show's constructed standing as a tantalizingly irreverent appropriation of its parent genres' dominant codes and conventions. In embracing in tandem the mystery story and the detective story's respectively centered and decentered realities, *Umineko no Naku Koro ni* enters the domain of the crime story as defined by Malmgren: i.e., an "oppositional discourse" capable of situating itself "in either the centered world of mystery fiction or the decentered world of detective fiction" and hence pitting itself "in opposition to either mystery or detective fiction" (p. 137). Bound neither by the imperative to force its clues to conform to a rationally planned agenda nor by an utterly subversive urge to erase all vestiges of meaning from its signs, *Umineko no Naku Koro ni* experiments with plural discursive identities, shifting from one to the other with the same iconoclastic glee with which many of its personae don disparate masks from arc to arc. In this matter, the anime is deeply loyal to the source form, the visual novel's principal attribute indubitably lying with its buoyant polymorphousness.

In the series, the concept of identity as a prismatic construct, on both the formal and the psychological planes, is deployed consistently as a means of eroding any prospect of reparative closure or plenitude, leaving viewers themselves to confront the precarious value of their interpretations of the drama's enigmas. The anime thus echoes William V. Spanos' delineation of the "anti-detective story" as a narrative that seeks to "evoke the impulse to 'detect' ... in order to violently frustrate it by refusing to solve the crime" (Spanos, p. 154). In this scenario, any faith in foundational principles designed to promote the solidity of human interaction and the reliability of the sign systems in which this is inscribed is radically questioned. A character's deviant behavior cannot be — either sympathetically or patronizingly — dismissed as a temporary aberration in an otherwise stable personality. In fact, it operates as a localized symptom of the inveterately fluid, unanchored, fragmentary and — above all — indecipherable — nature of the story's whole universe and informing zeitgeist. Furthermore, *Umineko no Naku Koro ni*'s cross-generic texture, allied to its proclivity to invite reflection on the processes through which stories are produced and consumed, draws the story into collusion with the domain of what Merivale and Sweeney have termed "metaphysical detective fiction" as a construct inclined to raise "profound questions" about "narrative, interpretation, subjectivity, the nature of reality, and the limits of knowledge" (Merivale and Sweeney, pp. 9–10). *Umineko no Naku Koro ni* adventurously embarks on precisely such an interrogative enterprise by throwing into relief the idea that the outcome of detection is not so much the solution of the crime or chain of crimes as a confrontation of the ineffable mystery of human selfhood and the limitations of human comprehension. Accordingly, if readers — or viewers — are also detectives, as suggested earlier in the discussion, it is also the case that they, too, must face up to the precariousness of their own identities and interpretations as integral components of the narrative weave. We are thereby enjoined to wonder what, if anything, we can actually presume to know, how we can unequivocally trust the reality of what we think we know, and how we can finally demonstrate that this amounts to anything more substantial and universal than a subjective — and therefore intrinsically imaginary — construction of the real.

The show's designation as metaphysical is most forcefully validated by Battler and Beatrice's experiences in an alternate reality plane, which afford them an apparently privileged stance as external observers and investigators. Yet, such a stance is inexorably undermined by the emphasis placed by the drama — discreetly, yet uncompromisingly — on the inevitable limitations of human perception and understanding. No matter how transcendental Battler and Beatrice's situation might be, it remains restricted and circumscribed: whatever grand theories they might dare to formulate in the face of chaos, their knowledge is delimited by the confines of their parallel dimension. In a sense, the two characters are akin to readers trapped in a huge library which may at first seem to provide them with any enthusiastic reader's ultimate Eden and to promise the prospect of boundless knowledge but can never fully appease their thirst for answers. That figurative library might be unthinkably vast and even approximate closely Jorge Luis Borges' or Umberto Eco's notion of a bookish cosmos stretching to infinity. Nevertheless, the readers lodged therein can only, everything considered, consult the volumes within their reach and make do with fragmentary, discordant and eventually unsatisfying information. Battler and Beatrice's experiences in their alternate realm metaphorically intimate that our bastions of order and knowledge are not, after all, necessarily or exclusively treasurehouses of truth.

As an anime adaptation spawned by an eminently pop cultural medium, *Umineko no Naku Koro ni* may be deemed to sit somewhat uneasily in the company of adaptations vaunting honorable descent from media of long established repute and academically respected worth. However, Kon's series demonstrates that virtually any medium (or indeed genre) holds immense dramatic potentialities which, if met and appropriated by an enterprising director, can reach actualization as thought-provoking and, most importantly, autonomous artifacts. Furthermore, as an adaptation of a visual novel as a particular subset of the videogaming megaverse, *Umineko no Naku Koro ni* is one of several anime released over the past decade utilizing as their source material a relatively recent development in the realm of popular entertainment, and specifically the videogaming industry. Several other anime have relied on a much older popular form: the comic book. Of course, countless anime are adaptations of manga, the Japanese equivalent of the comic book or the graphic novel (in a loose sense of the term), and it would be preposterous to assume that a comprehensive compendium could be provided in the present context — or indeed in anything other than an encyclopedic taxonomy. A more modest but still notable range of anime adaptations have drawn on comic books of the Western variety such as the ones immortalized by the Marvel Comics giant. An interesting development in the field, still under way as this study is being written, consists of the intended transposition to the anime screen by the illustrious studio Madhouse of Marvel Comics characters, appropriately reimagined so as to suit Japanese tastes and expectations through the infusion into the original yarns of some new elements and the excision of other motifs familiar to Western readers. Wolverine and Iron Man are the two main figures expected to reach the anime screen in the near future. Complementing this synergetic process, Marvel Comics are concurrently endeavoring to infiltrate the Japanese market through the creation of manga adaptations of comic books centered on the X-Men and Wolverine. This initiative finds a parallel in the Western market in the live-action *Batman* movies which, as Patrick Drazen comments, "were themselves based on new versions of the comic book, now gradually referred to as 'graphic novels,' some of which showed the influence of Japanese manga!" (Drazen, p. 13).

One of the most successful instances of adaptation to the anime screen of a comic-book series of Western parentage is *Witchblade* (TV series; dir. Yoshimitsu Ohashi, 2006), a show produced by Gonzo like *Gankutsuou: The Count of Monte Cristo*, here discussed in Chapter 3, and *Romeo x Juliet*, the case study covered in Chapter 5. *Witchblade* anticipates the later Madhouse projects cited above in editing its source material so as to satisfy specifically Japanese sensibilities. One of the most intriguing reorientations engineered by Gonzo consists of a subtle change in atmosphere, whereby the mood evoked by the original comic book is overlaid with genuine echoes of TV cop drama interleaved with supernatural imagery. The anime adaptation is faithful to the parent text in deploying as its sustaining structure the mythos of the Witchblade — a legendary weapon supposed to transcend time barriers and to endow its wielder, who must by definition be a woman, with supernatural faculties. Among the Witchblade's many eminent bearers rank the likes of Cleopatra and Joan of Arc but its current user is no more esteemed a figure than a simple NYC cop rather prosaically named Sara Pezzini. The anime does a superb job in exploring the heroine's troubled emotions and thus highlighting her intrinsic humanity despite the preternatural connotations of the status to which she inevitably ascends when the portentous weapon decides to latch itself onto her wrist. In this respect, the anime closely parallels *Umineko no Naku Koro ni*, where the more fantastical aspects of the adventure are never quite allowed to obfuscate the characters' affective intricacy, in keeping with the visual novel's well-documented devotion to the portrayal of intelligently nuanced personalities. Some of *Witchblade*'s most unforgettable moments consist of the relatively early sequences in which Sara discovers that the weapon is capable of both deflecting lethal bullets and effortlessly stabbing its foes but does not yet know how to communicate with it any more than tentatively. At a later stage, the protagonist will find out that the Witchblade also equips her with hypercognitive powers enabling her to perceive what has actually happened at a crime scene. Also remarkable, from a dramatic point of view, is Sara's interaction with the villain of the piece, the character of Kenneth Irons, a man driven by an insane desire to appropriate the Witchblade for himself as a result of an abortive attempt to wield the weapon in the remote past.

Chapter 7

A Tapestry of Courtly Life
The Tale of Genji

> *The Tale of Genji has become many different things to many different audiences through many different media over a thousand years, a position unmatched by any other Japanese text or artifact. It is also one of the few Japanese texts that, in the modern period, has had a global reach, coming to be recognized as part of world literature, earning acclaim as perhaps the world's first novel, and being placed alongside such modern masterpieces as Marcel Proust's À la recherche du temps perdu.*
> — Haruo Shirane 2008

The Tale of Genji, an eleventh-century narrative created by Lady Murasaki Shikibu and hailed as both one of the greatest classics of Japanese literature and one of the world's first novels, was first transposed from the page to the anime screen by director Gisaburou Sugii in 1987 in the form of a feature film. As noted in Chapter 2, Sugii also contributed in the capacity of art director to Eiichi Yamamoto's 1973 movie *Belladonna of Sadness*, and aspects of the style adopted by *The Tale of Genji* indeed echo the earlier anime. Sugii's preference for character and background designs of heightened minimalism and the emphasis on pure line are assiduously confirmed by *The Tale of Genji*. The 1987 film does not overtly resort to still images in the way *Belladonna of Sadness* does. Nevertheless, it strives to evoke an atmosphere of stillness by capitalizing on the unique powers of motionless — or motion-attenuated — drama by often emulating a stage play: a ruse abetted by the director's approach to lighting. The use of delicate, yet haunting, music and of traditional poetry and dance further intensifies the action's theater-oriented sensibility. As Kazuhiro Tateishi emphasizes, Sugii's anime focuses on the protagonist's "psychological struggle" to reconfigure the original narrative principally as "Genji's growth to independence," relying throughout on symbols as key constituents of his world and eschewing "explanatory speech" so as to appeal to the viewer "by direct visual and aural representation" (Tateishi, p. 315). One of the movie's most distinctive features is its highly deliberate pace: a frank dramatic correlative for the rhythm of court life in the Heian era (794–1185), where plots and feuds would often be proliferating at an alarming rate while remaining cloaked under a strictly codified semblance of order and almost ponderous quietude. (The period derives its designation from its capital Heian Kyou, and the word "Heian" itself is translatable as "peace and tranquillity.") Individual ambitions, in such a climate, would automatically become subsumed to the demands of a communal identity designed to communicate a sense of imperturbable stability. To sustain this ambience of depersonalized composure, the film keeps its characters stylized and somewhat devoid, at least on the surface, of personal urges, anxieties and yearnings. Lady Murasaki herself would have been enabled by numerous years of service with the royal dynasty to supply some candid insights into court life, its intrigues and its aesthetic tastes.

Adaptations of Lady Murasaki's text in various forms are so profuse as to defy comprehensive enumeration in the present context. Suffice it to mention that since the twelfth century, they have included literary works inspired by both its prose writing and its poetry, paintings meant either to symbolize court power or to adjust the story's message to the requirements of mass culture depending on the period, plays, commentaries, allegories, parodies, handbooks, textbooks, calligraphic works, games, book illustrations, and design patterns. In addition, as Haruki Ii points out, *The Tale of Genji* was held in high esteem as "a guide to moral ideals for rulers, a book of Confucian and Buddhist teachings, and a text for women's education" (Ii, p. 157). In subsequent phases of Japanese history, Lady Murasaki's saga was also harnessed to ideological agendas. Therefore, with the transfer of "political power ... from the aristocracy to the military class" in the Kamakura Period (1183–1333) and Muromachi Period (1392–1573), it inspired the development of the "new moral system" meant to serve as "the basis for warrior society," while the waning nobility could turn to *The Tale of Genji*'s representation of "the splendor of court culture ... for spiritual support" (p. 159). Thus, while the story's evocation of a society that no longer existed except in memory and imagination could easily have been overshadowed by the ascendancy of the samurai, it actually came to gain both their interest and their nostalgic respect. The cultural route traced by the ancient story's reception and transmutation over time persuasively proves that the text's worth does not consist of an immutable core but rather depends on the variable adaptive opportunities to which it has been liable at any one point in history.

Of special relevance to the present context are the two manga versions authored by Waki Yamato—*Asake yume mishi* (i.e., *Fleeting Dreams*, 1980–

1993)—and by Maki Miyako—*Genji monogatari* (1989). Yamato's manga is most remarkable at the aesthetic level, yielding graceful graphics that perfectly capture the courtly elegance of Genji's world and thus yield a modern adaptation of Heian scroll painting. Where Yamato focuses on the source text's ambience, Miyako is principally concerned with conveying *The Tale of Genji*'s erotic import, as evinced by her detailed, though not overtly pornographic, execution of sexual acts. Also worthy of attention are the two live-action movies bearing the original title helmed by Kouzaburou Yoshimura (1951) and by Kon Ichikawa (1966). As Tateishi explains, the 1951 movie "was epoch making in being the first publicly released film that deals with an imperial scandal and in which the emperor is portrayed by an actor, although he is visible only through bamboo blinds or from the back." While the screenplay was careful to avoid irreverence in the depiction of the imperial system and therefore represented the liaison between Genji and Fujitsubo as an "'open secret'" rather than a "clandestine affair," the film was banned as disrespectful toward the court during World War Two (Tateishi, p. 305). This example indicates that an adaptation does not only open the source text on which it draws to interpretation—and hence the possibility of metamorphosis over time—but is itself liable to changing perceptions dictated by ideological shifts in the contexts of its reception. The 1966 movie, for its part, is structurally more adventurous than its predecessor in that it is orchestrated primarily as an extended flashback through which Genji reflects upon various past relationships from an advanced stage in the original story. Although its critical reception was by no means uniformly complimentary, the film did meet with enthusiastic accolades of its artistic worth and technical daring. A very loose adaptation of Lady Murasaki's text, taking considerable liberties in the evocation of Heian culture, is offered by the live-action movie *Sennen no Koi—Hikaru Genji monogatari* (*A Thousand Years of Love—The Tale of Shining Genji*), directed by Tonkou Horikawa and scripted by Akira Hayasaka (2001). Although the film is rather formulaic in its adherence to gender-defined character stereotypes, it comes across as structurally inventive due its construction, as Tateishi comments, as "a story within a story, in which Murasaki Shikibu narrates her newly written tale to the young Empress Shoushi" (p. 316).

In a historical perspective, *The Tale of Genji*'s openness to adaptation is inscribed in the dynamics of cultural production and consumption typical of the epoch in which it came into being. Indeed, as Yukio Lippit argues, "the essentially modern notion of the work of art as a fixed entity" is irrelevant to Lady Murasaki's saga insofar as it "does not adequately capture the open-endedness and plural existence of the Heian literary object" resulting from the circulation of courtly narratives "in multiple copies" that would invariably be "subject to the type of creative scribal variation" attendant on "practices of manual reproduction" (Lippit, p. 51). Simultaneously, it is vital to remember that the act of reading itself was not considered private in the sense it is nowadays but actually constituted an eminently communal practice entailing not merely literary or technical expertise but also cultivated capacities in the fields of calligraphy, aural performance and the visual arts. Texts, therefore, existed as collective objects at the levels of both creation and reception. These factors, allied to the plethora of reincarnations spawned by *The Tale of Genji* over the centuries, makes the saga the very epitome of the adaptive spirit as described by Michael Emmerich: "Canonical works of literature do not remain canonical because they are continually being reproduced — although, no doubt, most of them are — but because they are continually being replaced" (Emmerich, p. 211). H. Richard Okada promulgates a cognate textual philosophy in arguing that "the impressive and ongoing flow of modern-day *Genji* scholarship attests to the fact that a final word on the text will never be written." By implication, it is unlikely that a conclusive adaptation of Lady Murasaki's saga — whatever medium or genre one may choose to invoke — will ever reach fruition and seize the work's essence so irreversibly as to foreclose the possibility of further adaptation. For a narrative like *The Tale of Genji*, Okada avers, "'final words are destined always to be inscribed on one of those 'magic slates' whose traces serve to remind us only that we can and must perform the act of writing yet again" (Okada, p. 292). The galaxy of adaptational moves to which *The Tale of Genji* has proved amenable likewise intimates that the existence of any one adaptation is ultimately a prompt to go on adapting.

It must also be noted that *The Tale of Genji* has had a far-reaching influence not only on Japanese art — and especially in the fields of poetry, theater, scroll painting, music and dance — but also on worldwide cultural production, profoundly affecting the codes and conventions of court fiction and the psychological novel over the centuries. Numerous readers have observed intriguing affinities, as intimated by the opening quotation, between Lady Murasaki's text and Marcel Proust's *Remembrance of Things Past*. According to Donald Keene, the text "occupies in Japanese literature the place of Shakespeare in English literature, of Dante in Italian literature, or of Cervantes in Spanish literature. It is also a monument to world literature, the first novel of magnitude composed anywhere" (Keene, p. 39). One of the first and most resonant paeans to Lady Murasaki's art within Western culture is undoubtedly Virginia Woolf's 1925 review of the opening volume of Arthur Waley's translation, where the author's unique flair for psychological insights of timeless cogency is brought to the fore: "To light up the many facets of [Genji's] mind, Lady Murasaki, being herself a woman, naturally chose the medium of other women's minds. Aoi, Asagao, Fujitsubo, Murasaki, Yuugao, Suetsumuhana ... one after another they turn their clear or freakish light upon the gay young man at the centre" (Woolf, p. 427).

The ensuing part of this chapter offers a detailed examination of Osamu Dezaki's version of *The Tale of Genji* (TV series; 2009) in relation to its source. It is important, on this point, to note that the full version of the original text composed by Lady Murasaki consists of a work of considerable length comprising fifty-four chapters (or books). The portion of the story adapted by Dezaki covers the period spanning the protagonist's birth to his exile (chapters 1–12). However, before embarking on a close study of the series, it is worth briefly considering another recent adaptation of the ancient narrative which, though orchestrated in a different medium, evinces some interesting affinities with Dezaki's anime: Yoshitaka Amano's artbook adaptation (2006) also bearing the title of Lady Murasaki's venerable text. Dezaki's anime and Amano's paintings are most pointedly linked by their rendition of the ancient narrative's specifically mythological flavor, which they capture in a graphically trenchant fashion even when they strike their most graceful and canorous chords. In a sense, both works posit the art of adaptation and the very spirit of myth as virtually inseparable to the extent that "the fundamental character of the mythical construct," as Roland Barthes stresses, "is to be appropriated" (Barthes 1993, p. 119). The appropriative process operates through the transgenerational and crosscultural communication of mythical "material which has *already* been worked on so as to make it suitable" for such a purpose (p. 110) but is repeatedly altered and recontextualized in accordance with distinctive historical, geographical and cultural milieux. In the process, myths "ripen" (p. 149) and thus fuel an ongoing amplification of the original discourses whence they emanate. In addressing contemporary relocations of Lady Murasaki's tale, for instance, we must ponder the implications of their adaptive moves no less than a millennium after the original text's production. Especially tantalizing, in this respect, is the use made by Dezaki's anime and Amano's artwork alike of the story's mythical essence in their own times to comment on current approaches to the ethics and politics of sexual pleasure.

Admired around the world for his luscious watercolor paintings and lyrical evocation of myriad facets of both Eastern and Western mythology and lore, Amano encounters fertile soil in Lady Murasaki's ancient text as the terrain on which to cultivate an intensely personal retelling of the classic saga of romance, longing and intrigue and thus infuse it with fresh life for the delight of contemporary audiences. As Matthew Alexander poetically observes, the volume allows "Amano's stunning art style" to stream "across the pages like a meandering brook late in the summer months before the first rains" (Alexander). Amano organizes his pictorial adaptation around a sample of Genji's lovers: Dezaki, as will be shown in detail later in this discussion, adopts an analogously selective approach. The artist subtly varies his colors in order to highlight the singularity of each persona and convey symbolically her emotional state, giving prominence to primary-based palettes to express energetic passion and pastel-based palettes to underscore moments of contemplation or languorous yearning. In prioritizing the original story's women, Amano pays homage not only to its female parentage and to the substantial percentage of female characters in Lady Murasaki's cast but also to the feminine ethos pervading various aspects of Heian culture.

Both Amano and Dezaki consistently evoke the relational nature of the characters' identities through the trope of intertwining or even overlapping bodies. While the image is logically consonant with the narrative's emphasis on eros, it also serves as a succinct cultural comment on Lady Murasaki's society: a world that allowed little, if any, real privacy. Even when other people's inquisitive gaze does not literally inspect Genji and his lovers so as to spawn rumors and feed courtly gossip, one gets the impression that the eye of etiquette follows them everywhere and at all times as an overarching system of surveillance. The collapse of individual boundaries suggested by both the artbook and the anime through the aforementioned strategy is additionally conveyed by their creators through a methodical blurring of framing and demarcating lines. Plumes of mist, dusky locales, vistas traversed by ceaselessly dancing blossom and snowflakes, alongside ubiquitous fans, veils and screens, bear witness to a deliberate avoidance of stark definition in favor of ambiguous or equivocal moods. At the same time, the original narrative's mythical dimension suits ideally the two artists' aesthetic preference for magical realism insofar as myth, in situating relatively ordinary actions in an extraordinary context, fosters the collusion of the natural and the supernatural, the down-to-earth and the esoteric, the phenomenal and the transcendental. Furthermore, stylistic similarities between Dezaki's series and Amano's paintings consistently invite reflection on their distinctive celebration of the visual image's storytelling powers. The momentous significance of visuality in *The Tale of Genji* per se is emphasized by Joan Stanley-Baker in her discussion of Japanese art of the Heian age.

Commenting on the earliest pictorial adaptation of Lady Murasaki's tale, the *Genji* scrolls (1120–1150), Stanley-Baker maintains that this "must have covered at least twenty separate scrolls with hundreds of illustrations and thousands of sheets of calligraphy.... The paintings were done by court ladies.... The influence of court women over the entire Heian cultural sphere has given the world the first full-blown fulfilment of feminine aesthetics since the spiritual and lyrical culture of Bronze Age Crete" (Stanley-Baker, p. 80). The style used for the scrolls of *The Tale of Genji* is known as "*onna-e*," i.e., "feminine painting" (p. 84). A pensive mood characterizes Lady Murasaki's narrative throughout its unfolding (and with a definite shift toward darkness in the second half of the saga) and this finds a close parallel in the text's ancient illustrations, where a sense of "nostalgia and melancholy for the passing of the old Heian order of poetry and peace" is ubiquitous (p. 81). Both Dezaki and Amano honor stylistic preferences harbored by the Heian artists themselves. These include the use of stylized facial attributes evocative of symbolic masks akin to the ones employed in Noh drama and the tendency to focus on the suspenseful build-up to action rather than on the action as such. Moreover, Dezaki and Amano alike appear to have inherited the Heian penchant for scenes that initially come across as placid but soon disclose undercurrents of tension or even turmoil. Items such as draperies and ribbons, veils and braided ropes, silk streamers and smoke wisps are often deployed to splendid effect as understated means of conveying a sense of dynamic ferment in even the most tranquil composition. Rumpled sheets or curtains in a state of relative disarray are also utilized as symbolic markers of emotive unrest, often reinforced by the adoption of tilted planes and daring perspectives. To communicate a feeling of affective isolation intended to magnify a scene's internal turbulence, architectural partitions such as sliding screens and room dividers are concurrently brought into play as major spatial forces. Bridges likewise serve symbolic purposes, alluding to prospects of connectivity and harmony but also exposing the characters' psychological suspension in a reality they can never take safely for granted — a reality, as *The Tale of Genji* keeps reminding us, no more durable than melting snow.

At the same time, both Dezaki and Amano reveal an acute awareness of the codes and conventions governing body language in the period in which *The Tale of Genji* is set, particularly in the treatment of almost sculpturally formalistic gestures, positions and expressions. They thus corroborate Stanley-Baker's contention that "Language, conduct and posture were so rigidly regulated in the eleventh and twelfth centuries that courtiers developed uncanny sensitivity to the slightest nuance of behaviour and situation allowing court paintings to depict scenes of great psychological intensity in compositions of apparent physical inertia" (p. 82). Accordingly, even though the explicit representation of emotional or psychological tension was proscribed by courtly etiquette, inner disquiet could nonetheless be summoned by symbolic means. Especially useful, in this matter, was the pictorial technique known as "*hikime kagihana* (line-eye hook-nose) which indicates features but does not identify individuals" (p. 81) and thus makes it possible to suggest highly polished "emotional nuances" through simple elements. For example, "eyebrows and eyes" may be "built up from many fine, straight lines into thick layers, with the eyebrows high on the foreheads," and the "pupils" rendered as "single dots, exactly placed along the eyeline" (p. 83). Calligraphy was concomitantly enthroned by Heian culture as a pictorial art in its own right. Dezaki's anime throws this idea into relief by exploiting the very nature of Japanese writing as a multilayered body of signs of pictographic derivation. In so doing, it foregrounds the concreteness of language even when it denotes abstract concepts, and thus underscores the material roots of narrative and drama alike in all their manifestations, as well as of other media likewise reliant on language in the broad sense of the term. *The Tale of Genji* therefore partakes of a specific semiotic sensibility eager to emphasize the performative nature of textuality — i.e., the power of words to operate as gestures and actions — by allowing writing to function as a kinetic instrument unrestrained by the limitations of the static physical page. Especially memorable, in this regard, are the shots used specifically by Dezaki to highlight various characters' calligraphic skills, where the *kanji* materialize on the screen stroke by stroke without the visible input of anybody's hand in so vibrant a mode as to appear not only tangible but even endowed with autonomous life. The written word, in this scenario, is elevated to the rank of an art form in its own right, intimately connected with the traditional Eastern practice of "wash painting" known in Japanese as *sumi-e* (墨絵).

In evaluating the significance of the pictorial dimension in *The Tale of Genji*, it is also important to observe that "pictures in the Heian era," as Joshua S. Mostow points out, appear to be invested with a "power" akin "to what is expressed in English by the verbal form 'to picture'— an active power to present and transform the real world" (Mostow, p. 1). This would entail that "the viewers of such pictures understood them to represent a magical world where time stood still" and could therefore experience them as "an escape from both mundane cares and the ravages of time" (p. 2). Painters, in this perspective, deserve praise for their knack of transcending ordinary reality through the vision of alternative scenarios. Pictures, moreover, can serve educational and documentary purposes and operate as tokens of eternity but also, in keeping with the period's melancholy sensibility, as somber mementoes of the inevitability of decline. On the subject of pictures, it is also noteworthy that the art of painting plays a prominent part in the anime's opening theme, Puffy AmiYumi's "Hiyori Hime," at the levels of both visuals and lyrics. More importantly, Genji's childhood bond to Fujitsubo, as the woman destined to occupy a unique position in his entire life, is symbolically sealed over their shared admiration for the art of scroll painting as Fujitsubo befriends the boy by showing him pictures inspired by indigenous landscape and lore, which she has brought from her parental home, just after her introduction to Genji by the Emperor.

The television version of *The Tale of Genji* helmed by Dezaki focuses even more pointedly than its feature-length predecessor on the quasi-mythological bildungsroman undertaken by its hero. In so doing, it studiously underscores the parent text's cultivation of a unique sensitivity to the ephemerality of beauty and pleasure, famously encapsulated by the aesthetic concept of *mono no aware* (物の哀れ). The first renowned critic of *The Tale of Genji*, Motoori Norinaga (1730–1801), views the narrative precisely as a poetic incarnation of *mono no aware*, emphasizing that this notion permeates Lady Murasaki's presentation of "what people feel" in response to disparate situations. These encompass "things both public and private, the best of things interesting, splendid, or awesome; there are also such things as flowers, birds, the moon, and the snow, appealingly described according to the season.... When the heart is heavy, then especially do the sight of the sky, the colors of the trees and grass, act to produce *aware*" (Norinaga, p. 203). Since "Nothing is felt more deeply by the human heart than love," in the logic of the tale, it is only natural that *aware* should be "experienced particularly profoundly, indeed unendurably, most often in love" (p. 213). Dezaki's anime, as we shall see, diligently evokes this world view, taking full advantage of the distinctive capacities held by the animated image as a means of expressing emotions directly associated with visual stimuli of the kind enumerated by Norinaga. In the process, it also maximizes the dialogue's lyrical propensities to paint the mystery of love without seeking to dissipate it through rational explication. Simultaneously, the anime seeks to replicate as closely as its medium allows the original work's impartial anatomy of Heian Japan: its decadent nobility, its intricate conspiracies and vendettas and, no less crucially, its unique take on concepts of style, elegance and etiquette.

The cultural connotations of the story outlined above will be examined in detail later in this chapter among other relevant concepts and motifs. An evaluation of the broad thematics articulated by Lady Murasaki and appropriated by Dezaki is first apposite. Dezaki's anime weaves a sumptuously embroidered tapestry of intertwined emotional adventures, chronicling the life and loves of Genji Hikaru (the "Shining Prince") and yielding equal doses of romance, psychological acuity, dynamic vibrance and pensive lyricism. In this respect, the show echoes faithfully its source text's own tenor and stylistic devotion to the ethos of indigenous *waka* poetry, where — as noted in a recent review of the series — thematic priority is consistently accorded to "the tyranny of time and the inescapable sorrow of romantic love" presented "within the context of man's relationship to nature" ("*Genji Monogatari Sennenki*"). The importance of poetry in *The Tale of Genji* will be also attended to in depth at a later stage in this discussion.

While Lady Murasaki brings into play over four-hundred characters across four generations, articulating her densely woven narrative through the collusion of their distinct personalities, Dezaki is required by his medium to concentrate much more closely on the immediate protagonist. In so doing, he is loyal to the original in depicting the titular hero as an Emperor's second son who, having been conceived by a concubine, has his status lowered to that of a commoner (albeit a clearly privileged one) in accordance with autochthonous customs of the epoch, and is employed as a courtly retainer. Even though Dezaki's series is eminently watchable and enjoyable even if one has not read its source text, some of the key events which Lady Murasaki posits as foundational narrative premises and structural mainstays deserve consideration for the sake of contextual cogency. Key to the ancient novel's opening part is the disclosure that despite her relatively humble status, the Emperor admires and respects Genji's mother, Kiritsubo, not solely as a sexual partner but also and no less importantly as a friend and advisor. This special position makes the lady prey to all sorts of pernicious rumors and acts: given the practice of polygamy at the Heian court, there was certainly no dearth of women so keen on advancing their personal causes as to strive quite unscrupulously to sully the name of any courtier to whom the Emperor might seem to be according exceptional attention or dedication. Kiritsubo's sufferings escalate, paradoxically, when she gives birth to Genji, a boy of unquestionably unparalleled beauty and charm whom the Emperor dotes upon as a finer child than the designated descendant to the throne, named Suzaku, and would gladly promote to that status instead. Although many of the courtly ladies criticize Genji's mother and do not hesitate to play some nasty tricks to aggravate her or even frighten her in the extreme, Lady Murasaki names one of Kiritsubo's persecutors in particular, Kikoden: as the mother of the selected crown prince, or Heir Apparent, she is the one who would be affected most adversely if the Emperor were to shift his allegiances to the lowly concubine and her son to the point of nominating Genji to the position of future Emperor instead of her own child.

However, since the Emperor could not possibly allow Genji to inherit the throne in preference to the official Heir Apparent without unleashing political turmoil, the best position the boy can hope for is that of an imperial underling. While this affords him an excellent education, stoked by Genji's unmatched versatility, intelligence, creativity and inquisitiveness, as well as a life of pleasure and unending romantic opportunities, the hero is haunted by a yearning which neither the Emperor nor any of the ladies he cherishes and cherish him in return have the power to fulfill and will eventually pave the way to his undoing. As Harold Bloom beautifully puts it, "The splendid Genji paradoxically is destroyed by his own incessant longing for the renewed experience of falling in love" (Bloom, p. 2). Utterly incapable of thwarting this dangerous addiction, Genji does not merely stand for erotic desire: he actually "*is* a state of longing" (p. 3). The idealized image of the woman Genji truly desires — as a lover, friend and all-time playmate in the game of life — is irrevocably beyond his reach. As a result, the original text tells us, on the "rare occasions" when "love did gain a hold upon him, it was always in the most improbable and hopeless entanglement that he became involved" (Lady Murasaki, p. 16). Dezaki follows his source closely in chronicling Genji's hopeless passion. The boy is seen to meet the object of his lifelong desire, Fujitsubo, at the age of nine, when she enters the imperial household as Genji's father's latest wife. This makes her, strictly speaking, the protagonist's fourteen-year-old stepmother. Nevertheless, Fujitsubo's young age and general disposition encourage the establishment of a relationship more akin to that of siblings than to that of mother and son. Genji makes it quite clear at an early stage that he does not regard the girl as either a parent or a sister and confirms his words with explicitly physical professions of love. Although there is every indication that Fujitsubo reciprocates Genji's feelings, she is restrained by their illicit character from giving them free rein. She finally resolves to snuff out the boy's "forbidden love" and distance herself from him once an for all upon his Coming of Age, coinciding with Genji's twelfth birthday, at which point she resolutely refuses even to let him gaze one last time at her lovely visage. As Genji officially becomes a man, he sheds his erstwhile infantile dress, loses his long locks, is barred access to the female quarters of his father's court and is engaged to the daughter of the Minister of the Left, Aoi — a girl four years his senior who shuns him as an inadequate suitor, as Dezaki emphasizes, having grown up to believe she would marry the heir to the throne.

The anime places great emphasis on the proposition that Genji's devotion to Fujitsubo never falters or wanes — as attested to by his habit of standing worshipfully in a secluded part of the imperial gardens whence to hear the lady's music as she plays the *koto* (the Japanese equivalent of the zither) once a month. Even though the Shining Prince struggles to stifle his pain by cruising through a seemingly interminable series of loves, his telltale eyes go on exhibiting the "faraway look," as Aoi's brother and Genji's closest friend Tou no Chuujou describes his expression in the screenplay, of one who is prey to "an unrequited love." According to Royall Tyler, the topos of unrequited love is axial to the story and emplaced as such right from the start through Kiritsubo's ordeal: "The major love-related elements in the introductory 'Kiritsubo' chapter ... foreshadow future developments. Genji's yearning for Fujitsubo ... remains alive for him until the end of his life. However, 'Kiritsubo' also evokes the political pressure that forces Genji's father, against his wishes, to appoint Suzaku rather than Genji heir apparent" (Tyler 2009, p. 3).

Due to the intractably unappeasable nature of Genji's one true passion, the joy exuded by the hero's exploits can never conclusively assuage the undercurrent of grief that courses his entire existence, sealing it in memory as the very quintessence of wistfulness. A story that could easily have amounted to no more than the mantra-like recitation of a philanderer's amours actually turns out to be an exquisitely profound and elegant record of the most intimate interpersonal relations and of their often tormented entanglement in a web of ethical, affective and societal tensions. It is from the protagonist's emotionally tormented personality and forever unsatisfied quest for physical and intellectual fulfillment — at times ostensibly verging on self-indulgence and a childish espousal of pleasure at any price — more than from any obvious dramatic complication that *The Tale of Genji* derives a psychological richness of veritably timeless appeal: not merely as a historical drama but also, and indeed more resonantly, as a meticulous dissection of desire and affective turmoil. The political machinations surrounding the hero's personal voyage are indubitably vital to the enhancement of the anime's narrative complexity but we are always invited to perceive them as metaphorically imbricated with Genji's experiences rather than reportorially documented independent events. This proposition is confirmed by the tale's treatment of the relationship between eros and politics. Genji's ambitiousness is inevitably conducive to the pursuit of political ascendancy. However, his society is so obsessed with style that it could not possibly tolerate any naked indications of a yearning for power in its supposedly finest specimen. Therefore, the hero's aspirations must be carefully dissimulated as the cultivation of ideals that transcend the sphere of petty procedures. Genji finds a perfect tool in eros: as most of his exploits tend to take an amorous turn, eroticism becomes the means through which political ambitions can be purified and sublimated. Erotic vicissitudes often operate as metaphors for fundamentally political conflicts, enabling both Lady Murasaki and Dezaki to present eros and politics as interacting forces. Accordingly, the personal and the social are relentlessly mapped onto each other as inseparable facets of being-in-the-world.

Dezaki stays faithful to Lady Murasaki's characterization of the titular hero, putting to maximum advantage his medium's distinctive capabilities and hence relying as far as possible on actions and wordless allusion to convey the Shining Prince's bodily and moral excellence rather than on verbal description. With its emphasis on the specifically visual dimension, the anime succeeds in capturing silently the content and tenor of Lady Murasaki's textual portrayal of her hero as a creature of "unrivalled beauty" (Lady Murasaki, p. 9), deemed by Korean clairvoyants to bear "the marks of one who might become a Father of the State" (p. 10). Genji is so conscious that his qualities could easily make him a victim of unwanted "scrutiny" and "jealous censure" as to feel "obliged to act with great prudence to preserve at least the outward appearance of respectability" (p. 16). It must be stressed, for the purpose of historical accuracy, that Genji's society would have readily interpreted his physical perfection as symbolic of his mental and ethical worth. In Heian culture, it would indeed be automatically assumed that a man endowed with bodily beauty would make a good ruler, for a comely outside must correspond to an admirable inside. The fortune-tellers (and physiognomists) who examine the boy at the Emperor's behest vividly convey this very message. The inextricability of body and mind promulgated by Lady Murasaki constitutes a time-honored lynchpin of Eastern thought and medicine in their multifarious and eclectic manifestations, reverberating throughout the teachings of the doctrine of *yin* and *yang*, the Chinese philosophy of the "Five Movements" (*Wu Xing*) and its Japanese counterpart in the system of the "Five Elements" or *godai* (which is redolent of Western alchemy), the Chinese divination practice of the *I Ching* and the geomantic tenets of *feng shui*.

When Genji grows so disenchanted with the world and its delights that his spiritual mettle weakens and his inner distinction becomes debatable, his body mirrors the state of his mind by contracting a mysterious illness of clearly psychosomatic proportions. The Shining Prince's vulnerability to penetration by malign natural agents visibly symbolizes his spiritual pollution. When, in the more advanced stages of the narrative, Genji's amative appetite is dispassionately exposed and his preference for unattainable lovers is accordingly revealed, Lady Murasaki seems keen on debunking her hero's godlike image to foreground his intrinsic humanity. Intriguingly, although Genji's deterioration cannot be openly witnessed until this point, there is already an ironical hint at the inner foibles that might feasibly mar even a man as fine as the Shining Prince in the passage, quoted earlier, where a clear difference is drawn between internal reality and external semblance. Thus, while indulging in her metafictional reflections, Lady Murasaki does not lose sight of her hero's spiritual fragility, and indeed underscores it in an utterly unsentimental manner. "Now at least we must suppose he was convinced that such secret adventures led only to misery," the narrator notes in the wake of amorous exploits that have left the protagonist in a state of hideous dejection. Lady Murasaki's clinical exposure of the hero's moral flaws reaches an intriguing peak as the narrator admits to being "very loath to recount in all their detail matters which he [Genji] took so much trouble to conceal," yet observes, in a further ironic flourish of her agile brush, that she cannot afford the luxury of discreetness. "I ... know that if you found I had omitted anything," she states, "you would at once ask why, just because he was supposed to be an Emperor's son, I must needs put a favorable showing on his conduct by leaving out all his indiscretions; and you would soon be saying that this was no history but a mere made-up tale designed to influence the judgment of posterity. As it is I shall be called a scandalmonger, but that I cannot help" (p. 80). By laying upon the reader full responsibility for the frank approach she adopts toward her subject matter, Lady Murasaki deploys irony to justify her depiction of situations and character traits that might have been commonly regarded by her society as incompatible with the dictates of decorum by claiming that failure to linger on such unpalatable aspects of the story would be tantamount to expediency, sycophantic flattery and, ultimately, sheer mendacity.

According to Okada, Lady Murasaki's narrative also interrogates the authority of historiography by focusing not on reportorial accuracy but on "the narrating itself, which continually locates us in its tenseless moment without any pretense of offering a detached, representational account of past events." Commenting specifically on the opening chapter titled after Genji's mother, where the narrator deliberately refrains from using precise historical dates and names, Okada shows how Lady Murasaki subtly succeeds in telling us that "what is now being narrated might really have happened" while also intimating that "its referent is not accurately determinable" (Okada, p. 183). The discrepancy between actual history and the course of events as officially recorded by historiography is thus subtly alluded to in a vein that brings to mind some of the chief preoccupations thrown into relief by the films discussed in Chapter 2 and, to a certain extent, by Mahiro Maeda's series *Gankutsuou: The Count of Monte Cristo* (Chapter 3). The narrative intrusions through which Lady Murasaki's narrator asserts her presence and endeavors to explain her rationale and objectives also serve to establish a strong, even conspiratorial, sense of intimacy between author and reader via the storytelling voice. In the anime, where analogous interventions would have felt quite out of place, a similar mood is created by a different means: that is to say, the employment in the capacity of narrator of the uniquely endearing persona of Murasaki, whom Genji adopts as a child, accommodates in his household as a surrogate little sister and eventually marries. Murasaki, incidentally, is also the character after whom the original author is named. Murasaki the character displays a fundamentally sympathetic attitude toward her beloved Genji, yet is not so blinded by her feelings as to fail to recognize and lay open his frailties and thus follows the model set by the original narrator with overall fidelity. The narrative ploys utilized by both the historical Lady Murasaki and her fictive namesake are axial in enabling the reader to empathize with Genji, on the one hand, and to take cognizance of his often lamentable shortcomings on the other. When the character coldly — though not ungallantly — rejects the women who long to share his bed while he chases obsessively those who play hard-to-get, it is sometimes tempting to despise him as a spoilt and arrogant youth. Yet, these are also the very situations in which his defenselessness in the face of unfulfillable yearnings and his abeyant dissatisfaction with a life of vaporous pleasures transpire most candidly and affectingly. The anime takes advantage of these moments, thus enhancing the original story's timeless cogency—and, specifically, its trenchant relevance to the sense of emptiness, anomie and directionlessness afflicting many contemporary cultures.

An episode in Genji's erotic escapades which paradigmatically illustrates Lady Murasaki's take on her hero's exploits is the one in which Fujitsubo falls ill and is forced by her condition to leave the palace for a while. Genji cannot help exploiting her temporary distance from the Emperor to pay her a clandestine visit. The action that ensues provides a brilliant instance of Lady Murasaki's ability to convey a potent sense of emotive tension and particularly the conflict between the young woman's guilt-ridden conscience, which causes her to look back upon her moments of intimacy with Genji "as something wicked and horrible" and to be filled with "torment" by their recollection, and the youth's frenzied longing to "vanish forever" with the beloved into a "dream" known to them alone (Lady Murasaki, p. 96). Shortly after the secret rendezvous has taken place, we are informed that Fujitsubo is pregnant and although there can be no doubt that the lady carries Genji's child, the precise circumstances in which the conception occurred are never explicitly disclosed. The narrative strategy based on the presentation of the effects of events that have not been mentioned before as though the reader could be expected to know all about them is diligently treasured by Lady Murasaki and eagerly emulated by Dezaki in his anime adaptation.

The director maximizes the dramatic potentialities inherent in this ploy to tailor them to the requirements of his own medium. Specifically, the freedom to present the results of incidents and occurrences that have not overtly featured on the screen before as and when the director deems apposite affords him plenty of scope for unexpected twists, narrative reorientations, shifts of perspective and even occasional coups de théâtre. At the same time, it squarely exonerates him from the strictures of chronological linearity. In the handling of temporality, both Lady Murasaki and Dezaki earnestly rely on foreshadowing and on the incremental accumulation of dramatic tension, dropping casual hints at later developments that gain intensity and significance as the story progresses. Much is implied and it is therefore up to the recipient of the written or filmic text to extrapolate certain meanings from mere clues. A good example is supplied, in the anime, by the installment in which the narrator states early on that Lady Rokujou will be required to reside with her daughter at the Ninomiya Shrine in Sagano for a year prior to the girl's assumption of her post as shrine maiden at Ise. Later in the episode, we see Genji rushing off to Sagano in the middle of a stormy night to bid Lady Rokujou farewell, having learnt that she is about to leave for Ise. This is a laconically effective way of suggesting that an entire year is meant to have elapsed between the beginning and end of the installment even though, on the surface, the events dramatized therein appear to have covered no more than a couple of days.

Axial to Lady Murasaki's literary vision is the firm belief in the value of fantasy as a means not merely of constructing entertaining worlds and thus providing escapist routes for their audiences but also — and far more crucially — of abetting people's understandings of their own worlds and ability to negotiate their intricacies. This point is lucidly encapsulated by a passage from Chapter 25 of the source text outlining the author's stance as a literary critic. In the passage, here quoted in Ivan Morris' translation, Genji remarks that although "romances" are not likely to accommodate a single "ounce of truth," it is precisely through texts ostensibly "full of fabrications" that "the emotion of things" is evoked "in a most realistic way" (Morris, pp. 308–309). We are here reminded of the message conveyed by Willy in *Romeo x Juliet* when he argues that fantastic tales play a key role in helping people deal with reality. (Please see Chapter 5.) In commenting, both elliptically and explicitly, on the function of literary fiction as a social, psychological and existential phenomenon, *The Tale of Genji* anticipates recent theoretical approaches to textuality eager to expose its inherent constructedness and thus explode the mimetic fallacy centered on the concept of the text as a transparent window onto reality. Such a stance finds eloquent confirmation in Dezaki's tendency to lay bare his adaptation's artificiality as an animated text, in keeping with both his medium's aesthetic proclivities and his own personal vision. As Richard Bowring points out, in his study of the original text, this strategy serves to "deliberately destabilise the reader, undercutting any decision on his or her part as to who may or may not be in the right at any one particular point." Never losing sight of its protagonist's consuming erotic longing, *The Tale of Genji* relishes in irony, ambiguity and even, at times, equivocation. Critical to this modus operandi is its tendency to engage with various characters' perspectives and viewpoints simultaneously, and thus invite us to guess the hidden motives lurking therein. In so doing, it embraces an incisively modern outlook. "As we are swung first one way and then the next," Bowring comments, "we come to appreciate the subjectivity of all vision" (Bowring, p. 63).

By looking at Genji's prismatic world through the eyes of various characters, Lady Murasaki is careful to diversify not only the moral and emotional tenor of their perspectives but also the intensity with which they typify a particular world view. Dezaki follows closely this approach in his selective retelling of the original tale. To undertake their multiperspectival project, both the writer and the director rely to a considerable extent on richly varied characterization. Therefore, whereas some personae (most notably, in the anime, Genji himself, Fujitsubo and Lady Rokujou) come across as fully rounded individuals through detailed psychological analysis, others (e.g., Yuugao, Aoi and Roku no Kimi) are more dependent on their situation within contingent predicaments as identity markers. There are also characters (e.g., Tou no Chuujou, Koremitsu) who, though undoubtedly appealing and insightful, exhibit steady attributes that render them more two-dimensional. Others still belong to the category of extras whose primary function is to augment the setting's authenticity — such as the urban crowds, the women in the Imperial Compound guarded by ubiquitous fans and screens, the innumerable servants and the unceasingly gossiping court retainers. Even such minor actors embody viewpoints of vital import to the story as a whole for they cast light, from the interstices of Heian society, on the aesthetic and ethical values underpinning that culture. No less importantly, they illuminate significant aspects of the main characters' personalities through their varyingly astute and shallow opinions. In addition, character is frequently revealed by means of contrasting mentalities and attitudes. For instance, the nurturing figure of Murasaki, capable of maternal affection and selfless behavior even when jealousy gnaws at her, is implicitly contrasted with Lady Rokujou, a woman of immense creativity, intelligence and charm whose jealousy, conversely, turns into the deadliest (and ultimately most self-destructive) of weapons. Uniting these diverse character typologies, in both the novel and the anime, is the pervasive feeling that life is governed by inscrutable forces wherein the metaphysical power of karma and the subjective power of unconscious desires blend and clash by turns. Much as the actors may look for happiness in the fleeting moment, they invariably find that any one instant of potential fulfillment is bound to lead to another instant along an endless chain of experiences that only ever leave them feeling incomplete, insecure, rudderless in the current of yearning.

According to Haruo Shirane, one of the most distinctive technical traits of Lady Murasaki's narrative is the substantial extent to which it "diverges from and works against literary conventions," thus providing something of "an ironic comment upon the *monogatari* tradition" (Shirane 1987, p. xix). This tendency is amusingly conveyed by passages, of the kind cited earlier, in which Lady Murasaki demystifies the notion of Genji as an exemplar. Concurrently, the notion of the Emperor's divine authority is also undermined, since the splendor that ought to be associated, in accordance with tradition, only with imperial charisma and hence the supreme ruler is actually presented by Lady Murasaki as an attribute of Genji the commoner and not of the heir to the throne. Dezaki's anime parallels the source narrative's good-humored tendency to puncture the conventions of its genre by repeatedly highlighting the hero's entrapment in an inescapable past. This motif serves to reinforce the tale's preoccupation with the ethos of *mono no aware*, congruously with the spirit of the Heian age, but also reminds us at virtually each turn that no narrative meant to elevate a human being and thus pave his path to literary immortality is truly viable in a world of forever broken promises and forever shattered dreams. The series' emphasis on the past finds an overt correlative in the parent text insofar as Lady Murasaki's story, much as it may appear to evolve organically from one stage to the next through a process of potentially endless metamorphosis, never loses sight of its building blocks even when they seemingly recede into oblivion. In fact, is allows past occurrences to gather meaning and importance incrementally as the saga unfolds.

In the source text, the gulf between Genji and Fujitsubo becomes conclusively insurmountable when the title of Empress is conferred upon the lady by her doting spouse. The Emperor, at this juncture, intends soon to resign the throne and would very much like to proclaim his new-born son Yuugiri (i.e., Genji and Fujitsubo's adulterous issue) as crown prince instead of Kokiden's boy. The situation witnessed earlier in relation to the protagonist thus reproposes itself in adapted guise later in the story vis-à-vis his son. As before, the Emperor is reluctant to enforce such a radical decision without a faction to support his move. After all, even the choice to pass over Kokiden, as the mature "mother of the Heir Apparent," for the sake of "a concubine aged little more than twenty" proves sufficient to cause "a good deal of discontent" as the "public" vociferously proceeds to "take Kokiden's side." However, as Fujitsubo is "installed" as the new Empress, Genji finally senses that she has "been raised so far beyond his reach that scarce knowing" what he is doing, he finds himself whispering "to himself the lines: 'Now upon love's dark path has the last shadow closed; for I have seen you carried to a cloud-land whither none may climb'" (Lady Murasaki, p. 150).

The anime reimagines these crucial components of the original narrative in a number of subtle ways while remaining faithful to their cumulative import. The show proposes that Genji, who has just returned to the capital following a protracted spell of depression occasioned by the sudden death of his beloved Yuugao and his attendant possession by demonic powers, engineers a nocturnal encounter with Fujitsubo on the outskirts of the imperial gardens, as the lady leaves the shrine in the woods where she has been secretly and tenaciously praying for his recovery. At this stage, the Shining Prince claims to be resolved to seal away his feelings for Fujitsubo and avert his gaze from her forever. This, he insists, is meant to be his very last trip to the grounds and shrine associated with his childhood and hence a symbolically final way of saying farewell to the past and its deceitful promises. However, Genji soon regrets his actions, wishing he had not put on a nonchalant and formally charming façade just to hide his true emotions. On a rainy night when Fujitsubo is staying at her parents' home, Genji effortlessly manages to access the lady's room as she inadvertently invites him in, believing the visitor to be her loyal attendant Myoubu (the title accorded to members of the Fifth Rank in the rigidly stratified Heian class system). It is on this "fateful" occasion that the passion haunting Genji and Fujitsubo from a young age is finally — and fleetingly — consummated and their child is conceived. It is now Fujitsubo that announces her determination to cut herself off from the Shining Prince for good, convinced that to bear the sin alone is written in her karma, and reflects upon her own doleful experience as a possible marker of broader gender politics: "Is it the fate of a woman," she wonders, "to live a life of sin?" Genji remains adamant, however, about the sanctity of their bond, trusting that it is neither tainted nor culpable, and dramatically declares: "If my love for you is forbidden, then there is no such thing as love in the world." The coup de théâtre coincides with the Emperor's announcement that he intends to hand the throne over to the current Heir Apparent and appointment of Genji as the guardian of his and Fujitsubo's new-born baby (much to the biological father's confusion). Wishing the child himself to ascend the throne upon reaching the appropriate age, the Emperor believes that Genji has the power to help him "pave the way for a new era."

From a cinematographical point of view, Dezaki's *The Tale of Genji* exhibits many of the technical and aesthetic preferences discussed in relation to the same director's adaptation of *The Snow Queen* in Chapter 4, and particularly, freeze-frame shots, segmented motion, split screens and stills displaying the original artwork. However, the later show's greater technical sophistication enables it to utilize additional tools to unprecedented effect. Modulating filters, intersecting slides and glittering overlays are among the most prominent. Pacing also plays a key role, being kept generally tight in Dezaki's capsulation of the source narrative through a keen focus on emotions and meditative excursions but appropriately varied as Genji moves from love to love, in keeping with the ancient art of scroll painting. In Heian scrolls, as Stanley-Baker stresses, every "painting has its own tempo, fast or slow, which engages our viewing to the extent of conditioning the speed at which we unroll the scroll. In the *Genji* scrolls, for instance, the pictorial sections are different paintings interleaved with a continuous calligraphic narrative" (Stanley-Baker, p. 97). Calligraphy itself, as Lippit explains, supplies a kind of visual "meter" whereby the artists could "choreograph the tempo and columnar flow of the writing" (Lippit, p. 59). An impression of acceleration can be conveyed, for example, by fluidly compressing a great number of characters in a vertical cascade — a technique used by Dezaki in the scene where his protagonist is depicted in the process of writing his farewell letters prior to his exile in order to lend urgency to his situation.

Concomitantly, Dezaki endeavors to capture the unique aesthetic sense treasured by Heian court civilization and attendant devotion to all manner of natural and artificial beauty. Hydrangea beds and wisteria trails so palpable as to reach, synesthetically, not only the eye but also the sense of olfaction, and swirls of fireflies redolent of fairy dust are among Dezaki's many gems. Gold-tinged sunsets and comely courtiers, swirling cherry blossom and snow flurries, melodious verse and fine garments, alongside mastery of music, dance, horse-riding, archery, calligraphy and, of course, the art of wooing, are held in high esteem by the Shining Prince's society as mutually interdependent facets of a single, holistic notion of the beautiful. The protagonist incarnates this ethos by excelling in all areas, thus epitomizing the notion of *miyabi* (雅) — i.e., "courtliness." In the rendition of costumes, traditional patterns are accorded pride of place, with the butterflies and peonies adorning the robes of the characters of Lady Rokujou and Roku no Kimi as particularly resplendent examples of Dezaki's artistry in their ability to detach themselves from the fabric and attain to a life of their own.

Dezaki's adaptation shares with its source a number of pivotal themes. The topos of supernatural phenomena is conspicuous among them and finds several expressions. References to demonic possessions, subjection to an evil influence, *mononoke* and magical agencies are frequent, as are the recurrent tropes inspired by traditional purifying and exorcizing rituals. Paradigmatic illustrations of the theme of the supernatural are supplied by the episodes in which Genji's mistress Yuugao and his wife Aoi are bewitched and killed by potent curses, ostensibly concocted by the jilted lover Lady Rokujou, here portrayed as a prototypical *hannya* (般若), or jealous woman, and hence as one of the most dreaded of Japanese demons. The Shining Prince himself is so profoundly affected by the malefic spell attendant upon Yuugao's death as to precipitate into a potentially fatal state of melancholia. What enables him to recover, apart from the scores of precious and salubrious gifts lavishly showered upon the royal retainer by his many admirers, is a sojourn at a mountain monastery where he engages in intensive praying and cleansing ceremonies. Several of the occurrences which both Lady Murasaki and Dezaki surround with an otherworldly aura may be explained in mundane ways. For example, Genji's state following Yuugao's departure could be interpreted clinically as a result of his inability to negotiate bereavement, and the monastic rites of which he partakes as a transition from paralyzing melancholia to resigned mourning. Relatedly, as Mary Dejong Obuchowski stresses, "it becomes increasingly clear through the novel that one is fundamentally responsible for his feelings and desires as well as for his acts, and that religious belief has firm grounding in common sense" (in *The Tale of Genji Study Guide*, p.182).

Moreover, regardless of Rokujou's necromantic skills, what the "cluster of stories" revolving around this character ultimately discloses is that sooner or later (and by whatever means), "hatred kills, directly or indirectly" (p. 181). One of the story's most enduring messages — and one which Dezaki is especially keen to promulgate in his own adaptation — is that "the religious elements of court ritual, exorcism and folk superstition, and themes of jealousy, guilt, and responsibility turn out to be so closely intertwined as to be inseparable" (p. 184). In evaluating the ethical and social implications of demonic possession, it is additionally useful to bear in mind Doris G. Bargen's contention that the instances of such a phenomenon depicted in *The Tale of Genji* could be read as attempts at female self-expression tied up with the sexual mores of Heian culture. Discussing specifically Yuugao's tragedy, the critic maintains that being "Of lower rank than her former and her present lovers," the girl "must consider herself fortunate to be favored by such high-ranking courtiers [i.e., Tou no Chuujou and Genji respectively]. At the same time, she has learned to be distrustful of uneven matches" (in *The Tale of Genji Study Guide*, p. 170). Concurrently, "it is important to see that the drama of Yuugao's possession is so powerful that Genji feels compelled to share her altered state and continues to do so," as suggested by his precipitation into a state of utterly debilitating forlornness. The Shining Prince is also presented as central to the supernatural experience, as though to indicate that while Yuugao might be trying to give voice to her repressed anxieties through her condition, her embryonic narrative is appropriated by her lover: "It is through Genji's feverishly involved perspective, at crucial times bordering on the hallucinatory, that Yuugao's rapid psychological and physical decline are first assessed" (p. 171).

In order to grasp the exact import of *The Tale of Genji*'s utilization of the supernatural, it is crucial to bear in mind that in Lady Murasaki's day, it was common for people to feel spiritually governed by superstitions more than by systematized religious doctrines. As Morris explains, some beliefs, "notably those related to witchcraft, necromancy, and other occult practice, were influenced by Shintoism, and represent the shamanistic strain in the native religion" (Morris, p. 123), whereas others, "including many that are concerned with ghosts and demons, appear to have derived from ancient native folklore whose origin is still obscure." Other superstitions strike their roots in Chinese culture, as most famously attested to by the influence of "omen lore based on *yin-yang* dualism and the five elements" (pp. 123–124). This composite body of beliefs is ever-present in Dezaki's adaptation — both explicitly, as demonstrated by the episodes concentrating on possessions, hauntings, exorcisms and divinatory practices — and implicitly, but more pervasively, as a shadow text stalking Genji's saga everywhere and imbuing it at all turns with somber poignancy. In the process, we are consistently reminded that the Heian world was "heavily populated with goblins, demons, spirits, and other supernatural beings" (p. 130).

A contemporary audience's appreciation of the full import of scenes such as the ones depicting Yuugao and Aoi's demonically engineered deaths or the later sequence centered on the ghost of Genji's father also requires, on a broader scale, recognition of the centrality of the subject of death to Japanese folklore and mythology. According to Michiko Iwasaka and Barre Toelken, death indeed constitutes "the *principal* topic in Japanese tradition" and this is attested to by the fact that "nearly every festival, every ritual, every custom is bound up in some way with the relationship between the living and the dead, the present family and its ancestors." While the ubiquity of death-related traditions can be explained largely on the basis of their ability to throw into relief pivotal tenets in the indigenous value system, such as "obligation, duty, debt, honor and personal responsibility" (Iwasaka and Toelken, p. 6), it also serves as a perfect trope to encapsulate the ethos of *mono no aware* seen to be axial to Genji's whole universe. Furthermore, the interpenetration of the domains of the breathing and the departed underpinning ghost lore posits the realm of the dead as intrinsically alive and animate by virtue of its impact on the beliefs and practices of the living world, and thus entails patterns of reciprocal responsibility connecting the two spheres. The death topos as dramatized in *The Tale of Genji* at the levels of both the source text and its anime version is rooted in a pluralistic approach to faith, ritual and life in general, which bears witness to the Japanese people's traditional tendency "to adopt, adapt, translate, reform and integrate the ideas and values of many cultures and religions into their own system" (p. 2). Therefore, *The Tale of Genji*'s take on spectral lore and, by extension, death in both the supernatural and mundane areas of existence partakes of a broader cultural attitude that could be described as the very epitome of the *adaptive* mentality — and hence as a forthright celebration of the focal concern pursued in this book in its entirety.

While it is important to acknowledge the role played by the supernatural, it is no less vital to appreciate the narrative's unwavering adherence to reality. As Keene stresses, even as Lady Murasaki appears to ideate Genji's world as something of a "refuge from the world in which she actually found herself, a transmutation of the prose of daily life at the court to the poetry of her imagination," she nonetheless derided the blatantly fantastic yarns unleashed by old folktales in their own deployment of otherworldly themes. The realm she portrays must therefore be grasped as "a sublimation" of her actual social reality, "not a never-never land" (Keene, pp. 18–19). Hence, Lady Murasaki's narrative also supplies a dispassionate dissection of social decline, and this constitutes another prominent theme which Dezaki's show shares with his source. The cultural climate inhabited by Genji is shaped by a fatalistic belief in the irreversibility of degeneration as a process affecting not only secular human affairs but even religion and its time-honored systems. Portraying the hero as a creature endowed with unrivaled beauty and urbanity is a circuitous way of suggesting that once humanity has reached such an apotheosis, everything that follows is bound to be inferior, marred, uninspiring. After all, the original narrator herself seems to find it surprising that a child as fine as Genji should have been conceived in what she terms "these latter and degenerate days" (Lady Murasaki, p. 3). According to Bloom, Lady Murasaki's "exaltation of longing over fulfillment throughout the novel" can itself be regarded as symptomatic of "a mingled spiritual and aesthetic nostalgia" that consistently "takes the place of a waning social order" (Bloom, p. 2). The anime closely echoes this proposition in its rendition of the theme of social decline, which Dezaki concurrently posits as inextricable from a wider world view. In this perspective, human existence at large is perceived as a fleeting occurrence on both "the main stage and the backstage," as the script evocatively puts it. With its telescoped reconfiguration of the original narrative, the anime trenchantly communicates this message by dramatizing the rapid intensification of the darkness ready to swallow Genji's gleaming aura as the story progresses. This is portrayed as a series of life-changing losses, as each of the three principal women in his life recedes from the scene and his father dies, leaving behind a disabling premonition of the impossibility of ever achieving any conclusive resolutions or absolutions.

The topos of social decline should also be understood in specific relation to the exhaustion of Heian civilization as such. Indeed, as Morris points out, numerous scholars have interpreted the demise of what stands out as one of Japan's most intriguing periods precisely as an outcome of ethical deterioration, highlighting "the growing self-indulgence and effeteness of the ruling class and their failure to observe Confucian principles of rectitude" (Morris, p. 5). James Murdoch is an exemplary case in point insofar as his *History of Japan* indeed brands the Heian upper echelons as an "ever-pullulating brood of greedy, needy, frivolous dilettanti—as often as not foully licentious, utterly effeminate, incapable of any worthy achievement, but withal the polished exponents of high breeding and correct 'form.'... Now and then a better man did emerge; but one such man is impotent to avert the doom of an intellectual Sodom.... A pretty showing, indeed, these pampered minions and bepowdered poetasters might be expected to make" (Murdoch, p. 230). Morris adopts an altogether less prejudiced take on Heian civilization, attributing its decline to a wide range of political and economic forces rather than a single ethical cause. However, he concedes that "an imbalance of energies poured into intellectual and artistic pursuits" at the expense of more pragmatic concerns would have been largely responsible for the erosion of that culture (Morris, p. 6). Relatedly, the historian is eager to emphasize the coexistence of the "delight in the aesthetic joys of the world" so characteristic of the Heian era with a no less ubiquitous apprehension of the "vanity of human pleasures" (p. 13).

Dezaki's anime vividly encapsulates this tension, dwelling on the passion for ceremonial grandeur typical of the hero's age with no dearth of descriptive details in the representation of magnificent tableaux exuding elegance and energy in equal measures, yet also showing how even the most splendid spectacle is destined to leave in its wake dark intimations of dislocation, evanescence and sorrow. No sooner has a feast, parade or ceremony left the screen than a dusky sense of foreboding seizes Genji's forever unsettled heart. Yet, the show is also keen to indicate that a truly accomplished Heian gentleman such as the Shining Prince would never allow the perception of *mono no aware* to ascend to the heights of sensationalist turmoil, since the maintenance of a sense of restraint is deemed critical to the display of genuine refinement. In this respect, Dezaki aptly employs his protagonist to document symbolically the spirit of a whole epoch. The season most suited to the capture of this mood is, unsurprisingly, autumn and Dezaki dutifully lingers on recurrent images of melancholy rain wreathed with veils of lacy vapor. The fading light of autumn is a perfect metaphor for humanity's vain pursuits and faltering visions.

A major factor to be taken into careful consideration while assessing *The Tale of Genji*'s melancholy contemplation of impermanence is the influence on Heian civilization of the teachings of Buddhism. Although that period, as indeed subsequent chapters in Japanese history, evinces a marked proclivity toward religious syncretism, allowing for the coexistence of Buddhism, Shintoism, Confucianism, Taoism and various beliefs rooted in both indigenous and Chinese lore, there can be little doubt that Buddhist principles predominate in the context of Lady Murasaki's narrative and its anime version alike. Thus, while Confucian beliefs impact significantly on the story's approach to family and clan, ancestor worship and filial respect, it is from Buddhism that *The Tale of Genji* derives its emphasis on the transience of earthly matters (*mujoukan*) and, relatedly, on the dreamlike character of life. The final chapter of Lady Murasaki's novel, importantly, is titled "The Bridge of Dreams" to emphasize the elusive quality of existence. Analogously, in Dezaki's final episode, Genji reflects on his life and concludes that it has all been merely "a dream"—or, in fact, something even "more fleeting than a dream." In addition, Dezaki makes frequent use of oneiric sequences and visionary experiences to convey the illusory nebulousness of the phenomenal domain.

As John R. Wallace argues, by injecting the Buddhist perception of life as insubstantial and transient into the ethos of aristocratic sophistication embodied by the concept of *miyabi*, Lady Murasaki "darkens the vision of beauty" so central to her work (Wallace, p. 311) by pointing to the "dark or infinite" world (p. 315) that underpins at all times the radiant card house of Heian courtliness. Savoir-faire, grace and pleasure cannot elude, due to their entanglement with the rhythms of fate and becoming, "the inevitability of the cycle of suffering" and "the essentially transitory nature of the object one finds beautiful or desirable" (p. 324). This proposition parallels Morris' aforecited account of the Heian era's schizoid vision. In this regard, *The Tale of Genji* could be said to anticipate Georges Bataille's contention that beauty can never unproblematically represent a flight from the ultimate shadow hosting the specters of sorrow, violation and death, since its existence is predicated upon the very possibility that "it may be befouled" (Bataille, p. 144). In portraying the metaphorically incestuous bond between Genji and Fujitsubo as pivotal to his adaptation, Dezaki reinforces this perspective insofar as he thereby posits any idealized notions of beauty and desire as inextricable from the murky reality of transgression, defilement and profanation. From an aesthetic point of view, it must also be remembered that the tendency toward meditative gloom so ingrained in the Heian age was tangentially fueled by the atmosphere of the typical upper-class dwelling of the time. As Morris comments, the aristocracy spent a substantial part of their lives in "semiobscurity" and its female members, specifically, "lived in a state of almost perpetual twilight. As if the rooms were not already dark enough, they normally immured themselves behind thick silk hangings or screens" (p. 34). Furthermore, as William J. Puette notes, "For the denizens of the capital, the actual world of daily activities was ... largely nocturnal" and "time was solely governed by the flow of events. People slept, ate, and committed their other quotidian duties around their social activities, which more often than not were conducted at night, till just before dawn" (Puette, p. 28).

A further topos of recurrent significance throughout the novel and the anime alike is the equation of human weakness to a lack of self-discipline and self-control, connotative of a loss of direction — and hence of a rupture in the natural equilibrium — and emblematized by overindulgence in earthly appetites. In using lack of restraint in the pursuit of sexual pleasure as the epitome of weakness, neither the original narrative nor the series are being stuffily moralistic: in fact, there is every indication that their authors are well aware of the dramatic potentialities inherent in that aspect of human existence and understandably keen to actualize them to the best of their abilities as a particularly effective way of communicating their existential message. Throughout the anime, all of the themes outlined above are often elaborated in a tersely economical, yet allusive, fashion through the interspersal of regular dialogue with snippets of poetry. In this respect, the show follows closely its source text, emulating its typically Heian devotion to the poetic word as the acme of artistic accomplishment and as a symbolic bridge between the human and spiritual realms. As Bowring explains, the poetic word "had from its beginnings been equated with divine speech, having the potential to bring into being that of which it spoke," and in Lady Murasaki's era, it had come to be automatically associated with "the realm of erotic possession/obsession." Hence, a "talented poet" was expected to be also a "talented lover" (Bowring, p. 66). This contention brings to mind the Platonic equation of the poet and the lover as vessels of a so-called fine (or divine) frenzy which, while enabling them to perceive levels of reality inscrutable by common eyes, also renders them unstable, unruly and irrational. This same idea resonates throughout Duke Theseus' famous speech at the beginning of the final act of Shakespeare's *A Midsummer Night's Dream*, where "the lunatic, the lover and the poet" are bracketed together as victims of an unbridled imagination capable of conjuring entire worlds out of their fantasies and delusions.

According to Morris, "The composition, exchange and quotation of poems was central to the daily life of the Heian aristocracy, and it is doubtful whether any other society in the world has ever attached such importance to the poetic versatility of its members" (Morris, p. 177). This is repeatedly confirmed by the ubiquitous use of poetry as a major component of the anime's textual repartee, and most pointedly by Genji's relationship with Lady Rokujou: a lady to whom he is at first drawn not only by rumors concerning her beauty but also by her reputation as a poet and calligrapher of unique caliber. The initial stages of the courtship are orchestrated almost entirely in lyrical form as exchanges of extemporaneous poems. Most importantly, Heian society expected poetry to thrive on allusiveness and obscurity, in the conviction that clarity and explicitness amounted to lack of refinement. In this matter, Lady Murasaki's culture parallels the world of the Western Renaissance courtier, where an accomplished individual's greatest asset was held to be the ability to convey an impression of effortless brilliance through studious effort in the deployment of cryptic imagery and densely layered allusions. The rule of *sprezzatura* (nonchalance) demanded the careful erasure of all traces of conscious toil. According to Yanping Wang, *The Tale of Genji* attests to the centrality of poetry in the Heian era insofar as the very "thematic frame" of Lady Murasaki's text depends on "*waka*" (和歌) — literally, "Japanese poem" — as "the language of love." The story's distinctive "poetics" is accordingly shaped by the aristocratic conception of eros as "an elaborate code of courtship" with stringent "rules of communion by poetry" (Wang, p. 35). Lynne K. Miyake argues that three main techniques govern *waka* poetry of the kind employed by Lady Murasaki — a discourse, it must again be stressed, that Dezaki's adaptation consistently enthrones as pivotal to its own dramatic structure. These encompass the use of polysemantic words (*kakerotoba*), linguistic associations grounded in culturally sanctioned diction and imagery (*engo*) and intertextual references to a wide range of poetic texts (*honkadori*). These strategies enjoin readers (or listeners) to engage in a collaborative exercise with the text by using their own imagination to actualize its potential meanings (Miyake, p. 79). The devices described by Miyake guide the dialogue between lovers resorting to poetry as their principal communicational vehicle. They thus supply a structure within which members of the two sexes, normally divided both by linguistic laws ratifying the utilization of different registers by men and women and behavioral codes prohibiting physical proximity, could establish and sustain powerful emotive connections.

Therefore, as Wang points out, the "medium" of "written poetry" and the "means" of "the hand-carried letter" containing the poetic word provided lovers with a "sign of presence" and hence a "physical substitute" comparable to "a fetish." This entails that in the context of *The Tale of Genji*, the "poetic letter" comes "to be privileged over presence itself" (Wang, p. 36). The ongoing translation of love and desire into aesthetically polished rituals, which in turn become embodied in poetic communication, makes Genji's world a perfect example of what Barthes terms an "empire of signs." In such a milieu, the critic contends, there is no such thing as a deep self since identity is constantly voided into urbane semiotic gestures (Barthes 1983). These ideas are paradigmatically borne out, in the series, by Genji's first meeting with Yuugao. Upon espying a flower he has never cast his eyes on before — the evening glory (or evening faces) whence Yuugao derives her denomination — Genji realizes that he cherishes its beauty even though it is not the kind of plant one would encounter in a patrician garden. Wishing to appease his master's aesthetic appetite, Koremitsu — Genji's chief retainer — seeks access to the residence disporting the object of his admiration and asks for an arrangement. He returns bearing a gracefully simple floral composition, placed upon a fan to ensure its integrity and accompanied by a piece of poetry. It is on the basis of this textual communication that the hero will soon enter one of the relationships destined to prove most influential in his psychological and moral evolution. The fact that Yuugao is capable of delivering beautiful lines even though she is but a humble city girl alludes to the power of poetry to transcend hierarchical barriers but there is little doubt that in reality, it was very much a prerogative of the Heian nobility.

Bowring confirms the existence of an intimate relationship between "poetic creation" and "sexuality" in Heian society, positing the composition of poetry as a means of gaining control over potentially unruly desires (Bowring, p. 14). The written word functions as a substitute for presence which, while inevitably signifying the absence of the desired object for which it stands, manages to rise to the status of a tangible reality unto itself. By "bridging the gap between self and other," the poetic sign temporarily plugs a "gap" that "itself is erotic" insofar as it is pivotal to the genesis of attraction and yearning (p. 15). The concept of the gap as an erotic element is corroborated by the popular trope of "*kaimami* or 'seeing through a gap in the hedge'" used in literature to allude to the frisson yielded by the experience of seeing and being seen surreptitiously" (p. 14). This idea brings to mind Barthes' tantalizing remarks on the topic: "Is not the most erotic portion of a body where the garment gapes? ... it is intermittence ... which is erotic: the intermittence of skin flashing between two articles of clothing ... between two edges ... it is this flash itself which seduces, or rather: the staging of an appearance-as-disappearance" (Barthes 1990, pp. 9–10). In Lady Murasaki's narrative, a paradigmatic illustration of *kaimami* is provided by the scene in which Genji catches his very first glimpse of Murasaki through a galvanizing gap in the fence. A mere peep is sufficient to allow him to detect the little girl's uncanny resemblance to Fujitsubo and to trigger in his mind a far-reaching chain of associations, culminating with the desire to bring her up to become his ideal wife. Dezaki's adaptation of Genji's initial encounter with Murasaki does not explicitly deploy the *kaimami* formula but does capitalize to considerable dramatic effect on Murasaki's presentation as the passive object of Genji's gaze: by the time the child comes face to face with the Shining Prince and finds herself instantly captivated by his gentle smile, the protagonist has already had the opportunity to study her behavior and formulate a preliminary assessment of her likely personality.

The scenes depicting Lady Rokujou in the act of writing enable Dezaki to throw into relief several key facets of traditional Japanese poetry as an art based on the interplay of what Shirane defines as "performance, visuality, and textuality" (Shirane 2005, p. 217). The character's alternately graceful and vigorous movements of hand and brush constitute a performance in the sense that they are choreographed in accordance with culturally endorsed codes and conventions enabling an audience to grasp them as actions endowed with ritualistic significance rather than an isolated event. The poem, as the physical entity yielded by that performance, stands out as both a written text amenable to reading and hermeneutic evaluation and a visual ensemble of artistically polished signs. In both its written and its visual dimensions, the poem rests on a substratum of collectively ratified assumptions in much the same way as the performance itself does. As the underpinning of Lady Rokujou's intellectual and erotic communion with Genji, her poetic texts call attention to the fundamentally dialogical nature of traditional Japanese poetry. As Shirane observes, "Modern readers tend to read poetry monologically, either in an expressive, lyrical mode, as an expression of a speaker's subjective state, or in a descriptive, mimetic mode, as a reflection of the external world as perceived by the speaker." In the context of "pre-modern or early modern Japan," by contrast, it "functioned dialogically, fulfilling socioreligious functions" (pp. 218–219).

When, in the opening moments of her first poetic dialogue with Genji, Lady Rokujou delivers hermetically brief poetic utterances, left deliberately suspended in the air so as to challenge her interlocutor to expand upon them, the anime points to another important aspect of traditional Japanese poetry: the expectation among cultured audiences that a respectable piece of poetry should always feel somewhat unfinished in order to enable its recipients to "participate in its production" (p. 221). Finally, the emphasis placed by the relevant scenes on both calligraphy and paper fully validates Shirane's contention that the aesthetic worth of the writing often exceeded in significance the quality of the content, while the materials employed in the process of composition were deemed likewise crucial. "A poor poem with excellent calligraphy," the critic explains, "was probably preferable to a good poem with poor calligraphy" and the "type, color, and size of the paper" upon which it was executed also carried critical weight. Furthermore, a writer could "add a sketch, attach a flower or leaf, or add incense or perfume to the poetry sheet" (p. 224) as a means of enhancing the medium's inherent attractiveness through the inspired inclusion of a personal touch of style. Given the immense value attached by Lady Rokujou to incense throughout the series (necromantic moments included), one can easily imagine the Lady applying a dab of her distinctive fragrance to the poetic messages issuing from her *sumi* well.

While Dezaki follows his source closely in the articulation of *The Tale of Genji*'s cardinal themes, he also reveals acute sensitivity to the story's original setting. No doubt reliant on punctilious historical research into the environmental and architectural attributes of Heian Kyou (now Kyoto), the anime portrays the capital as a thoroughly planned urban grid of great geometrical precision, traversed by uncommonly capacious streets, on which most aristocratic mansions would be situated, and by narrow alleys intersecting them across the city's chessboard, where the commoners' dwellings would cluster in close proximity to one another. The show draws attention on numerous occasions to the capital's natural location in an attractive rural region punctuated by numerous lakes and streams and surrounded by woods and mountains shrouded in hazy trails, where monasteries and shrines seamlessly coalesced with the habitat. The series is also faithful to Lady Murasaki's presentation of the Imperial Compound, which in turn closely mirrors its real-life counterpart. Hence, in both the source text and the anime, the characters' movements through the Compound are made to tally with the factual plan of the location as it stood at the time in which the story is set. Dezaki is also loyal to the original in the representation of Heian interiors as spaces shaped by Zen's dedication to an atmosphere of quiet composure devoid of redundant ornamentation and gaining their energy, in fact, from austerity and emptiness. The fluid interpenetration of the traditional Japanese dwelling and its environment is concurrently recorded — in particular, in the scenes where Genji enters his lovers' apartments by moving so effortlessly through the screens that separate them from the outside world as to seem to be crossing a barrier no more substantial than autumn mist.

Another aspect of the source narrative's cultural milieu which Dezaki captures with considerable accuracy is its rigid hierarchical approach to social organization. According to Morris, Heian culture made "court rank" the determining factor in the allocation of a person's "post in the government" and general affluence, which meant that "entry into the rank hierarchy was decided exclusively by one's family connexions" (Morris, p. 64). Concomitantly, the codes and conventions guiding aristocratic lifestyle were predicated on rank down to the minutest details of architectural, decorative and sartorial vogues. Dezaki's show is loyal to the parent text in stressing that "to determine a person's precise standing was no simple diversion but a matter of overriding importance" (p. 67). Thus, despite frequent claims advanced by classic historians regarding the nature of Heian civilization as an era of indolence and inaction, hierarchical priorities entailed that court life was often riven by turbulent tensions. In making the preservation of hierarchical barriers its priority, the set of stringent regulations governing daily existence at all levels of courtly intercourse inevitably led to discord. This is typified by *The Tale of Genji*'s opening as a veritable roster of tempestuous commotions unleashed by the Emperor's unorthodox attachment to a lowly concubine, which implies a violation of the very power basis on which the state thrives.

It is in its take on what Morris evocatively terms the "Cult of Beauty" that Dezaki's adaptation asserts its ability to mirror and appropriate its parent text's distinctive aesthetic with unmatched gusto. As the critic emphasizes, "refined standards of cultural appreciation and performance had become generally accepted values among members of the ruling class" (Morris, p. 170), to the point that lack of responsiveness to aesthetic matters rendered a Heian aristocrat as reproachable as a cowardly nobleman would be held to be in Western cultures of the same period (and indeed later epochs). Thus, "artistic sensibility" was held in higher esteem than "ethical goodness," while "style" was accorded precedence over "moral principles" and "good looks" ranked above "virtue" (p. 195). All facets of patrician Heian society corroborated this world picture, from architecture and interior design to vehicles and dress. The anime provides some of its most exquisite descriptive touches in the rendition of the accessories adorning the ladies' rooms, which are otherwise sparsely furnished in accordance with tradition. These include not only several painted screens that stand out as artworks in their own right but also writing equipment, incense burners, mirrors and musical instruments impeccably faithful to Heian style. It is in its approach to color that the aesthetic cultivation characteristic of Lady Murasaki's age proclaims itself most distinctively, evincing a passion for symbolic associations in all spheres of artistic production, as well as great sensitivity to the impact of the minutest nuances of chroma in the evocation of disparate moods.

The interplay of radiance and darkness is everywhere felt as a major factor in the Heian treatment of color, encapsulating the era's simultaneous devotion to pleasure and to the acknowledgment of its vaporousness. Dezaki's adaptation tirelessly demonstrates that it is in the domain of costume that the period's fascination with color is most palpably manifest, depicting hues that do not have exact equivalents in the Western world and of which not even contemporary Japanese audiences would necessarily know the names. The art of juxtaposing different shades in both male and female attire was of critical significance to the vestimentary sensibility of the age. In addition, the cult of beauty found ideal expression in the elaborate kind of kimono associated with court ladies of the era, which features pervasively in the anime and at times appears to infuse the duskiest of rooms with dancing iridescent light. Known as the *juunihitoe* (literally, "twelve-layer robe"), the garment came into fashion in the course of the tenth century. As the *Wikipedia* entry devoted to the *juunihitoe* explains, "The colours and the arrangements of the layers are very important. The colours have poetic names, such as 'crimson plum of the spring.' The only place where the layers are discernible is around the sleeves and the neck. The arrangements of the layers and their colours were a good indication to any outsider what taste and what rank the lady had" ("Juunihitoe"). In Heian fashion, a useful article on kimono history informs us, "Some two hundred rules were established which governed things like the combination of colors ... and how the colors of the outside and the lining should be harmonized. This resulted in certain colors being associated with November to February which were called *ume-gasane* or 'shades of the plum blossom.' Such kimonos were white on the outside and red on the inside. For March and April there was a combination called 'shades of wisteria,' a kimono with lavender outside and a blue lining. Winter and Spring had their own set with an outer garment of yellow and orange. The colors were set to mirror the seasons and their moods, showing just how closely the Japanese were attuned to the world of nature around them" ("Kimono History: The Heian Era").

Dezaki's anime respects these traditional rules throughout, to the point that any viewer acquainted with the basic chromatic conventions of the period would be in a position to guess in which season a particular scene is meant to take place by just looking at the colors of the female characters' costumes and without dwelling on the setting itself. Furthermore, the *juunihitoe* had an important part to play in the handling of gender relations in the Heian era: "Since a lady was not allowed to speak face-to-face to a male outsider, she could hold her sleeve up or use her opened fan to shield herself from inquiring looks. Communication to a suitor had to follow with her normally hiding behind the *sudare* (screen or blinds) in any case. The suitor could only see the sleeves of her *juunihitoe* that were peeking underneath the blinds" ("Juunihitoe"). One imagines that dressing and undressing must have constituted quite laborious tasks. The gracefully artless and fluid motion with which women's clothes tend to be shed in the context of Genji's trysts in the anime would seem to be something of a dramatic license on Dezaki's part. It should also be noted, however, that the director handles the act of dressing more realistically than its opposite — as evinced by the shots in which Roku no Kimi robes herself again at the end of a night of passion.

According to Wang, the profound significance held by colors in the Heian era is fully demonstrated by *The Tale of Genji*'s use of various hues as symbolic markers of the hero's lovers: "Genji's affection for his women is multi-color love.... His colors of love are individualized as green love for Fujitsubo, (idealistic, romantic impulsive symbolized by peacock, rain and tree), black love for Yuugao, (creative, mystic, transcendental symbolized by owl, night, dream and death) ... brown love for Murasaki, (heterogeneous, aggressive, passionate and paternal symbolized by horse, pyramid and mountain)." Furthermore, diverse hues are consistently associated with flowers that "stand as metaphors signifying different colors of love and erotic transformations." Genji also links his particular colors of love with flowers by ideating for each of the ladies "a floral name based on his artistic tastes." Thus, the color of love associated with Murasaki, brown, is identified by Genji with "red lotus," while her name designates "his most favorite flower" (Wang, p. 47). One witnesses an almost constant rhetorical movement from Genji's women to colors, from colors to flowers, from flowers to names, and from the names back to the women themselves in a pattern as cyclical as the rhythms governing the Heian era's Buddhist cosmos. In the original narrative, flowers also operate as a symbolic means of fostering harmony and concord among potentially adversarial figures.

This is borne out by the portion of the story in which Genji moves to a large estate, the Rokujou mansion: a magnificent palace where he can comfortably accommodate various ladies who have acquired special positions in his life and indeed bring together disparate strands of his experiences up to that point. These include Murasaki, Lady Rokujou's daughter Akikonomu, Genji's daughter by the Akashi Lady (a character not included in Dezaki's anime) and Tamakazura, Yuugao and Tou no Chuujou's daughter. An exemplary symbol of floral cordiality is provided by the scenes wherein Murasaki and Akikonomu exchange poems in their respective gardens, the spring garden and the autumn garden. The anime underscores the emblematic association of diverse female characters with flowers in its own fashion and chiefly through the presentation, in smooth succession, of frames of a female character and of the flower connected with her. Thus, the early flashback to Kiritsubo, emphasizing that her beauty was so proverbial that she was often compared to moonlight, intercuts images of Genji's mother and shots of candid moonflowers (a.k.a. morning glories). Analogously juxtaposed are the frames depicting Yuugao and the evening glory after which she is named, and Fujitsubo and the luxurious wisteria surrounding the pavilion to which she owes her own designation. (Aoi, though this point is not explicitly made in the anime, is named after the heartvine.)

While hues are undoubtedly accorded a privileged role in Heian culture, likewise vital is the part played by scents. As Brian Moeran maintains, the Heian era regarded the sense of smell as "a cultural pursuit" invested with "spiritual and aesthetic qualities." Insofar as "the kind of incense a nobleman or woman created" was generally held to mirror or even accentuate his or her intrinsic personality, "olfaction was also a moral construction of reality.... In general, Japanese believe that fragrance calms the spirit (which makes sense, given that it is also used to communicate with and soothe the ancestral spirits)" (Moeran, p. 4). The sense of smell has been conventionally relegated to the lowliest rank in the sensorium because it is held to be more intimately associated with the body's materiality than any of the other senses. In the West, in particular, the enduring legacy of ocularcentrism has served to perpetuate this trend. Heian attitudes to olfaction demonstrate that this sense may in fact rise to the status of an aesthetically sophisticated and culturally esteemed expressive vehicle. Women's garments were punctiliously imbued with delicate incense blends meant to communicate the wearer's individuality through her metonymic connection with a specific fragrance. Hence, while a female member of the aristocracy and royal retinue would not, as a rule, exhibit her face in public, she could assert her distinctive presence by means of the olfactory trail that followed her — a somewhat inevitable corollary of the custom whereby the same robes were often donned and even slept in for protracted periods of time. Dezaki's anime eagerly throws into relief the importance of smell in Genji's world by recourse to recurrent visual tropes. The most intriguing of these consists of frames in which the pattern on a woman's robe appears to detach itself from the fabric and to drift through space as a swarm of butterflies or a flowery cloud, suggestive of the particular scent exuding from the wearer's body in the form of inebriating plumes of multicolored mist. Another frequent image operating as a punctuating refrain throughout the series is the image of the incense burner — an item of interior design invested with great significance in the sparsely furnished rooms typical of traditional Japanese architecture. Although the image itself is insistently reiterated, repetition always entails an element of difference, and each of the frames devoted to the object dwells on a subtly individualized vessel. The uniqueness of the scent associated with each of Genji's lovers — and, by implication, of each of the women themselves — is succinctly encapsulated by the images of the censers located in their respective apartments. Impalpable aromas are thereby embodied as tangible icons.

In an article evocatively titled "A Wisp of Smoke. Scent and Character in *The Tale of Genji*," Aileen Gatten comments on the enduring importance of olfaction in Japanese culture with reference to the practice of the "incense ceremony," or Genji *kou* (香): a ritualized parlor game combining "the matching of rare sensations" with "easy sociability." This practice harks back to Heian culture, with its enthroning of the art of smell as an axial component of aristocratic etiquette requiring no less schooling and competence than calligraphic, poetic and musical pursuits. The critic underscores the imbrication of olfactory experience with gender politics in unequivocal terms, arguing that given Heian society's pronounced sexual segregation, "one of the few means of forming an opinion of one's companion was the scent emanating from his or her quarters" (Gatten, p. 36). Dezaki's smell-centered shots capture this atmosphere with unsurpassed visual dexterity, deploying the synesthetic powers of the animated image to evoke sensations normally unattainable by the eye alone. Just as the colors used in the assemblage of the *juunihitoe* match the symbolic connotations of different seasons, so the Heian codification of the language of olfaction relies on six fundamental fragrances, each of which is equated to a different season. "Plum Blossom is linked with spring, Lotus Leaf with summer, Chamberlain with the autumn wind, and Black with deepest winter" (p. 37). As Liza Dalby explains, the participants in an incense ceremony express their evaluations of particular fragrances by means of a "scoring system" using "a set of symbols coded to 52 of the 54 chapters of *The Tale of Genji*." Thus, a potent cultural connection can again be seen to obtain between Lady Murasaki's eleventh-century milieu and the incense ceremony, even though this practice actually originated in a ludic ritual formalized "in the fourteenth century." The symbols used to describe the olfactory experience are now well-established "design motifs" with autonomous ornamental value and consist of "combinations of five vertical bars joined at the top by horizontal bars in different combinations" (Dalby).

The foregoing analysis will hopefully have made it quite clear that both Lady Murasaki's novel and Dezaki's adaptation of it accord axial significance to gender relations in all three forms these could assume in Heian culture: i.e., marriage as primary wife, marriage as concubine and casual affair. *The Tale of Genji*'s historical situation in the Heian era provides the basis for this thematic emphasis insofar as its women, as long as they belonged to the upper echelons, held a central position in the cultural sphere even though they were still routinely excluded from political affairs. Stanley-Baker, as noted earlier in this chapter, posits the Heian era's cultivation of a distinctively feminine aesthetic as an almost unprecedented phenomenon. Tyler argues that what is most remarkable about the treatment of gender relations in *The Tale of Genji* is that even though Genji's world is a male-dominated society in which a woman's "main concern, and that of her entire household, was that she should escape the gaze of any unrelated male," it is nonetheless the case that "gender relations in *The Tale of Genji* ... are humane in tone. There is no trace of physical violence against women, nor is there any unreasonable insistence on purity, virginity, and so on. Men expect women to overlook many things, but they may also do their best to reciprocate" (Tyler 2002).

Several factors militated in favor of women's cultural ascendancy. Especially important among them, given Lady Murasaki's particular vocation, was the introduction of a specifically Japanese script that enabled women to engage in literary composition despite their exclusion from the scholarly realm of Chinese letters—the sole available medium up to that point in history. According to Shirane, prose writing employing the indigenous script and the vernacular was not taken seriously at first, largely due to its uncertain status at both the thematic and the formal levels, resulting in "a hybrid form that seemed to be reinvented at every stage in its development" and related assumption that it was just "a frivolous pastime" for "women and children who could not read Chinese" (Shirane 1987, p. xvi). Nevertheless, the form—broadly termed *monogatari* (物語)—did hold the undeniable advantage of supplying female writers with a way into the practice of literature. Moreover, when Lady Murasaki's narrative was finally recognized as a work of great richness and sophistication, it was not held in esteem simply as a story but also, more significantly, as an eminent "sourcebook for poets" and "a guide to poetic diction" (pp. xvi-xvii), which contributed vitally to the consolidation of the author's standing despite her traditionally marginalized gender. Hence, the emancipatory potentialities of linguistic reform must not be ignored for they played a key part in the redefinition of women's lives in the Heian era. Okada further reinforces the connection between femininity and the *monogatari* tradition, arguing that with the advent of a distinctively Japanese script, "women eagerly and skillfully occupied the subject positions of writing in a linguistic medium named after them. Known by the term 'feminine hand' (*onna-de*), which signified *hiragana* writing, their discourse employed one of the two types of phonetic syllabary developed to transcribe the sounds of the native language. The term contrasted with 'masculine hand' (*otoko-de*), which signified Chinese writing practised in Japan" (Okada, p. 160). It is also crucial to note that "in addition to their own discursive mode," aristocratic ladies in Lady Murasaki's age also owned "their own discursive space" in the guise of the "salon": a place in which women could gather, within a thoroughly "organized" system, "around an imperial princess, empress, or other high-ranking woman" to write and engage in critical debates (p. 162).

However, we must not forget, as Morris points out, that "despite the relatively favorable social and economic situation of Heian women, the conditions of polygamy made their actual position precarious" (Morris, p. 241). Although a woman was entitled to the inheritance and retention of property, she could not hope to manage it in the absence of male assistance, and this rendered her highly dependent on the imperative to obtain and maintain a man's protective love regardless of how many other women might also feature in his life. According to Tyler, it is also worth observing that "in *The Tale of Genji* the simple existence of another wife or quasi-wife may not alarm a lady too seriously. What matters more is the other woman's intrinsic rank.... A formal wife seems to have been prepared to accept the existence of other wives or quasi-wives as long as none threatened her own standing with her husband" (Tyler 2002). These ideas are profoundly relevant to both Lady Murasaki's novel and Dezaki's series insofar as the familial power struggles of which Genji's mother is a helpless victim form the story's main premise and indirectly pave the way to many subsequent developments in the protagonist's own life. The most eloquent plea for the sanctity of true love in contrast with socially sanctioned bonds is voiced by Genji's elder half-brother Suzaku shortly after his ascent to the throne. Although the hero's half-brother is obviously not blessed with the charisma proverbially associated with the sparkling Genji, he is consistently depicted by Dezaki as magnanimous and sensitive. This is most memorably evinced by his clement treatment of Genji when Kikoden craftily masterminds his downfall. Suzaku is even willing to condone his wife Roku no Kimi's amorous involvement with Genji in the belief that fond as he is of the lady, he has no right to legislate where her heart lies.

Lady Murasaki's work, in this perspective, does not constitute simply one instance of Heian female writing among many. Its take on both established forms and genres (the *monogatari*, the courtly romance, the bildungsroman) and myriad sociohistorical facets of her epoch in fact indicates that *The Tale of Genji* represents a radical intervention in the field. As Bowring argues, in Lady Murasaki's milieu, it was common for female texts to bear the marks of sexual discrimination. Unlike their male counterparts, they tended to contain "few dates, few names, no references to political realities," as though their authors were trying to "cut away that part of the world" in which women could not hold any authority. Lady Murasaki, by contrast, engages adventurously with "history and politics," thus standing out as the first female author in her culture capable of breaking free from "the autobiographical straitjacket that her contemporaries had so successfully created for themselves" (Bowring,

p. 17). What is most impressive about both Lady Murasaki's attitude to her hero's exploits and Dezaki's adaptive take on the ancient narrative is their shared ability to draw the modern reader or viewer into the psychological dimension of gender politics, allowing us to experience it intimately and affectively rather than merely as a social reality or historical phenomenon. This strategy is instrumental in dispelling the prejudicial reservations of audiences inclined to doubt the ancient text's current relevance and accessibility. The representation of jealousy as the direst of human afflictions is a prime example of Lady Murasaki's psychological acuity. The anime itself resonantly validates this contention in the dramatization of Genji's tortuous relationship with Lady Rokujou and of its wide-ranging repercussions not only on the protagonist's personal existence but also on the destinies of other women he loves. Dezaki articulates his personal vision of gender relations in the Heian period by focusing on a relatively small selection, over its eleven installments, of the women loved by Genji in the corresponding portion of Lady Murasaki's novel (i.e., as noted, chapters 1–12). This strategy enables the director to concentrate closely on the influence exerted by those ladies on the shaping and evolution of the hero's identity without diluting its significance through the incorporation of digressive episodes — something in which the original author was, by contrast, free to indulge due to the massively greater breadth of her own work. Tyler maintains that while it is important to acknowledge that Genji is central to the story, this recognition ought not to induce us to overlook "the experience and importance of the women whose absorbingly difficult relationships with him give the work its most accessible appeal," for "Genji and the tale's female characters of course stand in a reciprocal relationship to each other, as do living men and women" (Tyler 2009, pp. 7–8).

At the same time, in examining the subtle balance of power in which the Shining Prince and his lovers operate, it is crucial to appreciate both the magnitude of the hero's striving and the overall integrity evinced by his treatment of women. According to Donald Evans, Genji "predates Tristan. The modern era is filled with such stories of reckless, hopeless romance. Importantly, Genji is not a cad. Unlike Don Juan, his interest is never in the conquest. Unlike Don Giovanni, who humiliates Donna Elvira for belaboring their affair, Genji never forgets any woman he has loved" (in *The Tale of Genji Study Guide*, p. 156). Relatedly, Genji does not function simply as a narrative device deployed to string together a chain of erotic exploits, since the parts he plays in relation to his numerous lovers vary significantly from case to case, and several of his entanglements carry a significance that evidently transcends romantic boundaries. The most blatant instance is the hero's liaison with Fujitsubo: a dramatic complication that cannot be dismissed purely as an instance of amorous extravagance due to its far-reaching social implications:

"The major issue," Tyler contends, "is not outrageous behavior by a son toward his father, although this is bad enough. Rather, it is the implied possibility of a break in the legitimate imperial line" (Tyler, "*Genji Monogatari* and *The Tale of Genji*").

Dezaki's reconfiguration of his source delivers a number of structural alterations based on the adoption of telescoping, capsulation and synthetic collage. It is hence worth considering in some detail the anime's approach to Lady Murasaki's text at the principally organizational level. (Please note that even when plot details are outlined, there is no danger of incurring in spoilers in this instance, since the series does not depend on the withholding of outcomes for dramatic effect but frankly anticipates the likely consequences of its characters' actions from the outset.) As intimated earlier in this discussion, Lady Murasaki begins her narrative *ab ovo* in keeping with Heian literary tastes, describing Kiritsubo's relationship with the Emperor and victimization by jealous courtiers, Genji's birth and his mother's premature demise, Fujitsubo's introduction into the imperial household as a concubine and the protagonist's development up to his Coming of Age and betrothal to Aoi. The structure to which Lady Murasaki adheres in the opening segment of the saga is fundamentally linear and chronological — although, it must be stressed, this approach is by no stretch of the imagination dominant in *The Tale of Genji* as a whole, where conventional syntagmatic ordering is in fact repeatedly shunned in favor of crosstemporal leaps. In Dezaki's anime, conversely, the opening installment moves back and forth in time between Genji's childhood and the present. This format demonstrates the director's preference for a multitemporal approach to storytelling, while offering him scope for reflection on the enduring impact of the past and its emotive legacy upon the entire course of the hero's life. Genji's mother features only in the context of flashbacks and is said to have perished shortly after the child's birth. Like Lady Murasaki, Dezaki allows some time to elapse between Genji's delivery and Kiritsubo's departure — supposedly, because Heian Japan believed that dying at childbirth was a heinous sin.

Again in keeping with Heian preferences in literary matters, Lady Murasaki then devotes a substantial section to the so-called conversation-on-a-rainy-night set piece, a subset of the "judgment" (*sadame*) formula, wherein Genji and his male associates discuss the characteristics of various stereotypes of femininity. This segment of the novel is followed by the narrative's first direct engagement with Genji's amorous habits as it portrays the hero's insistent — and vain — pursuit of the character ot Utsusemi ("Lady of the Locust Shell"). The anime adaptation skips these occurrences. However, its opening episode is sufficient to give the audience a clear sense of Genji's "diverse and magnificent" erotic palate — as the character of Tou no Chuujou ironically describes it. Thus far, the only woman accorded unequivocal prominence by the series is Fujitsubo. Aoi is also ushered into the action but solely to indicate the coldness pervading her relationship with Genji and with no hint at her future importance in the story. Lady Rokujou, the next lady to whom Dezaki draws dramatic attention by means of practically a whole installment, is almost casually introduced by the source text with the information that the protagonist has been seeing her for some time, just before launching into a comprehensive elaboration of Genji's doomed relationship with Yuugao. When, having devoted ample space to Lady Rokujou, Dezaki turns to Yuugao, the anime's handling of the events centered on this young female closely mirrors their treatment by Lady Murasaki. Yuugao's sudden death as a result of an evil spirit's intervention (putatively at the behest of a jealous rival) and Genji's resulting depression are accordingly chronicled in detail. Like the source text, the show is eager to emphasize the fascination with vulnerability and innocence as a major trait of Genji's personality. (Both Lady Murasaki's narrative and the anime make it also possible to extrapolate, at this juncture, the ages of various key personae — it is therefore safe to assume that Genji is now seventeen while Yuugao is nineteen, which makes Lady Rokujou twenty-five, Fujitsubo twenty-two and Aoi twenty-one.)

In both the original story and the series, Genji meets another female destined to play a pivotal role in his overall life trajectory just as he begins to recover from his long illness: Murasaki. A child around ten years of age, Murasaki is immediately revealed by Lady Murasaki's narrative to be the daughter of Fujitsubo's elder brother, Prince Hyoubu, which makes it incontrovertibly obvious why the kid should remind Genji of Fujitsubo. The novel also tells us that Genji wishes to adopt the child but is not allowed to do so by protective agents who automatically suspect that he wishes to exploit her sexually. Genji is finally in a position to take charge of Murasaki upon the death of her grandmother, who has been looking after the girl in the aftermath of her expulsion from the paternal home due to the interference of an evil stepmother (a popular topos in Heian romantic prose). A final obstacle arises when Prince Hyoubu resolves to take Murasaki back after all but Genji draconianly overcomes it by simply abducting her. In the anime, we do not meet Murasaki again, following her initial encounter with the protagonist, until a fairly advanced stage in the drama, by which time she is already established in Genji's household. It is even later in the show that the reason for Murasaki's stunning resemblance to Fujitsubo is disclosed.

The two characters are also connected by their names, Fujitsubo meaning "Lady of the Wisteria Pavilion" and Murasaki "lavender" or "purple"— i.e., a color deemed highly fashionable in Heian society, produced by grinding gromwell roots. It is also worth stressing, in this regard, that in the eminently color-oriented aesthetic sensibility of the Heian age, purple played an especially important role. It covered an impressive variety of hues which ranged, as Norma Field elucidates, "from the palest of lavenders or pinks to the deepest red, almost black, blues" (Field, p. 161) and strict rules dictated that "only the highest-ranking of the aristocracy could wear purple, the dark hues being restricted to princes of the blood of the fourth order or above and officials of the second and third ranks. It also connoted imperial rule, Buddhist law, and even the Taoist paradise" (p. 162). An occurrence of momentous consequence in Genji's character development, Murasaki's introduction into the story is handled by Dezaki with fidelity to the source text. In the anime, as in the parent narrative, the girl enters the action with an emotive vocal eruption triggered by her playmate Inuki's malicious release of her pet sparrow from its makeshift home in the incense basket. Genji's gaze is instantly captivated by the sight of a child that bears an uncanny resemblance to his beloved. As Field observes, the connection between Murasaki and Fujitsubo perceived by Genji upon this accidental sighting is so potent as to cause something of a magical "transubstantiation (of niece into aunt, of copy into original, or metonymy into metaphor)" (p. 160). Bloom proffers an analogous hypothesis in arguing that "Lady Murasaki, more than nine hundred years before Freud, understood that all erotic transferences were substitute-formations for earlier attachments" (Bloom, p. 5).

Murasaki clearly stands, to a significant degree, as a replica of Fujitsubo in Genji's love life in much the same way as Fujitsubo herself stands as a replica of Kiritsubo in the Emperor's love life. It would be erroneous to assume, however, that the two women's shared role as duplicates — or adaptations — makes them in any way inferior to either the models they are supposed to repeat or other members of the hero's metaphorical harem. In fact, they carry substantial weight as principal and autonomous dramatis personae in both the novel and the anime. As argued earlier, Lady Murasaki questions the conventional subordination of fiction to historiography, based on a doxastic trust in the de facto reliability of official records, with a unique alloy of irony and grace. In enthroning two characters of replicative standing as key dramatic agents, she advances a cognate philosophy insofar as this ploy enables her to debunk the presumed superiority of the original over its adaptation, and thus implicitly provide validation for the independent import of subsequent adaptive works taking *The Tale of Genji* as their launchpad — of which Dezaki's series is a resplendent contemporary instance. In this respect, Murasaki and Fujitsubo could be regarded as incarnations *en abyme* of the very notion of adaptation as a textual formation that does not occupy a secondary, parasitical position vis-à-vis its source but actually holds individual signifying value. The original author suggests that the nature of Genji's attraction to Murasaki, shaped as it is by the bizarre logic of displaced yearning, is sexual from the start, although she also shows that the protagonist has the decency to wait until she turns fourteen before taking her as his bride and consummating the bond. The anime subtly redefines the original perspective. Murasaki, as the dispossessed princess of classic fairy tale, sees Genji as something of a Prince Charming or Knight in Shining Armor, while to Genji, she epitomizes the childhood innocence he has never known. It is not until the final portion of the anime that the erotic dimension of Genji and Murasaki's connection becomes manifest and even then, its onscreen rendition remains fundamentally Platonic. Significantly, the relationship between Genji and Murasaki grows increasingly intimate in inverse proportion to the hero's ever-decreasing involvement in public affairs caused by his steep fall from grace toward the end of the series.

Both the novel and the show devote their next crucial moments to the dramatization of the events leading to the conception and birth of Genji and Fujitsubo's child, with the differences outlined earlier. The novel does not univocally follow the revamping of Genji and Fujitsubo's impossible relationship: in fact, it takes time to meander on the outskirts of the sprawling empire of its hero's erotic pursuits by chronicling Genji's abortive affair with the pathetic Suetsumuhana ("Sunflower" or "Safflower"). The anime, by contrast, only shifts its focus from that crucial relationship to develop another bond bound to grow in importance as the story progresses. It accordingly devotes a brief, yet very poignant, sequence to Genji and Aoi's achievement of unprecedented intimacy, as a result of which yet another child fathered by the protagonist will soon come into the world. The show then exhibits one of its most proficient feats of adaptive editing as Dezaki integrates the occurrences portrayed in two of the novel's key chapters (7 and 8) into a single and vibrantly paced episode. These are the segments devoted by Lady Murasaki to the Festival of the Red Leaves, where the Emperor proclaims Fujitsubo Empress and announces that her newborn child will become crown prince once Kokiden's son has ascended the throne, and the Festival of the Cherry Blossoms, where Genji's lust paves the way to his debacle as he seduces Kokiden's sister Oborozukiyo ("Misty Moon of Spring"). In the anime, the key event is the Festival of the Cherry Blossoms and is said to be held to celebrate the birth of the Emperor's (in fact, Genji's) son. On this occasion, the protagonist gives a magnificent display of his excellence of both body and mind by performing the traditional dance known as "Waves of the Blue Sea." At the end of the night, inebriated by drink and the spell of the misty moon, Genji embarks on a dangerous liaison with Kokiden's sister, here referred to as Roku no Kimi, the "Sixth Princess," with no inkling of her status. (Please note that in the original, Oborozukiyo and Roku no Kimi are two separate characters.) Whereas in the parent narrative Kokiden has been known to the reader from the start, in the series, the formidable lady does not make an overt appearance until this stage in the action, at which point we are also informed that Roku no Kimi is betrothed to the Heir Apparent. The reasons for the unique dangerousness of Genji's affair with Roku no Kimi thus gain urgency, in the anime, through their sudden and roller-coaster exposure. In the source text, by contrast, they come as a logical consequence of factors we are already familiar with.

In Lady Murasaki's text, the events that ensue travel fluidly between the political and the personal in the space of four more chapters (9–12). These chronicle Genji's father's abdication and half-brother Suzaku's ascent to the throne, Lady Rokujou's grudge against Aoi, resulting from a tragic incident held to have insulted the older woman's standing and conducive to yet another lethal curse, and Aoi's death shortly after her son's delivery. (A decorous time gap is again inserted between birth and death for the aforementioned reason.) It is at this point that Genji abruptly turns to Murasaki with the intention of becoming a good husband and hence, ideally, a better man altogether. Shortly after Aoi's demise, the only two key women left in Genji's life also recede from the scene, as Lady Rokujou relocates to Ise, where her daughter is due to take the post of priestess, while Fujitsubo takes the vows as a Buddhist nun and enters a life of stark self-denial. As Shirane observes, whereas "the social romance could be regarded as a movement in which an alienated or lost individual is reintegrated in society, the spiritual quest moves in the opposite direction" (Shirane 1987, p. 185). Lady Murasaki is keen to emphasize that Genji cannot reinvent himself from one day to the next by depicting his rekindling of the nefarious affair with Oborozukiyo and, as a result of his being caught in the act by her father the Minister of the Right, his persecution by Kokiden who is hell-bent on the Shining Prince's disgrace having resented his very existence from the moment he left Kiritsubo's womb. It is as a direct outcome of his ruthless demonization by Suzaku's mother that Genji, now aged twenty-six, resolves to sail to the rustic and wind-swept region of Suma with just a handful of loyal attendants. This aspect of the original yarn reflects a well-documented historical reality since, as Bowring emphasizes, the "dominant political fact" in Heian society "was that the Emperor, at the spiritual and psychological centre, was politically impotent and under the influence of whichever aristocratic family happened to be in a position to take decisions" (Bowring, p. 1). The anime script throws this idea into relief through Tou no Chuujou, who comments that while Genji's father was on the throne, the Minister of the Left (i.e., Tou no Chuujou's own father) held an influential position, yet never presumed to steer governmental policies to personal advantage, whereas Suzaku's ascension has signaled the advent of the Minister of the Right (i.e., Kokiden and Roku no Kimi's father) as a major force and this nobleman's aggressive tactics result in his faction's unscrupulous interference with imperial governance.

Women's paradoxical position as simultaneously active and passive presences in the Heian political system is paradigmatically communicated by Fujitsubo's part in both the source text and the anime. This character is accorded a far more prominent role in the anime than it is in the original saga. The greater temporal breadth of Lady Murasaki's text enables it to trace the character's significance over a more protracted trajectory, culminating with Fujitsubo's emplacement as an influential agent in her son's court and the recipient of all the privileges of a retired ruler. Yet, her overall presence is understated and situated in the margins of visibility rather than at its focal point, and thus posited as stationary rather than explicitly active, as if to intimate that the clandestine nature of her bond with the hero makes it imperative to shield her privacy. Making the most of the emphatically visual and dynamic qualities of his medium, Dezaki chooses to enthrone Fujitsubo as a dramatic fulcrum from beginning to end. Importantly, the last dialogical sequence presented by the anime pivots on this character and her active voice as she professes undying love for Genji. The very final shot is devoted to the hero himself but divests him of language, featuring instead an allusively brief voiceover spoken by the narrator. In positing Fujitsubo as a pivotal presence, Dezaki foregrounds the source text's preoccupation with what Field describes as the dichotomy of "sacred and profane" (Field, p. 22). As intimated, the imperial system is predicated on the myth of the supreme ruler as the incarnation of the sacred. Nevertheless, this supposedly superior reality cannot totally divorce itself from the realm of the secular and the mundane since "The issue of succession, implicated in the political machinations revolving around women (i.e., potential mothers) forever betrays the presence of the profane at the heart of divine rule" (p. 23). Dezaki's presentation of the affair involving Genji and Fujitsubo as an axial component lends special weight to these issues. It indeed stresses that the sacred and the profane are inextricably intertwined by not only highlighting the infiltration of the former by the latter as a result of a woman's instrumentality in the politics of succession but also polluting the transcendental purity of imperial authority through adultery and metaphorical incest. Although critics are divided over the issue of whether or not Genji and Fujitsubo's relationship should be considered incestuous, the anime screenplay explicitly refers to Fujitsubo as Genji's "older sister and mother."

Dezaki's show follows quite faithfully the events presented by Lady Murasaki as the trigger of Genji's downfall, yet with the infusion of editing and cinematic maneuvers that enable the director to impart his anime with a distinctive flavor of its own. Particularly remarkable, in this regard, is

Dezaki's knack of varying the action's tempo. Thus, while the episode introducing Roku no Kimi is by and large deliberately paced, the segment that follows exhibits a rapid accumulation of dexterously intercut occurrences. Like the original text, Dezaki's anime alternates between the public and the private. In the political sphere, we see the Emperor abdicate and Genji's guardianship of his little boy conclusively ratified. In the personal domain, Aoi's pregnancy is announced, while Lady Rokujou's mounting frustration with Genji's protracted absence from her residence is concurrently exposed. The two dimensions intersect when the new Emperor, who admires Genji deeply even though he is well aware of his own inferiority in the face of the Shining Prince's polyhedric talents, appoints the hero as Imperial Messenger for the Summer Festival and this celebration, in turn, marks the genesis of Lady Rokujou's grudge against Aoi. In the course of the splendid procession where everybody hopes to catch a glimpse of the charismatic Imperial Messenger, a quarrel erupts between the bearers of Aoi's and Lady Rokujou's carriages, culminating with the ungallant remark that the "mistress" must give way to the "wife," and the older woman's vehicle is overturned, thus inflicting on its occupant an unpardonable insult. As Lady Rokujou's resentment grows, the malign spirit that seems to function as her doppelganger throughout the series gains control of her psyche and engineers Aoi's possession, long illness and eventual death shortly after the delivery of her and Genji's baby boy Yuugiri. Dezaki's depiction of Lady Rokujou at this critical juncture in the series finds a perfect match in Field's vivid portrayal of Genji's arguably most complicated lover. The critic emphasizes Lady Rokujou's "distinguished" standing as a "possessing spirit" within a "tradition rich in ghosts" and views "this manifestation of her character" as a wellhead of "abiding interest, even now when the darkness of Heian estates, so conducive to the play of spirits, has given way to well-lit rooms" (p. 45). Most importantly, as far as the anime's diegesis is concerned, it is what Field terms the character's "bifurcated self" that enables Lady Murasaki to realize "a concentration of being unreplicated by other heroines" (p. 61). The character's knack of branching off into discordant personalities that may coexist harmoniously one moment and clash catastrophically the next supplies Dezaki with an invaluable pivot through which the protagonist's ordeal can be smoothly imparted with psychological and dynamic coherence.

Once it has become incontrovertibly obvious that Genji's fall from grace is inevitable due to his illicit liaison with Roku no Kimi, the anime's pace slows down to a considerable degree. This is achieved principally through the displacement of action as a cinematographical priority in favor of meditative and dialogical scenes. Those devoted to Genji's final farewells to Lady Rokujou and Fujitsubo, specifically, could be said to emblematize the very essence of *mono no aware*, suggesting that Genji has reached a stage in his life whence no turning back is possible. Once again, the show moves smoothly between personal and collective preoccupations, with poignant moments of emotional intimacy centered on Genji and Murasaki at one end of the spectrum, and tense exchanges between rival political forces (i.e., the supporters of the Minister of the Left and the Minister of the Right) at the other. Despite its overall preference for dialogical drama, the final part of Dezaki's series is not in any way stagnant. In fact, the few action sequences it does contain are endowed with scintillating dynamism. The fight in which Genji and Tou no Chuujou vanquish quite effortlessly a gang of thugs keen to seize the hero to ingratiate themselves with the authorities is especially notable as an instance of kinetic ebullience. In the episodes leading to Genji's departure for the desolate shores of Suma following his spiritual marriage to Murasaki in the blissful light of the full moon, the most memorable sequences are arguably the ones revolving around Genji and Suzaku. Although the new Emperor has no choice but to demote his half-brother, he is only too eager to be as lenient as possible toward him and goes on respecting Genji as a man of unequaled worth despite his apparent flaws. For Suzaku, Genji could never cease to be the Shining Prince. A paradigmatic illustration of this aspect of the adaptation is the scene — also flooded by moonlight — in which Suzaku, modestly conceding that his terpsichorean skills are paltry, asks Genji to perform with him in private the aforecited "Waves of the Blue Sea." As the Emperor and the disgraced retainer harmonize their bodies to the dance, the entire hierarchical structure at the core of the Heian system appears to collapse as though it were no more substantial than a decrepit paper screen.

An intriguing structural aspect of the anime, which closely mirrors the source text's orchestration and simultaneously marks its eschewal of formats more typical of Western prose and drama, lies with Dezaki's handling of narrative progression. This does not pivot on intimate interplay within a cast of fixed personae but rather on the juxtaposition of relatively discreet strands. Lady Murasaki, argues Shirane, likewise "conceived of the *monogatari* as a changeable entity built on the autonomy of each part" (Shirane 1987, p. 155). The foregoing analysis will hopefully have succeeded in showing that the series posits five female characters and the emotional travails associated with them as axial to Genji's bildungsroman: namely, Fujitsubo, Lady Rokujou, Yuugao, Aoi and Murasaki. However, these threads are not systematically interwoven. In fact, the key ladies are not seen to interact dramatically with one another as the action progresses. Lady Rokujou and Aoi do come into contact at the time of the notorious carriage mishap but even though the accident leads to lethal consequences, the two characters do not meet face to face. Similarly, an important connection is said to exist between Fujitsubo and

Murasaki but the two women never communicate or feature in the same scene. Thus, Dezaki seems primarily interested in presenting his narrative blocks as components of a horizontal arrangement open to multifarious ramifications, not in subordinating them to a vertical hierarchy intended to culminate in clear-cut resolutions. The director is, however, keen to highlight internal correspondences between different characters as a means of braiding together distinct portions of the story. An especially critical parallel can be seen to obtain between Kiritsubo and Fujitsubo as favorite concubines. In addition, Dezaki throws into relief Genji's tendency to fall for women of inferior social standing (e.g., Yuugao) and, in so doing, implicitly uncloaks the hero's propensity to follow closely in his father's footsteps when it comes to a dangerous disregard for rank. These parallels could be seen as an ineluctable outcome of Genji's psychological shaping by his forebears' actions, and specifically by an immoderate passion deemed illicit by the Heian imperial system. Although Genji's tactics of constant deferral as he shifts from love to love and involvement in the contingent sphere of politics help him keep the legacy of the past at bay, his actions actually end up replicating submerged events dating back to his conception and infancy, with his premature loss of a uniquely significant female figure as the critical factor. While the Shining Prince might appear to have adequately negotiated orphanhood and learnt to live with loneliness, the reiteration of his primal trauma upon relinquishing Fujitsubo figuratively reactivates the infantile shock with intensified vigor. It is in response to this twin experience of severe emotional deprivation that Genji embarks on an amorous career which, due to the ephemeral nature of each of its stages, seems subliminally designed to repeat the drama of loss ad infinitum, feasibly in a desperate effort to bind its negative affects and hence come to terms with its inexorability. It is as if Lady Murasaki's — and, by extension, Dezaki's — hero were striving to reconcile the life drive that fosters love above all else and the death drive that declares love all but unthinkable, and thus transmute the agony caused by the remembrance of traumatic experiences into a cathartic journey of both the imagination and the senses.

The most dramatic correspondence established by Lady Murasaki's narrative is the fatalistically painful analogy between the climax of Genji's emotional life in his youth — the consummation of his love for Fujitsubo and resulting conception of a son destined for the throne — and the events surrounding the protagonist's eventual downfall (chapters 34–41). These events find inception with the Shining Prince's marriage to the Third Princess, Emperor Suzaku's most treasured daughter, upon Suzaku's retirement and monastic renunciation of the world. When Genji leaves his mansion to visit the ailing Murasaki, one more victim of spirit possession, the young Kashiwagi (Tou no Chuujou's son) entertains a clandestine liaison with the hero's new wife and makes her pregnant. Thus, Genji's transgression against his father is here replicated with tragic irony by Kashiwagi's affair with the Third Princess. As in the previous case, the truly unpardonable crime does not lie so much with the breach of marital fidelity as with the potential violation of the political system implied by the act. Moreover, Genji's own origins and early stages of character formation eerily presage many of the subsequent events in his life—and particularly the ones destined to lead to the gravest and most irreversible repercussions for both the hero and his whole society. At the beginning of the narrative, we are informed that the Minister of the Left has chosen Genji as his daughter Aoi's future husband in preference to the Heir Apparent despite the younger brother's uncertain standing. We also learn, as mentioned, that Suzaku is the son of an especially ambitious and vindictive imperial spouse, Kikoden, and that the latter detests Genji due to the Emperor's fondness for both the boy himself and his late mother Kiritsubo. When Suzaku asks Genji to marry the Third Princess, he symbolically wreaks an unconscious revenge on his half-brother by roping him into a catastrophic relationship. Such a move should only, it must be emphasized, be regarded as unconscious, for Suzaku seems genuinely attached to Genji despite the Shining Prince's superiority in all areas—an aspect of the source text to which the anime is pointedly faithful—and to derive no pleasure from Genji's debacle. The correspondence here outlined demonstrates that despite its apparent structural looseness, Lady Murasaki's text is so scrupulously orchestrated that Genji's end is directly connected with his beginnings, and each narrative fragment has a distinct and unique place within the text's overall puzzle.

In choosing to end the series with Genji's journey to Suma, and hence an adaptation of events presented in the twelfth chapter of Lady Murasaki's work, Dezaki makes quite an imaginative choice. Indeed, it is so common for editions of *The Tale of Genji* destined for both students and the general public to encompass just the first nine chapters of the original saga that one could easily have expected the director to follow suit. In stretching the drama's span to the hero's exile, the anime gives itself a chance to reflect on crucial aspects of Japanese thought directly informed by Buddhist ideals: namely, the value of self-detachment from materialistic pursuits as the crux of a person's spiritual journey. This concept complements dialectically the aesthetic principle of *mono no aware*. As Shirane maintains, while the latter entails "a sensitivity to all, particularly love and nature, that gives rise to deep emotions," self-detachment "demands resolution, stoicism, selflessness." Yet, this does not render the two concepts adversarial, let alone incompatible: "instead of simply being at odds with *mono no aware*, the drama of renunciation reveals once more the emotional depth, the sensitivity, and the vulnerability of the individual" and thus confirms *The Tale of Genji*'s overarching preoccupation with "the aesthetics of pathos, fragility, weakness, and uncertainty" (Shirane 1987, p. 201). In extending his show's purview to moments in the source text that signal the saga's descent into darkness, Dezaki is in a position to harness his medium to the exploration of humanity's murkier connotations instead of encouraging the viewer to bask unreflectively in the Shining Prince's ephemeral aura.

Furthermore, while the departure for Suma occurs in Lady Murasaki's twelfth chapter, the narrative of renunciation dramatized by Dezaki in his closing installment also captures, albeit obliquely rather than through overt onscreen adaptation, major preoccupations evinced by the original author at several points in her text. The two key moments recording Genji's contemplation of his spiritual fate — and the prospect of damnation to which a life spent exclusively in the service of carnal delights is likely to have paved the way — take place early in the episode. The first is the pre-credit sequence chronicling a dream set in a bleak snow-swept landscape. This sequence harks back to a previous oneiric passage capturing Fujitsubo's delirious vision just as she is about to give birth. This also staged in the context of a snow storm and dramatizes Fujitsubo and Genji's vain attempt to flee the reality of court life and give their love free rein, when it is clearly already too late. In the subsequent snowy sequence, Genji struggles through the blizzard, his heart already pierced by two arrows and about to be penetrated by one more fatal bolt, and chances upon Fujitsubo and Myoubu in their monastic garb. Genji tells the holy women that he is beyond salvation and therefore deserves the severest of punishments. When his beloved encouragingly advises him to pray to Amida Buddha, the protagonist ripostes that he has no hope of redemption as long as the mere thought of an unclothed body is sufficient to lead his senses astray. Moreover, he is still powerless to suppress his "forbidden love" and would welcome eternal damnation in exchange for just one chance to embrace his beloved again. In fact, he would even be willing to accept rebirth as an Asura — a demon possessed by extreme passions that thrives on carnage. The second key sequence revolves around Genji's visit to his late father's funerary monument, traditionally constructed out of a huge stone, just before leaving for Suma. The former Emperor materializes before Genji in a truly classic scene paying full homage to Japanese culture's inveterate fascination with ghostly matters. (Like any respectable indigenous specter, he has invisible feet.) The supernatural entity makes it incontrovertibly clear, in this scene, that Genji's sole hope of salvation ultimately rests not with external absolution but with the young man's preparedness to *forgive himself*.

The strictest forms of Buddhism maintain that to interrupt the ceaseless revolution of the wheel of karma, it is necessary to cut oneself off from desire as the ultimate root of all human afflictions through intense discipline and, by embracing the doctrine that the self is non-existent, eventually access the enlightened state of nirvana beyond the rhythms of Eternal Recurrence. Although, in principle, all human beings can aspire to nirvana, it is quite clear that in classic Buddhism, only few special beings possess the intellectual resources and perseverance needed to achieve that goal. However, as Bowring points out, "The kind of Buddhism (Mahayana) that lies at the heart of the *Genji* was more compassionate and was based on a shift from enlightenment for the few to salvation for all; a shift from meditation to devotion" (Bowring, p. 9). In this religious perspective, the karmic cycle is not seen as utterly unbreakable by ordinary people and salvation is therefore attainable even by those who have not undertaken rigorous training intended to lead to the haven of illumination. Of the various characters populating Buddhist mythology that are held to have achieved nirvana but to have chosen to abide among common humans to assist their quest for salvation, the figure of Amida was accorded a privileged place in Lady Murasaki's days. Amida was said to have "promised eventual salvation to all who simply trusted him and had faith," Bowring explains. "His paradise (known as the Pure Land) was not nirvana itself but ... was certainly outside the karmic wheel and once gained there was no backsliding. This quickly became the paradise to which all aspired ... and when people talk of devotion in the *Genji* it is mainly with Amida in mind" (p. 10).

Dezaki's adaptation of the most salient events chronicled in the first twelve chapters of his source text reveals a consistent commitment to the principle of repetition, where Fujitsubo's experiences echo Kiritsubo's fate, Aoi's tragedy replicates Yuugao's ordeal, and both Kokiden and Lady Rokujou, driven by jealousy, reenact analogous crimes. Repetition on the structural plane of the show emulates the rhythm of the rolling seasons on the basis of which the action's settings are defined. Concomitantly, it parallels the Buddhist concept of Eternal Recurrence embedded in the original tale's cultural context. Dezaki's introduction of the themes of sin, forgiveness, penance and redemption at the close of his series enables him to foreshadow events chronicled by Lady Murasaki's narrative beyond the twelfth chapter, and specifically in Chapters 13–21, where those very themes are invested with paramount significance. In that portion of the saga Genji's self-imposed relinquishment of the glamorous world of the capital constitutes a cleansing rite of passage entailing a process of death and rebirth. Its culmination coincides with the protagonist's pious undertaking of a lustration ceremony through which he symbolically washes his sins away by sending off an effigy of himself in a boat. Once again, the personal and the political are seen to coalesce, for Genji's private self-purification paves the way to important public developments. These are marked by the hero's eventual return to the capital and rapid rise to the status of a full-fledged politician. However, Genji's redemption is not conclusive — any more than human life can ever be presumed to be in a cosmos governed by cyclical patterns and rhythms. Thus, even when the hero asserts himself in the political arena, accepts the prestigious title of Honorary Retired Emperor and holds ascendancy over his son's government, he is still cursed by an ethical makeup that prevents him from drawing satisfaction from his accomplishments and compels him to overreach himself, to strive for newer and better ends. The outcome, as with so many Faustian figures, is catastrophe: a fate here sealed, as noted, by Genji's entanglement in an emotional and political triangle akin to the one previously engendered by his affair with his father's favorite wife.

What renders Lady Murasaki's narrative so compellingly modern despite its historical remoteness — and allows Dezaki to take it as the springboard for an animated drama of great contemporary relevance — is above all its dramatization of the evolution of interiority through a focus on the processes attendant upon the genesis of consciousness itself. Genji's self-imposed exile constitutes the critical point in the parable. The topos of a hero's separation from society as a result of a transgressive act and ensuing state of guilt-ridden alienation could indeed be described as a seminal concern of the novel form. The self, in this scenario, is ineluctably sculpted out of seclusion and loneliness in the face of a world proverbially ungenerous in the dispensation of answers regarding the meaning and purpose of existence. Faithful to the source text's core philosophical message throughout its diegesis, Dezaki's anime does not fail to close with a sobering reflection on the ultimate vapidity of any promise of lasting fulfillment, to remind us that this pales to near insignificance in the face of both the anguish and the glory of incessant longing.

The revamping of ancient materials comparable to Lady Murasaki's eleventh-century novel informs one of the most revered anime productions of all times dating back to the medium's early history and renowned as the very first full-color animated movie to be released in Japan: the feature film *Hakujaden* (a.k.a. *The Legend of the White Serpent*) helmed by Kazuhiko Okabe and Taiji Yabushita (1958). Based on a venerable Chinese fairy tale, the movie chronicles the tortuous love relationship between a girl named Bai Niang and a boy named Xu Xiang. However, Bai Niang also happens to be a snake spirit and hence invites the unsolicited attention of a zealous demon-fighting wizard, Fa Hai, who believes she is a vampire and condemns her to hard labor in a remote town to protect Xu Xiang. In a suspenseful and lush drama portraying the struggle between the seemingly doomed protagonists and the wizardly monk with a tasteful avoidance of cut-and-dried decisions about the ethical superiority of either party, *Hakujaden* abounds with vividly rendered references to Oriental lore. The characters of Xu Xiang's panda pets Panda and Mimi — both of whom are varyingly endowed with magical or supernatural connotations — come across as especially unforgettable, in this regard. The fantastic action sequences triggered by a plucky all-animal team mustered by Panda and Mimi to attack the magician and further the protagonists' romance are most remarkable, not only in dramatic terms but also from a purely technical point of view when one takes into consideration the film's historical situation. Some of *Hakujaden*'s marine visuals, incidentally, foreshadow Hayao Miyazaki's movie *Ponyo on the Cliff by the Sea* (2008), here briefly discussed in Chapter 4, confirming Miyazaki's youthful infatuation with the seminal anime production and self-conscious acknowledgment of its profound influence on his own output. Most importantly, in this context, *Hakujaden* could be said to foreshadow *The Tale of Genji* in its recent configurations through its ability to imbue an ancient story with tantalizingly contemporary appeal.

Filmography

Primary Titles

Belladonna of Sadness (1973)

ORIGINAL TITLE: *Kanashimi no Beradona*. STATUS: movie. DIRECTOR: Eiichi Yamamoto. ORIGINAL CREATOR: Jules Michelet. SCREENPLAY: Yamamoto, Yoshiyuki Fukada. MUSIC: Masahiko Satoh, Nobuhiko Sato. ART DIRECTOR: Kuni Fukai. ANIMATION DIRECTOR: Gisaburou Sugii.

Gankutsuou: The Count of Monte Cristo (2004–2005)

ORIGINAL TITLE: *Gankutsuou: The Count of Monte Cristo*. STATUS: TV series (24 episodes). EPISODE LENGTH: 24 minutes. DIRECTOR: Mahiro Maeda. ORIGINAL CREATOR: Alexandre Dumas. SCREENPLAY: Natsuko Takahashi, Tomohiro Yamashita. SCENARIO: Takahashi, Yamashita. MUSIC: Jean Jacques Burnel, Koji Kasamatsu, Reiji Kitazato. CHARACTER DESIGNER: Hidenori Matsubara. ART DIRECTORS: You Sasaki, Yusuke Takeda. ANIMATION DIRECTOR: Takaaki Wada. BACKGROUND ART: Masanori Kikuchi. SOUND DIRECTOR: Yota Tsuruoka. SOUND EFFECTS: Yoshiki Matsunaga. SPECIAL EFFECTS: Shin Inoie. SPECIAL 3DCGI ANIMATOR: Akira Suzuki. TEXTILE CONVERTER: Sayuri Okada. TEXTILE DESIGNER: Yasufumi Soejima. COLOR DESIGNER: Eriko Murata. ANIMATION PRODUCTION: Gonzo. PRODUCTION: Gonzo. SOUND EFFECTS PRODUCTION: Rakuonsha. MUSIC PRODUCTION: Future Vision Music.

Grave of the Fireflies (1988)

ORIGINAL TITLE: *Hotaru no Haka*. STATUS: movie. DIRECTOR: Isao Takahata. ORIGINAL CREATOR: Akiyuki Nosaka. SCREENPLAY: Takahata. MUSIC: Masahiko Satoh, Michio Mamiya. CHARACTER DESIGNER: Yoshifumi Kondou. ART DIRECTOR: Nizo Yamamoto. ANIMATION DIRECTOR: Kondou. PRODUCER: Toru Hara. BACKGROUND ART: Eiji Hirakawa, Eiko Sudo, Fukiko Hashizume, Junko Ina, Mutsuo Koseki, Noriko Higuchi, Seiki Tamura, Shuichi Hirata, Tooru Hishiyama, Youji Nakaza, Yoshinari Kinbako. EDITOR: Takeshi Seyama. SOUND DIRECTOR: Yasuo Uragami. SOUND EFFECTS: Michihiro Ito, Noriyoshi Oohira. SPECIAL EFFECTS: Kunji Tanifuji. ANIMATION PRODUCTION: Studio Ghibli. PRODUCTION: Studio Ghibli. SOUND EFFECTS PRODUCTION: E & M Planning Center.

Like the Clouds, Like the Wind (1990)

ORIGINAL TITLE: *Kumo no You ni, Kaze no You ni*. STATUS: TV movie. DIRECTOR:

Hisayuki Toriyumi. ORIGINAL CREATOR: Ken'ichi Sakemi. SCREENPLAY: Akira Miyazaki. MUSIC: Haruhiko Maruya. CHARACTER DESIGNER: Katsuya Kondou. ART DIRECTOR: Yuji Ikeda. ANIMATION DIRECTOR: Kondou. EDITOR: Takeshi Seyama. SOUND DIRECTOR: Kan Mizumoto. PRODUCTION: Studio Pierrot, Yomiko Advertising, Inc.

Romeo x Juliet (2007)

ORIGINAL TITLE: *Romeo x Juliet*. STATUS: TV series (24 episodes). EPISODE LENGTH: 30 minutes. DIRECTOR: Fumitoshi Oizaki. ORIGINAL CREATOR: William Shakespeare. SERIES COMPOSITION: Reiko Yoshida. SCREENPLAY: Kurasumi Sunayama, Miharu Hirami, Natsuko Takahashi, Reiko Yoshida. MUSIC: Hitoshi Sakimoto. CHARACTER DESIGNER: Daiki Harada. ART DIRECTOR: Masami Saito. PRODUCER: Touyou Ikeda. EDITOR: Seiji Hirose. SOUND DIRECTOR: Tomohiro Yoshida. COLOR DESIGNER: Toshie Suzuki. ANIMATION PRODUCTION: Gonzo. PRODUCTION: CBC, G.D.H., Gonzo, SKY Perfect Well Think Co., Ltd. SOUND PRODUCTION: Rakuonsha.

The Snow Queen (2005–2006)

ORIGINAL TITLE: *Yuki no Jo-Oh*. STATUS: TV series (39 episodes). EPISODE LENGTH: 25 minutes. DIRECTOR: Osamu Dezaki. ORIGINAL CREATOR: Hans Christian Andersen. SERIES COMPOSITION: Masashi Sogo. SCREENPLAY: Makoto Nakamura, Michiru Shimada, Sukehiro Tomita, Tomoko Konparu. MUSIC: Akira Chisumi. CHARACTER DESIGNER: Akio Sugino. ART DIRECTOR: Jirou Kouno. ANIMATION DIRECTOR: Kenji Hachizaki. PRODUCERS: Hideaki Miyamoto, Tadao Matsumoto. BACKGROUND ART: Mayumi Okabe. SOUND DIRECTOR: Tomoaki Yamada. SOUND EFFECTS: Yukiyoshi Itokawa. COLOR DESIGNER: Junko Ito. ANIMATION PRODUCTION: TMS Entertainment. PRODUCTION: NHK.

The Tale of Genji (2009)

ORIGINAL TITLE: *Genji Monogatari Sennenki*. STATUS: TV series (11 episodes). EPISODE LENGTH: 30 minutes. DIRECTOR: Osamu Dezaki. ORIGINAL CREATOR: Lady Murasaki Shikibu. SERIES COMPOSITION: Tomoko Konparu. SCREENPLAY: Dezaki, Konparu. MUSIC: S.E.N.S. CHARACTER DESIGNER: Akio Sugino. ART DIRECTOR: Jirou Kouno. ANIMATION DIRECTOR: Sugino. MUSIC DIRECTOR: Seiji Suzuki. ANIMATION PRODUCTION: Tezuka Productions, Tokyo Movie (TMS Entertainment). PRODUCTION: Tokyo Movie Shinsha.

Umineko no Naku Koro ni (a.k.a. *When Seagulls Cry*; 2009)

ORIGINAL TITLE: *Umineko no Naku Koro ni*. STATUS: TV series (26 episodes). EPISODE LENGTH: 23 minutes. DIRECTOR: Chiaki Kon. ORIGINAL CREATOR: Ryukishi07. SERIES COMPOSITION: Toshifumi Kawase. SCREENPLAY: Fumihiko Shimo, Tatsushi Moriya, Toshifumi Kawase. CHARACTER DESIGNER: Yoko Kikuchi. ART DIRECTOR: Junichi Higashi. CHIEF ANIMATION DIRECTORS: Yoko Kikuchi, Yukiko Ban. PRODUCERS: Hiroyuki Oomori, Mika Nomura, Takema Okamura. BACKGROUND ART: Akiko Manabe, Asami Saito, Etsuko Abe, Hyun Chul Won, Hyun Soo Kim, Junko Shimizu, Kayoko Haruhara, Kenta Shimizu, Kim Soon Ja, Miho Sugiura, Minami Usui, Misuzu Noma, Rie Kikuchi, Sachie Endou, Seung Hyeon Lee, Sin Hye Lee, So Young Kim, Sun Hee Ban, Takamasa Honma, Tetsuo Imaizumi, Toshie Honda, Won Suk Choi, Yayoi Okashiwa, Yuka Ohashi, Yuki Maeda. 3D DIRECTOR: Akira Inagaki. EDITOR: Masahiro Matsumura. SOUND DIRECTOR: Hozumi Gouda. SOUND EFFECTS: Noriko Izumo. SPECIAL EFFECTS: Masakazu Uehara. COLOR DESIGNER: Eiko Kitazume. COLOR KEY: Eiko Kitazume, Yui Azumi. TEXTURE DESIGNER: Emi Akiba. Animation Production: Studio DEEN. Production: Frontier Works. SOUND PRODUCTION: Dax Production.

Secondary Titles

Anne of Green Gables (TV series; dirs. Isao Takahata and Shigeo Koshi, 1979)
The Dagger of Kamui (movie; dir. Rintaro, 1985)
A Dog of Flanders (TV series; dir. Yoshio Kuroda, 1975)
The Hakkenden (OVA series; dirs. Takashi Anno and Yuki Okamoto, 1990–1991 [Part 1]; 1993–1995 [Part 2: *Shinsho*])
Hakugei: The Legend of Moby Dick (TV series; dir. Osamu Dezaki, 1997–1999)
Hakujaden (a.k.a. *The Legend of the White Serpent*) (movie; dirs. Kazuhiko Okabe and Taiji Yabushita,1958)
Heidi, Girl of the Alps (TV series; dir. Isao Takahata, 1974)
The Melancholy of Haruhi Suzumiya (TV series; dir. Tatsuya Ishihara, 2006)
One Thousand and One Arabian Nights (movie; dir. Eiichi Yamamoto, 1969)
Ponyo on the Cliff by the Sea (movie; dir. Hayao Miyazaki, 2008)
Puss in Boots (movie; dir. Kimio Yabuki, 1969)
Sennen no Koi — Hikaru Genji monogatari (a.k.a. *A Thousand Years of Love — The Tale of Shining Genji*; dir. Tonkou Horikawa, 2001)
The Stingiest Man in Town (TV special; Katsuhisa Yamada, 1978)
The Tale of Genji (movie; dir. Kouzaburou Yoshimura, 1951)
The Tale of Genji (movie; dir. Kon Ichikawa, 1966)
The Tale of Genji (movie; dir. Gisaburou Sugii, 1987)
Tsuyokiss — CoolxSweet (TV series; dir. Shinichiro Kimura, 2006)
Witchblade (TV series; dir. Yoshimitsu Ohashi, 2006)

Additional Titles Cited

The Adventures of Tom Sawyer (TV series; dir. Hiroyoshi Saitou, 1980)
Aesop's Fables (TV series; dir. Eiji Okabe, 1983)
The Alcoa Hour (TV series; dirs. Kirk Browning, Herbert Hirschman *et al.*, 1955–1957)
Andersen Stories (TV series; dir. Masami Hata, 1971)
Animal Treasure Island (movie; dir. Hiroshi Ikeda, 1971)
Animated Classics of Japanese Literature (TV series; dir. Fumio Kurokawa, 1986)
Black Jack (OVA series; dirs. Osamu Dezaki and Fumihiro Yoshimura, 2006)
Cinderella (TV series; dir. Hiroshi Sasagawa, 1996)
The Count of Monte Cristo (movie; dirs. Francis Boggs and Thomas Persons, 1908)
The Count of Monte Cristo (movie; dirs. Joseph A. Golden and Edwin S. Porter, 1913)
The Count of Monte Cristo (TV series; dir. Henri Pouctal, 1918)
The Count of Monte Cristo (movie; dir. Henri Fescourt, 1929)
The Count of Monte Cristo (movie; dir. Rowland V. Lee, 1934)
The Count of Monte Cristo: Ière époque: Edmond Dantès (movie; dir. Robert Vernay, 1943)
The Count of Monte Cristo (movie; dir. Robert Vernay, 1955)
The Count of Monte Cristo (TV series; dirs. David MacDonald and Sidney Salkow, 1956)

The Count of Monte Cristo (movie; dir. Claude Autant-Lara, 1961)
The Count of Monte Cristo (TV series; dir. Peter Hammond, 1964)
The Count of Monte Cristo (a.k.a. *Under the Sign of Monte Cristo*; movie; dir. André Hunebelle, 1968)
The Count of Monte Cristo (movie; dir. David Greene, 1975), *The Count of Monte Cristo* (TV miniseries; dir. Denys de La Patellière, 1980)
The Count of Monte Cristo (TV miniseries; dir. Josée Dayan, 1998)
The Count of Monte Cristo (movie; dir. Kevin Reynolds, 2002)
Gulliver's Space Travels: Beyond the Moon (movie; dir. Yoshio Kuroda, 1965)
Howl's Moving Castle (movie; dir. Hayao Miyazaki, 2004)
Iron Man (currently in production at Madhouse Studio)
The Jungle Book (movie; dir. Wolfgang Reitherman, 1967)
Kiki's Delivery Service (movie; dir. Hayao Miyazaki, 1989)
Rascal the Raccoon (TV series; dirs. Hiroshi Saitou, Seiji Endou, Shigeo Koshi, 1977)
Romanoff and Juliet (movie; dir. Peter Ustinoff, 1961)
Rome and Jewel (movie; dir. Charles Kanganis, 2006)
Romeo and Juliet (movie; dir. George Cukor, 1936)
Romeo and Juliet (movie; dir. Renato Castellani, 1954)
Romeo and Juliet (movie; dir. Franco Zeffirelli, 1968)
Romeo and Juliet (movie; dir. Baz Luhrmann, 1996)
Romeo and Juliet: Sealed with a Kiss (movie; dir. Phil Nibbelink, 2006)
Romeo Must Die (movie; dir. Andrzej Bartkowiak, 2000)
Romie-0 and Julie-8 (TV special; dir. Clive A. Smith, 1996)
The Sex Lives of Romeo and Juliet (movie; dir. Peter Perry, Jr., 1969)

Shakespeare in Love (movie; dir. John Madden, 1998)
Snedronningen (movie; dirs. Jacob Jørgensen and Kristof Kuncewicz, 2000)
Snezhnaya Koroleva (movie; dir. Lev Atamanov, 1957)
Snezhnaya Koroleva (movie; dir. Gennadi Kazansky, 1966)
The Snow Queen (TV movie; dir. Andrew Gosling, 1976)
The Snow Queen (short movie; dirs. Marek Buchwald and Vladlen Barbe, 1992)
The Snow Queen (movie; dir. Martin Gates, 1995)
Snow Queen (TV movie; dir. David Wu, 2002)
The Snow Queen (TV movie; dir. Julian Gibbs, 2005)
The Snow Queen's Revenge (movie; dir. Martin Gates, 1996)
Snow White and the Seven Dwarfs (movie; dirs. David Hand, William Cottrell, Wilfred Jackson, Larry Morey, Perce Pearce and Ben Sharpsteen, 1937)
The Story of Pollyanna (TV series; dir. Kouzou Kuzuha, 1986)
Swiss Family Robinson (TV series; dir. Yoshio Kuroda, 1981)
Tales from Earthsea (movie; dir. Goro Miyazaki, 2006)
Three Thousand Miles in Search of Mother (TV series; dir. Hayao Miyazaki, 1975)
Tromeo and Juliet (movie; dir. Loyd Kaufman, 1996)
Uznik zamka If (a.k.a. *The Count of Monte Cristo* or *The Prisoner of If Castle*; movie; dir. Georgi Yungvald-Khilkevich, 1988)
Veta (movie; dir. Kodanda Rami Reddy A., 1986)
West Side Story (movie; dirs. Jerome Robbins and Robert Wise, 1961)
Wolverine (currently in production at Madhouse Studio)

Bibliography

Alexander, M. 2006. "*The Tale of Genji* Review." *Dark Horse*. <http://www.darkhorse.com/Reviews/369/Tale-of-Genji>.

Amano, Y. 2006. *The Tale of Genji*. Text by A. Itou and J. Imura. Trans. R. Nacht. Milwaukee: Dark Horse Press.

Andersen, H. C. 1911. *Stories from Hans Andersen with Illustrations by Edmund Dulac*. London: Hodder & Stoughton.

_____. 1924a. *Hans Andersen's Fairy Tales*. Illustrations by K. Nielsen. London: Hodder & Stoughton.

_____. 1924b. *Hans Andersen's Fairy Tales*. Illustrations by A. Anderson. London: Collins.

_____. 1997. *The Snow Queen*. Trans. and adapted by A. Bell. Illustrations by B. Watts. New York: North-South Books.

_____. 2001. *The Snow Queen and Other Tales*. Trans. M. Ponsot. Illustrations by A. Segur. New York: Golden Books.

_____. 2002. *The Snow Queen*. Illustrations by T. Pym. London: Everyman's Library.

_____. 2004. *Tales of Hans Christian Andersen*. Trans. N. Lewis. Illustrations by J. Stewart. London: Walker Books.

_____. 2005. *The Snow Queen*. Retold by N. Raven. Illustrations by Y. Yerko. Dorking, Surrey: Templar Publishing.

_____. 2007. *The Snow Queen*. Trans. N. Lewis. Illustrations by C. Birmingham. London: Walker Books.

_____. 2009. *The Snow Queen*. Retold by C. Peachey. Illustrations by P. J. Lynch. London: Andersen Press.

Andrew, D. 1984. *Concepts in Film Theory*. Oxford: Oxford University Press.

_____. 2000. "Adaptation." In *Film Adaptation*, edited by J. Naremore. New Brunswick: Rutgers University Press.

Ascari, M. 2009. *A Counter-History of Crime Fiction*. Basingstoke and New York: Palgrave Macmillan.

Auster, P. 1987. *City of Glass*. New York: Penguin.

Bargen, D. G. 1986. "Yuugao: A Case of Spirit Possession in *The Tale of Genji*." *Mosaic*, vol. XIX, no. 3, Summer, pp. 15–24. Extract in *The Tale of Genji Study Guide*. BookRags. <http://www.bookrags.com/studyguide-talegenji/>.

Barthes, B. 1983. *Empire of Signs*. Trans. R. Howard. London: Jonathan Cape.

Barthes, R. 1990. *The Pleasure of the Text*. Trans. R. Miller. Oxford: Basil Blackwell.

_____. 1993. [1972.] *Mythologies*. Trans. A. Lavers. London: Vintage.

Bataille, G. 1986. *Eroticism: Death and Sensuality*. Trans. M. Dalwood. San Francisco: City Light Books.

Baudrillard, J. 1988. *Selected Writings*. Edited by M. Poster. Cambridge: Polity Press.

Belsey, C. 1994. *Desire: Love Stories in Western Culture*. Oxford: Blackwell.

_____. 2001. "The Name of the Rose in *Romeo and Juliet*." In *Romeo and Juliet*, New Casebooks Series, edited by R. S. White. Basingstoke and New York: Palgrave.

Benjamin, W. 1969. *Illuminations*. Trans. H. Zohn. New York: Schocken Books.

Berger, J. 1972. *Ways of Seeing*. London and Harmondsworth: BBC and Penguin.

Bettelheim, B. 1975. *The Uses of Enchantment: The Meaning and Importance of Fairy Tales*. London: Thames & Hudson.

Bloom, H. 2004. "Introduction." In *Murasaki Shikibu's The Tale of Genji*, edited by H. Bloom. Philadelphia: Chelsea House Publishers.

Bowring, R. 2004. *Murasaki Shikibu—The Tale of Genji*. Second Edition. Cambridge: Cambridge University Press.

Buckminster Fuller, R. *The Quotations Page*. <http://www.quotationspage.com/quote/34494.html>.

Callaghan, D. 1994. "The Ideology of Romantic Love: The Case of *Romeo and Juliet*." In *The Weyward Sisters: Shakespeare and Feminist Politics*, edited by D. Callaghan, J. Helms and J. Singh. Oxford: Blackwell.

Calvino, I. 2009. [1965, 1967.] "The Count of Monte Cristo." In *The Complete Cosmicomics*. Trans. W. Weaver, T. McLaughlin and T. Parks. London: Penguin.

Carter, A. 1990. *The Virago Books of Fairy Tales*. London: Virago.

Cartmell, D., and I. Whelehan. 2007. *The Cambridge Companion to Literature on Screen*. Cambridge: Cambridge University Press.

Cavallaro, D. 2002. *The Gothic Vision: Three Centuries of Horror, Terror and Fear*. London and New York: Continuum.

Chesterton, G. K. "Gilbert Keith Chesterton Quotes." <http://www.worldofquotes.com/author/Gilbert-Keith-Chesterton/1/index.html>.

Cixous, H., and C. Clément. 1997. *The Newly Born Woman*. Trans. B. Wing. I B Tauris & Co.

Costanzo Cahir, L. 2006. *Literature into Film: Theory and Practical Approaches*. Jefferson, NC: McFarland.

"The Count of Monte Cristo (film)." *Wikipedia—The Free Encyclopedia*. <http://en.wikipedia.org/wiki/The_Count_of_Monte_Cristo_(film)>.

Crowfoot. <http://www.quoteworld.org/quotes/3295>.

Dalby, L. "Genji kou." *Tale of Murasaki*. <http://www.lizadalby.com/LD/TofM_Genjiko.html>.

Davis, L. 2001. "Desire and Presence in *Romeo and Juliet*." In *Romeo and Juliet*, New Casebooks Series, edited by R. S. White. Basingstoke and New York: Palgrave.

Deleuze, G. 1990. "Plato and the Simulacrum." In *The Logic of Sense*, edited by C. V. Boundas. New York: Columbia University Press.

———. 1994. *Difference and Repetition*. Trans. P. Patton. London: Athlone Press.

Demko, G. J. "Mysteries in the Land of the Rising Sun." *G. J. Demko's Landscapes of Crime*. <http://www.dartmouth.edu/~gjdemko/japan.htm>.

Derrida, J. 1978. *Writing and Difference*. Trans. A. Bass. London: Routledge.

———. 1985. *The Ear of the Other: Otobiography, Transference, Translation*. Trans. P. Kamuf. New York: Shocken Books.

———. 1992. "Aphorism Countertime." In *Acts of Literature*, edited by D. Attridge. London: Routledge.

Desmond, J. M., and P. Hawkes. 2005. *Adaptation: Studying Film and Literature*. New York: McGraw-Hill.

Dickens, C. 2000. [1843.] *A Christmas Carol*. Retold by J. Parker Resnick. Illustrations by C. Birmingham. London: Kingfisher Publications.

Doyle, A. C. 1963. "The Crooked Man." In *The Memoirs of Sherlock Holmes*. New York: Berkley.

Drazen, P. 2003. *Anime Explosion: The What? Why? & Wow! of Japanese Animation*. Berkeley, CA: Stone Bridge Press.

Dumas, A. 1955. [1845–1846.] *The Count of Monte Cristo*. Introduced by R. Church. London and Glasgow: Collins.

Ebert, R. 2004. "Interview." *Grave of the Fireflies* Double Disc Special Edition, Disc Two. Optimum Releasing.

Edison, T. A. "Thomas Alva Edison Quotes." <http://thinkexist.com/quotes/thomas_alva_edison/>.

Elliott, K. 2003. *Rethinking the Novel/Film Debate*. Cambridge: Cambridge University Press.

Ellis, J. 1982. "The Literary Adaptation: An Introduction." In *Screen* 23(1).

Emmerich, M. 2008. "The Splendor of Hybridity." In *Envisioning the Tale of Genji—Media, Gender, and Cultural Production*, edited by H. Shirane. New York: Columbia University Press.

Eno, B. "Manipulating Quotes." <http://www.brainyquote.com/quotes/keywords/manipulating.html>.

Evans, D. 2001. *Epics for Students*. Andover: Gale. Extract in *The Tale of Genji Study*

Guide. *BookRags*. <http://www.bookrags.com/studyguide-talegenji/>
Field, N. 1987. *The Splendor of Longing in The Tale of Genji*. Princeton: Princeton University Press.
Fischlin, D., and M. Fortier. 2000. *Adaptations of Shakespeare: A Critical Anthology of Plays from the Seventeenth Century to the Present*. London: Routledge.
Frazer, J. G. 1992. [1913–1920.] *The Golden Bough: A Study in Magic and Religion*. Third Edition. New York: Macmillan. Electronic edition: *Bartleby.com*. 2000. <http://www.bartleby.com/196/>.
Freud, A. 1946. *The Ego and Its Mechanisms of Defense*. New York: International University Presses.
Fukushima, D. H., Jr. "Hotaru no Haka." <http://www2.hawaii.edu/~dfukushi/Hotaru.html>.
Gage, J. 1993. *Colour and Culture*. London: Thames & Hudson.
Gankutsuou: The Count of Monte Cristo Complete. 2005. Tokyo: Media Factory.
Gatten, A. 1977. "A Wisp of Smoke. Scent and Character in *The Tale of Genji*." *Monumenta Nipponica*, vol. 32, no. 1, Spring, pp. 35–48. Sophia University.
Gaudreault, A. and Marion, P. 2004. "Transécriture and Narrative Mediatics: The Stakes of Intermediality." In *A Companion to Literature and Film*, edited by R. Stam and A. Raengo. Oxford: Blackwell.
Genette, G. 1997. [1988.] *Palimpsests: Literature in the Second Degree*. Trans. C. Newman and C. Doubinsky. Lincoln: University of Nebraska Press.
"Genji Monogatari Sennenki." 2009. *Anime-Wiki.org*. <http://en.anime-wiki.org/wiki/Genji_Monogatari_Sennenki>.
Geraghty, C. 2007. *Now a Major Motion Picture: Film Adaptations of Literature and Drama*. Lanham, MD: Rowman & Littlefield.
Gill, R. 2008. "Introduction." In *Romeo and Juliet— Oxford School Shakespeare*. Oxford: Oxford University Press.
Gillies, J. "Grave of the Fireflies." *Apollo Movie Guide*. <http://apolloguide.com/mov_fullrev.asp?CID=4516&Specific=5303>.
Gombrich, E. H. 2006. *The Story of Art*. Sixteenth Edition. London: Phaidon.
Grella, G. 1980. "The Formal Detective Novel." In *Detective Fiction: A Collection of Critical Essays*, edited by R. W. Winks, pp. 84–102. Englewood Cliffs: Prentice-Hall.
Guida, F. 2000. *A Christmas Carol and Its Adaptations: Dickens' Story on Screen and Television*. Jefferson: McFarland.
Hazlitt, W. 1996. *Hazlitt's Criticism of Shakespeare: A Selection*, edited by R. S. White. Lewiston, Queenstown, Lampeter: Edwin Mellen Press.
Heyden, L. 2008. "Christmas Fairies." *Suite 101*. <http://paganismwicca.suite101.com/article.cfm/christmas_fairies>.
Hoban, R. "Russell Hoban Quotes." <http://thinkexist.com/quotation/language_is_an_archaeological_vehicle-the/263125.html>.
Hoffmann, E. T. A. "E. T. A. Hoffmann Quotes." <http://www.brainyquote.com/quotes/authors/e/e_t_a_hoffmann.html>.
Hubert, H., and M. Mauss. 1964. *Sacrifice: Its Nature and Function*. Trans. W. D. Halls. Chicago: University of Chicago Press.
Hutcheon, L. 2006. *A Theory of Adaptation*. London and New York: Routledge.
Ii, H. 2008. "Didactic Readings of *The Tale of Genji*." In *Envisioning The Tale of Genji—Media, Gender, and Cultural Production*, edited by H. Shirane. New York: Columbia University Press.
"Interview with Nosaka Akiyuki and Isao Takahata." *Animerica, Anime and Manga Monthly* vol. 12, no. 11. <http://www.geocities.com/ronin_tigris/nosakainterview.html>.
Iwasaka, M., and B. Toelken. 1994. *Ghosts and the Japanese: Cultural Experience in Japanese Death Legends*. Logan: Utah State University Press.
Joyce, J. 2008. [1922.] *Ulysses*. Oxford: Oxford World's Classics.
"Juunihitoe." *Wikipedia—The Free Encyclopedia*. <http://en.wikipedia.org/wiki/Juunihitoe>.
Kawai, H. 1988. *The Japanese Psyche: Major Motifs in the Fairytales of Japan*. Dallas, TX: Spring Publications.
Keene, D. 2004. "The Tale of Genji." In *Murasaki Shikibu's The Tale of Genji*, edited by H. Bloom. Philadelphia: Chelsea House Publishers.
Kidnie, M. J. 2009. *Shakespeare and the Problem of Adaptation*. London and New York: Routledge.

"Kimono History: The Heian Era." <http://www.bookmice.net/darkchilde/japan/khist4.html>.
Kristeva, J. 2001. "*Romeo and Juliet*: Love-Hatred in the Couple." In *Romeo and Juliet*, New Casebooks Series, edited by R. S. White. Basingstoke and New York: Palgrave.
Lady Murasaki. 2000. *The Tale of Genji*. Trans. A. Waley. Mineola, New York: Dover Publications.
Lederer, W. 1986. *The Kiss of the Snow Queen: Hans Christian Andersen and Man's Redemption by Woman*. Berkeley: University of California Press.
Legg, M. C. 2003. "Snow Queen." *Suite 101*. <http://www.suite101.com/article.cfm/fairytales_myths_fables_&legends/105068> and <http://www.suite101.com/article.cfm/fairytales_myths_fables_&legends/105068/2>.
_____. 2004. "*Snow Queen*: The Old Woman's Garden-Flower Talk." *Suite 101*. <http://www.suite101.com/pages/article_old.cfm/fairytales_myths_fables_&legends/106388> and <http://www.suite101.com/article.cfm/fairytales_myths_fables_&legends/106388/2>.
Leitch, T. 2008. "Adaptation Studies at a Crossroads." *Adaptation* vol. 1, no. 1. Oxford: Oxford University Press.
Lippit, Y. 2008. "Figure and Facture in the *Genji* Scrolls — Text, Calligraphy, Paper, and Painting." In *Envisioning The Tale of Genji — Media, Gender, and Cultural Production*, edited by H. Shirane. New York: Columbia University Press.
Macherey, P. 1995. "Creation and Production." In *Authorship: From Plato to the Postmodern: A Reader* edited by S. Burke. Edinburgh: Edinburgh University Press.
Malmgren, C. D. 2001. *Anatomy of Murder*. Bowling Green: Bowling Green University Popular Press.
Marc. 2003. "*Grave of the Fireflies*." <http://animeworld.com/reviews/graveofthefireflies.html>.
Martin, T. 2006. "Review — *Gankutsuou: The Count of Monte Cristo* — DVD 2: *The Count of Monte Cristo*. Anime News Network. <http://www.animenewsnetwork.com/review/gankutsuou/dvd-2>.
Merivale, P., and S. E. Sweeney. 1998. *Detecting Texts: The Metaphysical Detective Story from Poe to Postmodernism*. Philadelphia: University of Pennsylvania Press.
Michelet, J. 1939. [1862.] *Satanism and Witchcraft: A Study in Medieval Superstition*. Trans. A. R. Allinson. New York: Lyle Stuart/Citadel Press.
Miyake, L. K. 1993. "The Narrative Triad." In *Approaches to Teaching Murasaki Shikibu's The Tale of Genji*," edited by E. Kamens. New York: The Modern Language Association of America.
Moeran, N. 2007. "Making Scents of Smell: Manufacturing Incense in Japan." *Creative Encounters* Working Paper # 1. June.
Morris, I. 1994. *The World of the Shining Prince: Court Life in Ancient Japan*. New York, Tokyo and London: Kodansha International.
Mostow, J. S. "'Picturing' in *The Tale of Genji*." *The Journal of the Association of Teachers of Japanese*, vol. 33, no. 1, pp. 1–25.
Murdoch, J. 1949. *A History of Japan, Volume I*. London: Kegan Paul.
Naremore, J. 2000. "Introduction: Film and the Reign of Adaptation." In *Film Adaptation*, edited by J. Naremore. London: Athlone Press.
Norinaga, M. 1969. *Gengi Monogatari Tama no Ogushi. Motoori Norinaga Zenshuu*, edited by S. Ohno, vol. 4. Tokyo: Chikuma Shobo.
Obuchowski, M. D. 1976. "Religious Threads and Themes in *The Tale of Genji*." *CLA Journal*, vol. XX, no. 2, December, pp. 185–94. Extract in *The Tale of Genji Study Guide*. BookRags. <http://www.bookrags.com/studyguide-talegenji/>.
Oizaki, F. 2009. "Interview." *Romeo x Juliet: Romeo Collection*. FUNimation.
Okada, H. R. 1991. *Figures of Resistance: Language, Poetry, and Narrating in The Tale of the Genji and Other Mid-Heian Texts*. Durham: Duke University Press.
Okri, B. "Ben Okri Quotes." <http://thinkexist.com/quotation/only_those_who_truly_love_and_who_are_truly/152945.html>.
Olson, D. 2007. "Little Burton Blue." *MP: A Feminist Journal Online*, June.
Ong, M. L. 2007. "*The Snow Queen* — Andersen's Classic Fairy Tale About Overcoming Depression." *Suite 101*. <http://fairytales.suite101.com/article.cfm/the_snow_queen>.

Peary, G., and R. Shatzkin. 1977. *The Classic American Novel and the Movies*. New York: Frederick Ungar.

Porter, D. 1981. *The Pursuit of Crime: Art and Ideology in Detective Fiction*. New Haven: Yale University Press.

Pratchett, T. 1992. *Witches Abroad*. London: Corgi Books.

Princess Skye. 2009. "When does a princess become a queen?" *The Princess Portal*. <http://princessportal.com/archives/1301>.

Puette, W. J. 1983. *Tale of Genji: A Reader's Guide*. Tokyo, Rutland, VT and Singapore: Tuttle Publishing.

Rapoport, A. 1999. *Two-Person Game Theory*. New York: Dover Publications.

Reeve, J. 2006. *Japanese Art in Detail*. London: The British Museum Press.

Romeo x Juliet Destiny of Love Visual Fan Book. 2008. Tokyo: Gonzo/CBC-GDH-SPWT.

Rushdie, S. 2001. *Haroun and the Sea of Stories*. London: Puffin.

Sanders, J. 2006. *Adaptation and Appropriation*. London: Routledge.

"Satan as Hero in *Paradise Lost*." *Romantic Criticism*. <http://67.104.146.36/english/gothic/works/satanhero.html>.

Shirane, H. 1987. *The Bridge of Dreams: A Poetics of "The Tale of Genji."* Stanford: Stanford University Press.

_____. 2005. "Performance, Visuality, and Textuality: The Case of Japanese Poetry." *Oral Tradition*, 20/2, pp. 217–232.

_____. 2008. "*The Tale of Genji* and the Dynamics of Cultural Production: Canonization and Popularization." In *Envisioning The Tale of Genji — Media, Gender, and Cultural Production*, edited by H. Shirane. New York: Columbia University Press.

The Snow Queen 1 and 2. 2005–2006. Tokyo: NHK.

Soliman. 2009. "La pittura nel cinema: Giulietta e Romeo." *Abbracci e pop corn*. <http://abbracciepopcorn.blogspot.com/2009/12/la-pittura-nel-cinema-giulietta-e-romeo.html>

Spanos, W. V. 1972. "The Detective and the Boundary: Some Notes on the Postmodern Literary Imagination." *Boundary 2*, 1, 1, pp. 147–168.

Stam, R. 2000. "Beyond Fidelity: The Dialogics of Adaptation." In *Film Adaptation*, edited by J. Naremore. London: Athlone Press.

Stanley-Baker, J. 2000. *Japanese Art*. London and New York: Thames & Hudson.

Symons, J. 1985. *Bloody Murder: From the Detective Story to the Crime Novel: A History*. New York: Viking.

Tanizaki, J. 2001. [1933.] *In Praise of Shadows*. Trans. T. J. Harper and E. G. Seidensticker. London: Vintage.

Tateishi, K. 2008. "*The Tale of Genji* in Postwar Film — Emperor, Aestheticism, and the Erotic." In *Envisioning The Tale of Genji — Media, Gender, and Cultural Production*, edited by H. Shirane. New York: Columbia University Press.

Todorov, T. 1977, *The Poetics of Prose*. Trans. R. Howard. Ithaca: Cornell University Press.

Turner, J. P. 1950. *The North-West Mounted Police: 1873–1893*. Ottawa: Edmond Cloutier, King's Printer.

Tyler, R. 2002. "Marriage, Rank and Rape in *The Tale of Genji*." *Intersections: Gender, History and Culture in the Asian Context* Issue 7, March. <http://intersections.anu.edu.au/issue7/tyler.html>.

_____. 2009. *The Disaster of the Third Princess — Essays on The Tale of Genji*. Canberra: ANU E Press — The Australian National University.

_____. "*Genji Monogatari* and *The Tale of Genji*." Japan Foundation Sydney. <http://www.jpf.org.au/omusubi/profile/royalltyler-genji-lect-english.pdf>.

Valter. 2008. "Dead as Michelet." *Documents*. <http://surrealdocuments.blogspot.com/2008/05/dead-as-michelet.html>.

Wallace, J. R. 2004. "Tarrying with the Negative: Aesthetic Vision in Murasaki and Mishima." In *Murasaki Shikibu's The Tale of Genji*, edited by H. Bloom. Philadelphia: Chelsea House Publishers.

Wang, Y. 2002. "Poetry: The language of Love in *The Tale of Genji*." *NUCB JLCC*, 4, 2.

White, R. S. 2001. "What is this thing called love?" In *Romeo and Juliet*, New Casebooks Series, edited by R. S. White. Basingstoke and New York: Palgrave.

Woolf, V. 1967. [1925.] "*The Tale of Genji*, The First Volume of Mr. Arthur Waley's Translation of a Great Japanese Novel by the Lady Murasaki." In "Virginia Woolf and Lady Murasaki." *Literature East and West*, vol. II, no. 4, pp. 421–427.

Wullschlager, J. 2005. "Hans Christian Andersen." *Illustrated Exhibition Guide.* London: The British Library. <http://collectbritain.co.uk/onlinegallery/features/andersen/pdf/essay.pdf>.

"Yuki-onna." *Wikipedia—The Free Encyclopedia.* <http://en.wikipedia.org/wiki/Yuki_onna>.

Zipes, J. 1994. *Fairy Tale as Myth: Myth as Fairy Tale.* Lexington: University of Kentucky Press.

Index

À la recherche du temps perdu (*Remembrance of Things Past*) 149
The Adventures of Tom Sawyer 66
Aesop's Fables 66
Akiyuki, N. 27, 29
The Alcoa Hour 62
Alexander, M. 150
Amanda, L. 57
Amano, Y. 150–151, 152
Andersen, H.C. 9, 63, 64
Andersen Stories 65
Anderson, A. 93
Andrew, D. 7–8
Animal Treasure Island 66
Animated Classics of Japanese Literature 27
Anne of Green Gables 66, 98
Anno, T. 35
Art Nouveau 57
As You Like It 114
Asake yume mishi (a.k.a. *Fleeting Dreams*) 147–148
Ascari, M. 132, 139–140
Atamanov, L. 96
Auster, P. 132

Badel, A. 57
Bakin, K. 35
Barbe, V. 96
Barge, P. 58
Bargen, D.G. 166
Barthes, R. 150, 172, 173
Bartkowiak, A. 122
Bass, J. 62
Bataille, G. 25, 170
Baudelaire, C. 25, 43
Baudrillard, J. 3, 12
Beardsley, A. 20
Beauty and the Beast 76

Belladonna of Sadness 9, 10, 20–26, 31, 36, 37, 146
Bellini, G. 120
Belsey, C. 108, 117
Benjamin, W. 3, 11
Berger, J. 11
Bernstein, L. 121
Bettelheim, B. 65
Birmingham, C. 63, 91–92, 93, 94, 95
Black Jack 94
Blake, W. 25, 42–43
Bloom, H. 155, 168, 185
Borges, J.L. 144
Botticelli, S. 120
Bowring, R. 161, 170–171, 172–173, 181–182
Brasseur, P. 58
Brontë, E. 25
Brooke, A. 100–101
Brown, F.M. 123
Browning, K. 62
Bruegel the Elder, P. 94
Buchwald, M. 96
Buckminster Fuller, R. 31
Bunbury, H.W. 122
bunraku 27
Byron, Lord G.G. 43

Calderon, P.H. 123
Callaghan, D. 126
Calvino, I. 58–59
Carpaccio, V. 120–121
Carter, A. 65
Cartmell, D. 7
Castellani, R. 120
Cavallaro, D. 138
Caviezel, J. 58
Cervantes, M. 149
Chagall, M. 93, 123
Chamberlain, R. 58

Chesterton, G.K. 128
Chiranjeevi 58
A Christmas Carol 62–63
Church, R. 48, 52
Cinderella 66
Cixous, H. 20
Clément, C. 20
Coker, P., Jr. 62
Coleridge, S.T. 53–54
Conan Doyle, A. 133
Costanzo Cahir, L. 6, 7
Costras, D. 123
Cottrell, W. 96
The Count of Monte Cristo (novel) 39
The Count of Monte Cristo (1980 miniseries) 58
The Count of Monte Cristo (1998 miniseries) 58
The Count of Monte Cristo (1908 movie) 57
The Count of Monte Cristo (1913 movie) 57
The Count of Monte Cristo (1929 movie) 57
The Count of Monte Cristo (1934 movie) 57
The Count of Monte Cristo (1943 movie) 57
The Count of Monte Cristo (1955 movie) 57
The Count of Monte Cristo (1961 movie) 57
The Count of Monte Cristo (1968 movie) 58
The Count of Monte Cristo (1975 movie) 58
The Count of Monte Cristo (2002 movie) 58
The Count of Monte Cristo (1918 series) 57
The Count of Monte Cristo (1956 series) 57
The Count of Monte Cristo (1964 series) 57
Crowfoot 26
Cukor, G. 120
Curtis, T. 58

The Dagger of Kamui 35
Dalby, L. 179
Dante 149
D'arc: Histoire de Jeanne D'arc 31
Davis, L. 124–125, 126
Debussy, C. 55
A Defense of Poetry 43
Delacroix, E. 23
Deleuze, G. 10–11,12
Demko, G.J. 131–132
Depardieu, G. 58
Derrida, J. 11–12, 115–116, 117
de Sica, V. 30
Desmond, J.M. 7
Dezaki, O. 61–62, 64–98, 150–196
Dickens, C. 62–63
Dicksee, Sir F. 123
Disney, W. 96
A Dog of Flanders 66, 98

Dominczyk, D. 58
Donat, R. 57
Donizetti, G. 55
Drazen, P. 145
Dulac, E. 20
Dumas, A. 9, 39, 40, 43, 44, 47, 51, 59, 60

Ebert, R. 29
Eco, U. 144
Edison, T.A. 1
Elliott, K. 8
Ellis, J. 19–20
Emmerich, M. 149
The Emperor's New Clothes 68, 73
Endou, S. 66
Eno, B. viii
Ephesiaca 100
Evans, D. 183

Faust 195
Fescourt, H. 57
Field, N. 185, 188, 189
Fini, L. 120
Fischlin, D. 100
Fisher, H. 108
Fitzgerald, F.S. 54
The Flying Trunk 67, 68, 69, 70
Fortier, M. 100
Frazer, J.G. 25
Freud, A. 77
Fukai, K. 21
Fukushima, D.H., Jr. 29
Füssli, J.C. 22

Gage, J. 109
Gankutsuou: The Count of Monte Cristo 10, 38–62, 137, 145, 159
Gates, M. 96
Gatten, A. 179
Gaudreault, A. 94
Genet, J. 25
Genette, G. 17, 99
Genji monogatari (manga) 148
Genji Scrolls 151
Geraghty, C. 10, 17
Ghirlandaio, D. 121
Gibbs, J. 96
Gill, R. 100–101, 121
Gillies, J. 28, 30
The Goblin at the Grocer's 67
Gombrich, E.H. 108–109
Gosling, A. 96
Goya, F. 22
Gozzoli, B. 94, 120

Index

Grave of the Fireflies (film) 8, 26–30, 33, 36, 37, 107
Grave of the Fireflies (novel) 27
Grella, G. 140
Guida, F. 63
Gulliver's Space Travels: Beyond the Moon 66

The Hakkenden 35, 36
The Hakkenden: Shinsho 35
Hakugei: The Legend of Moby Dick 61–62
Hakujaden (a.k.a. *The Legend of the White Serpent*) 195
Hamlet 110, 111, 123
Hand, D. 96
Harada, D. 119–120
Hata, M. 65
Hawkes, P. 7
Hayasaka, A. 148
Heidi, Girl of the Alps 66, 97
Hirschman, H. 62
Hoban, R. viii
Hoffmann, E.T.A. 99
Holbein, H. 93
Holt, E. 96
Horikawa, T. 148
Howard, T. 120
Howl's Moving Castle 66
Hubert, H. 25
Hutcheon, L. 6, 18, 60, 106

Ihara, S. 131
Ii, H. 147
Ikeda, H. 66
Impressionism 20
Inner Palace Harem Story 31
Ishihara, T. 34
Ito, N. 31
Iwasaka, M 167

Jackson, W. 96
Jade, C. 58
Jayaprada 58
Joan of Arc 20
Jørgensen, J. 96
Jourdan, L. 57
Joyce, J. 19
Juliet (1888) 123
Juliet (1898) 123
Julius Caesar 110, 111
The Jungle Book 96

Kadono, E. 66
Kafka, F. 25
Kanganis, C. 121

Kaufman, L. 122
Kawai, H. 22–23
Kazansky, G. 96
Keene, D. 149, 167
Kemp, L. 123–124
Kidnie, M.J. 106–107
Kiki's Delivery Service 66
Kimura, S. 116–117
King Lear 112, 123
Klimt, G. 20, 55–56
Kon, C. 130–144
Kondou, K. 31
Koshi, S. 66, 98
Kristeva, J. 126–127
Kuncewicz, K. 96
Kuroda, Y. 66, 98
Kurokawa, F. 27
Kurosawa, A. 102
Kuzuha, K. 66

Lederer, W. 75–76, 77
Legg, M.C. 77, 78
Leighton, Lord F. 123
Leitch, T. 7
Lewis, N. 66–67, 89
Liberty Leading the People (La Liberté guidant le peuple) 23
Like the Clouds, Like the Wind 8, 31–33, 34, 35, 36, 37
Lippit, Y. 148–149, 164
La Litterature Et Le Mal (*Literature and Evil*) 25
The Little Match Girl 69, 80
The Little Mermaid 68, 69, 80
Louis XIII 39
Louis XVI 40
Louis XVII 40
Louis XVIII 40
The Love Suicides at Sonezaki 27
Luhrmann, B. 121
Lynch, P.J. 92, 93, 94

Macbeth 123
Macherey, P. 122
Madden, J. 121–122
Maeda, M. 38, 44–47, 49, 52–56, 60, 159
Malmgren, C.D. 139–140, 141, 142
Mantegna, A. 120–121
Marais, J. 57
Marc 28
Marion, P. 94
Marquis de Sade 25
The Marriage of Heaven and Hell 43
Martin, T. 48, 50

Index

Martini, S. 94
Marvel Comics 144–145
Mathot, L. 57
Matthau, W. 62
Mauss, M. 25
The Melancholy of Haruhi Suzumiya 34–35
Melville, H. 62
The Merchant of Venice 111
Merivale, P. 136, 143
Meyerbeer, G. 55
Michelet, J. 20, 24–25, 26
A Midsummer Night's Dream (pantomime) 124
A Midsummer Night's Dream (play) 110, 123, 171
Milton, J. 42, 43
Miyake, L.K. 171–172
Miyako, M. 148
Miyazaki, G. 66
Miyazaki, H. 31, 65–66, 196
Mizuno, J. 21
Moeran, B. 178
Monzaemon, C. 27, 28
Morey, L. 96
Morris, I. 161, 166, 168, 170, 171, 175, 181
Mostow, J.S. 153
Much Ado About Nothing 111
Munch, E. 20
Murasaki, Lady Shikibu 146–195
Murdoch, J. 168
Muti, O. 58

Nansou Satomi 35
Napoleon Bonaparte 39–40
Naremore, J. 61
Nelligan, K. 58
Nibbelink, P. 122
Nielsen, K. 92
The Nightingale 69
Noh Theatre 21, 152
Norinaga, M. 154

Obuchowski, M.D. 165
Ohashi, Y. 145
Oizaki, F. 99–129
Okabe, E. 66
Okabe, K. 195
Okada, H.R. 149, 159, 180
Okamoto, Y. 35
Okri, B. 64
Olson, D. 87
One Thousand and One Arabian Nights (movie) 26

One Thousand and One Nights (a.k.a. *Arabian Nights*) 26, 41
O'Neill, J. 57
Ong, M.L. 76–77
Othello 110, 123

Parry, N. 57
The Pea Blossom 80
Pearce, G. 58
Pearce, P. 96
Peary, G. 60
Perry, P., Jr. 122
Peterson, T. 123
Piero della Francesca 120
pinku 21
Plato 3, 10
Poe, E.A. 137
Ponyo on the Cliff by the Sea 66, 196
Porter, D. 142
Pratchett, T. 5
Pre–Raphaelites 20
The Princess and the Pea 67, 89
Prokofiev, S. 96
Proust, M. 25, 149
Puette, W. 170
Puffy AmiYumi 153
Puss in Boots 66, 96
Pym, T. 93, 95

Rachmaninoff, S. 55
Rackham, A. 20
Rankin, A., Jr. 62
Rapoport, A. 139
Rascal the Raccoon 66
Rathbone, B. 62
Raven, N. 81, 93
The Reconciliation of the Montagues and Capulets Over the Dead Bodies of Romeo and Juliet 123
The Red Shoes 80
Reeve, J. 1, 20–21
Reitherman, W. 96
Remembrance of Things Past (*À la recherche du temps perdu*) 149
Renoir, P.-A. 21
Revelations: Persona 96
Richard III 110
Richard-Willm, P. 57
Richelieu, Cardinal 39
Rintaro 35
Robbins, J. 121
Romanelli, C. 58
Romanoff and Juliet 122
Romanticism 42–44, 57

Index

Rome and Jewel 121
Romeo and Juliet (artbook) 118–119
Romeo and Juliet (contemporary paintings) 123
Romeo and Juliet (1936 movie) 120
Romeo and Juliet (1954 movie) 120
Romeo and Juliet (1968 movie) 121
Romeo and Juliet (1996 movie) 121
Romeo and Juliet (1870 painting) 123
Romeo and Juliet (1884 painting) 123
Romeo and Juliet (1964 painting) 123
Romeo and Juliet (play) 99, 100, 110, 111, 112, 113, 114, 115, 116, 120, 121, 122, 123, 124, 126
Romeo and Juliet: Sealed with a Kiss 122
Romeo and Juliet with Friar Lawrence 122
Romeo Must Die 122
Romeo x Juliet 10, 13, 85, 99–129, 137, 145, 161
Romie-0 and Julie-8 122
Rossellini, R. 30
Rushdie, S. 5

Saitou, H. 66
Sakemi, K. 31, 32
Sakimoto, H. 109
Sanders, J. 6, 19–20, 23, 24, 36, 64, 99, 100
Sasagawa, H. 66
Schumann, R. 55
Segur, A. 92–93
Sennen no Ko—Hikaru Genji monogatari (a.k.a. *A Thousand Years of Love—The Tale of Shining Genji*) 148
The Sex Lives of Romeo and Juliet 122
Shakespeare, W. 9, 78, 99, 100, 101, 104, 105, 106, 107, 110, 111, 112, 113, 114, 120, 121, 124, 171
Shakespeare in Love 121–122
Sharpsteen, B. 96
Shatzkin, R. 60
She Was Good for Nothing 80
Shearer, N. 120
Shelley, P.B. 43
Shirane, H. 146, 162, 173–174, 180, 187, 190, 192–193
Smith, C.A. 122
Snedronningen 96
Snezhnaya Koroleva (animated movie) 96
Snezhnaya Koroleva (live-action movie) 96
The Snow Queen (American animated short) 96
The Snow Queen (anime) 10, 64–98, 137, 164
The Snow Queen (British animated movie) 96
The Snow Queen (British animated TV movie) 96
The Snow Queen (British hybrid movie) 96
The Snow Queen (English National Ballet) 96
The Snow Queen (fairy tale) 64–98
The Snow Queen (live-action TV movie) 96
The Snow Queen—Ballet Redefined... 96
The Snow Queen's Revenge 96
Snow White and the Seven Dwarfs (fairy tale) 76
Snow White and the Seven Dwarfs (movie) 58
Soliman 120–121
Sondheim, S. 121
La Sorcière 20, 25
Spanos, W.V. 142
Stam, R. 60
Stanley-Baker, J. 151–152, 164
The Steadfast Tin Soldier 67, 68, 69
Stevenson, R.L. 66
Stewart, J. 90–91, 94, 95
The Stingiest Man in Town (animated special) 62–63
The Stingiest Man in Town (musical) 62
The Story of Pollyanna 66
Studio Ghibli 31
Studio Gonzo 13, 145
Studio Pierrot 31
Sugii, G. 21, 146
Sui, A. 53
Surrealism 57
Sweeney, S.E. 136, 143
Swift, J. 66
Swiss Family Robinson 66
Symbolism 20, 57
Symons, J. 138

Takahata, I. 27, 29, 66, 97, 98
The Tale of Genji (anime, 1987) 21–22, 146–147
The Tale of Genji (anime, 2009) 3, 10, 137, 150–196
The Tale of Genji (artbook) 150–152
The Tale of Genji (live-action movie, 1951) 148
The Tale of Genji (live-action movie, 1966) 148
The Tale of Genji (novel) 146–195
Tales from Earthsea 66
The Taming of the Shrew 111
Tanigawa, N. 31
Tanizaki, J. 2

Tarot 20
Tateishi, K. 146–147, 148
Tchaikovsky, P.I. 55
The Tempest 111, 112
Thalberg, I. 120
The Three Musketeers 39
Three Thousand Miles in Search of Mother 66
Through the Looking-Glass, and What Alice Found There 76
Thumbelina 68
The Tinder Box 68
Titus Andronicus 111
Tobin, R.M. 96
Todorov, T. 140–141
Toelken, B. 167
Toriyumi, H. 31
Tsuyokiss — CoolxSweet 116–117
The Tragicall History of Romeus and Juliet 100
The Traveling Companion 80
La Traviata 107
Tristan and Isolde 107
Tromeo and Juliet 122
Twelfth Night 111
Tyler, R. 156, 180, 181, 182, 183

The Ugly Duckling 68, 69, 70, 80
Umineko no Naku Koro ni (anime) 9, 10, 130–145
Umineko no Naku Koro ni (videogame) 128–130
Ustinoff, P. 122
Uznik zamka If (a.k.a. *The Count of Monte Cristo* or *The Prisoner of If Castle*) 58

Valter 25
Verdi, G. 107
Veta 58

Waley, A. 149
Wallace, J.R. 169–170
Wang, Y. 171, 172, 177
Waterhouse, J.W. 123
Watts, B. 93, 95
Weber, J. 58
West Side Story 121
Whelehan, I. 7
White, R.S. 107, 120, 121
Wilde, O. 54
The Winter's Tale 78, 111
Wise, R. 121
Witchblade 145
Woolf, V. 149–150
World Masterpiece Theater 66
Wu, D. 96
Wullschlager, J. 73

Xenophon of Ephesus 100

Yabuki, K. 66, 96
Yabushita, T. 195
Yamada, K. 62, 63
Yamamoto, E. 20, 23, 26, 146
Yamato, W. 147–148
Yano, T. 35
Yerko, V. 93–94, 95
Yoshimura, F. 94, 148

Zeffirelli, F. 121
07th Expansion 128, 130, 131
Zipes, J. 65

www.ingramcontent.com/pod-product-compliance
Ingram Content Group UK Ltd.
Pitfield, Milton Keynes, MK11 3LW, UK
UKHW041958140426
5217IPUK00015B/858